Hannah Arendt
and the Jewish Question

For Carol
Again and Always

Hannah Arendt
and the Jewish Question

Richard J. Bernstein

The MIT Press
Cambridge, Massachusetts

First MIT Press edition, 1996
© 1996 Richard J. Bernstein

This book was printed and bound in the United States of America.

Library of Congress Cataloging-in-Publication Data

Bernstein, Richard J.
  Hannah Arendt and the Jewish question / Richard J. Bernstein.
     p.   cm.
  Includes bibliographical references and indexes.
  ISBN 0-262-02406-3 (hardcover: alk. paper).—ISBN 0-262-52214-4 (pbk.: alk. paper)
  1. Arendt, Hannah—Views on Jewish history. 2. Jews—History—1789–1945—Historiography. 3. Holocaust, Jewish (1939–1945)—Historiography. I. Title.
DS143.B55   1996
909'.04924—dc20   96-11506
                                                                          CIP

What is the subject of our thought? Experience! Nothing else!
And if we lose the ground of experience then we get into all kinds
of theories. When the political theorist begins to build his
systems he is also usually dealing with abstraction.

"Hannah Arendt on Hannah Arendt," 1972

I have always believed that, no matter how abstract our theories
may sound or how consistent our arguments may appear, there
are incidents and stories behind them which, at least for
ourselves, contain as in a nutshell the full meaning of whatever
we have to say. Thought itself – to the extent that it is more than
a technical, logical operation which electronic machines may be
better equipped to perform than the human brain – arises out of
the actuality of incidents, and incidents of living experience must
remain its guideposts by which it takes its bearings if it is not to
lose itself in the heights to which thinking soars, or in the depths
to which it must descend.

"Action and 'The Pursuit of Happiness'," 1962

I have refused to abandon the Jewish question as the focal point
of my historical and political thinking.

Letter to Karl Jaspers, 1946

Contents

Preface

Hannah Arendt loved to tell stories, and storytelling is woven into the fabric of her thinking. It seems appropriate, therefore, to tell my own story of how I came to write this book. For I did not (consciously) intend to write *this* book. It happened as a result of a series of fortunate contingencies. Several years ago I was invited to give a series of lectures on a Jewish theme at a major university. At first I thought this invitation was a mistake. Although I had written about a variety of contemporary philosophers and intellectual issues, I had never dealt explicitly with Jewish issues. The individual who had extended the invitation was aware of this, but said that the idea of the series was to provide an occasion for persons who had contributed to other intellectual areas to think about Judaism and Jewishness. Because I was busy preparing *The New Constellation* for publication, I was unable to accept the invitation. But I was also unable to forget a phrase in the letter I received – "to write the one 'Jewish' book that you always wanted to write." That phrase struck a deeply resonant chord. I realized that there *was* a 'Jewish' book I wanted to write. I wanted to explore the ways in which several major twentieth-century thinkers who were Jews confronted their Jewishness. In what ways, if any, did such a confrontation affect and shape their own cultural contributions? The idea was to select several twentieth-century thinkers and examine the range of different understandings and responses to a Jewish identity. In the early stages of the project, I thought of writing about Arendt, Freud, Scholem, Benjamin, Derrida, and Lévinas. Because writing has always also been a personal quest, I thought of this project as a way of exploring my own relation to my Jewish heritage and how it has influenced (or not influenced) my intellectual concerns.

I decided to begin with a first chapter on Hannah Arendt. I had already written about several aspects of her work and taught courses dealing with her thought. I felt that I understood the main themes and tensions of her thinking. Since the time when I first met Hannah Arendt in the early 1970s, she has been a living presence for me.

I had a slight familiarity with Arendt's so-called Jewish writings, but had never studied them seriously. Like many others, I tended to think of them as marginal and quite separate from her major works dealing with totalitarianism, the human condition, revolution, and the life of the mind. As I began immersing myself in these writings, reading her correspondence, rereading her book on Rahel Varnhagen, and acquainting myself with the biographical details of her life before she published *The Origins of Totalitarianism*, I felt that I was not only rediscovering the richness and nuances of her thinking, but reading her for the first time – like a second first reading. I was guided and helped by the growing number of excellent studies that focused on Arendt's confrontation with the Jewish question, as well as the incidents and living experiences that grounded her own thinking.[1]

A phrase from a review by Ann Lane struck me as exactly right: "Arendt's self-consciousness as a thinker, writer and actor involved her Jewish heritage. Until that fact is understood, most judgments of her will be off the mark."[2] This is reinforced and amplified by a comment that Hanna Pitkin makes in an extremely perceptive paper dealing with the concept of society in Arendt's work:

> Only when the highly abstract, remote, Grecophile concepts of *The Human Condition* are traced back to their roots in Arendt's life does their true political significance and contemporary relevance emerge. One must, as my colleague Michael Rogin once put it "look through the Greeks to the Jews."[3]

I was struck by the fact that Arendt's Jewish concerns, her own grappling with the Jewish question, left their mark on all her thinking.

So, what started out to be a chapter in a book turned out to be this book itself.

I have entitled my book *Hannah Arendt and the Jewish Question*. The phrase "the Jewish question" may sound a bit archaic and quaint today. I vividly recall that when I was a teenager growing up in Brooklyn (during the Second World War), there were many local jokes about "the Jewish question." "The Jewish question and ——" was a formula where one could simply, imaginatively fill in the blank. The idea was that there was a "Jewish angle" on any subject – for example, "The Jewish question and the Brooklyn Dodgers." It was only later that I realized that this sort of joking was a defense mechanism for screening out the incomprehensible horrors of the Holocaust, which were only gradually sinking into our consciousness after the Second World War. It was only much later that I discovered how important the expression "the Jewish question," "die Judenfrage," "la question sur les Juifs," had been both for Jews and non-Jews from the late eighteenth century through "the final solution" and the destruction of European Jewry. Despite the persistent use of the definite article, "the Jewish question" never referred to a single, well-defined, determinate issue or question. On the contrary, it was used to designate a whole series of shifting, loosely related, historical, cultural, religious, economic, political, and social issues, ranging from what rights were due to the Jews as citizens of nation-states to whether the Jews constituted a distinctive people, race, or nation.

Furthermore, "the Jewish question" – an expression that initially gained popularity in the writings of anti-Semites, and was used only later by Jewish intellectuals – takes on very different shading depending upon the specific historical context in which it is used.[4] In the twentieth century, the Jewish question became not only a focal point of concern for Zionists, but also ominous with the Nazi anti-Semitic ideology that demanded a final solution to the Jewish question – the extermination of European Jewry. In our post-Wittgensteinian age, in which there is so much suspicion of any form of essentialism, it seems reasonable to say that "the Jewish question" is a signifier for quite disparate questions which are only related by "family resemblances." But this dissolution is a bit too facile. For it is not accidental that "the Jewish question" should have become a major concern from the eighteenth century to the present. Like a red thread running through its many different and sometimes even incompatible uses, there has been an underlying anxiety about the fate of the Jewish people in the modern age. This is how Arendt herself thought about the Jewish question, and it gives special poignancy to her declaration: "I have refused to abandon the Jewish question as the focal point of my historical and political thinking."

Acknowledgments

In acknowledging one's debts there is an opportunity to pause and recognize how much of one's thinking builds upon the work of others. This is especially true with regard to this book. Since Hannah Arendt's death many scholars have helped to recover the importance of Arendt's Jewishness and her struggle with the Jewish question in order to understand the full range of her independent thinking. I indicate some of the most important contributions in the Introduction. I have been especially fortunate to benefit from intense conversations with colleagues who have a passionate interest in Arendt. These have included Andrew Arato, Seyla Benhabib, Teresa Brennan, Keith David, Bernard Flynn, Judith Friedlander, Jeffrey Goldfarb, Agnes Heller, James Miller, and Reiner Schürmann. I want to single out my debt to Jerome Kohn, with whom I have taught several courses on the work of Hannah Arendt. Jerry, one of Arendt's last research assistants, who has edited several of her works, has a comprehensive and subtle understanding of the total range of Arendt's thinking. His intellectual generosity and sensitivity embody Hannah Arendt's enduring legacy. I had the good fortune to read Elisabeth Young-Bruehl's biography, *Hannah Arendt: For Love of the World*, when it was still an unpublished manuscript. I recall my excitement when the Hannah Arendt that I knew during the last few years of her life came alive on the pages of Elisabeth's biography. In writing my own book, I have come to appreciate her book even more. I have returned to it many times for guidance and insight.

I have been blessed with a humane, dedicated, caring secretary, Claire Martin, who has helped in ever so many ways. She enabled me to carry out my responsibilities as Chair of the Department of Philosophy and protected my time so that I could write this book. Brent Hopkins and Lynne Taddeo, my research assistants, have been cheerful and patient in attending to the many technical details of preparing a book for publication. Jean van Altena of Polity Press made many helpful suggestions for improving the text. I want to express my appreciation to John Thompson of Polity Press. He is the ideal editor, whom every author dreams about – intelligent, perceptive, enthusiastic, and encouraging.

Chapter 7 is a revision of "Did Hannah Arendt Change Her Mind?: From Radical Evil to the Banality of Evil," forthcoming in *Hannah Arendt: 20 Years Later*, ed. Larry May and Jerome Kohn (Cambridge, Mass.: MIT Press, 1996). Chapter 8 is a revision of " 'The Banality of Evil' Reconsidered," forthcoming in *Hannah Arendt and the Meaning of Politics*, ed. Craig Calhoun and John McGowan (Minneapolis: University of Minnesota Press, 1996).

Abbreviations

Hannah Arendt
and the Jewish Question

Introduction

> I have always regarded my Jewishness as one of the indisputable factual data of my life, and I have never had the wish to change or disclaim facts of this kind. There is such a thing as a basic gratitude for everything that is as it is; for what has been *given* and was not, could not be *made*.
>
> Arendt, Letter to Gershom Scholem

When Hannah Arendt died in 1975 at the age of 69, she had achieved limited fame and a great deal of notoriety. Her books, especially *The Origins of Totalitarianism, The Human Condition, On Revolution,* and her well-crafted essays collected in *Between Past and Future* and *Men in Dark Times* were known to a reading public that extended beyond the academy. In the United States (and to a lesser extent in Germany) Arendt was recognized as an outspoken and controversial intellectual. Her notoriety was due to several heated controversies provoked by her writings, especially the controversy surrounding her *Eichmann in Jerusalem: A Report on the Banality of Evil.*[1] When it was published in 1963, there was a storm of protest. Arendt was damned, vilified and criticized (primarily by members of the Jewish community) for what she was presumed to have said and how she had said it. The controversy raged until her death – and long after.

Although there have always been a small group of thinkers who admired her writings and have been inspired by them, Arendt was considered to be a marginal thinker. She did not fit into any of the mainstream academic disciplines or categories. She was always something of an outsider – "a conscious pariah." In the 20 years since her death – and especially during the past few years – there has been an explosion of interest and intensive discussion of her writings. Prizes named in her honor, conferences, books, and articles about her are appearing everywhere. There is a new generation of young intellectuals who are discovering and rediscovering her. What is so impressive about this renaissance of interest is how international it is – from Poland to Brazil, from Italy and France to Australia and China. As we approach the final years of the twentieth century, Hannah Arendt is being recognized as one of the major political thinkers of this century. How is one to account for the interest and excitement that her writings are generating? What is it about her work that is so appealing, provocative, and fertile? I do not think there is a single explanation or reason. Rather, there are a plurality of concerns that help to explain why she is such an important thinker for us – and a variety of approaches to her diverse writings.

Arendt first became widely known when she published *The Origins of Totalitarianism* in 1951 at the age of 45. The book was immediately recognized as a landmark. Unfortunately it was read (or rather seriously misread) as a "cold war" treatise.[2] But with the collapse and disintegration of Communist ideology, there is now a growing realization of how prescient Arendt had been in laying bare the inner structure and dynamics of totalitarian ideology, terror, and domination. Even more important, Arendt's reflections about how power can appear spontaneously, grow "from below," and topple regimes that seem all-powerful and impenetrable, anticipated some of the unprecedented events that took place in Eastern Europe during the 1980s.

In 1958 Arendt wrote, with great enthusiasm, about the abortive 12-day Hungarian revolution. She declared that it was a "true event whose stature will not depend upon victory or defeat." Although she recorded the tragedy by which the Soviet system was able to survive, she had the perspicacity to observe that this fleeting event might very well be the beginning of a series of events that hold out the promise of "a sudden and dramatic collapse of the whole regime [rather] than a gradual normalization" (OT_2, 480, 510). It was not Arendt's prescience that was so impressive, but her critical reflections on power, action, and the appearance of "islands of freedom" in what otherwise seem to be bleak, desolate landscapes. Arendt became a heroine for many East European dissidents during the 1980s (just as she was a heroine for many Americans in the 1960s during the early days of the civil rights movement). Arendt, especially in her attempt to recover the lost treasure of the revolutionary spirit, was read as a political thinker of *hope*, who understood the possibilities, dangers, joys, and fragility of human beings spontaneously arising and creating public spaces in which freedom becomes a tangible worldly reality. Arendt was never a naive optimist. She knew that these "islands of freedom" disappear as quickly as they appear. She also knew how persistent and dangerous the tendencies toward "tribal nationalism" and racist ideology are in the twentieth century.

But I do not think that Arendt's insights into totalitarianism and post-totalitarianism are the primary reason for the current interest in her work. With the growing disenchantment with all ideologies and all "-isms," Arendt's intellectual and political appeal becomes more evident. It is her steadfast independence that is so luminous – her refusal to accept conventional categories, classifications, and clichés. The most persistent theme in Arendt's writings is that the horrendous events of the twentieth century have called into question all traditional standards and criteria for judgment. The task of the thinker is to forge new concepts in order to comprehend these events. Arendt's independence is typified by an exchange that took place between her and the distinguished political scientist Hans Morgenthau at a conference dedicated to her work which was held in 1972, a few years before her death. Morgenthau asked her bluntly "What are you? Are you a conservative? Are you a liberal? Where is your position within contemporary possibilities?" Arendt's forthright reply is revealing.

> I don't know. I really don't know and I've never known. And I suppose I never had any such position. You know the left think that I am conservative, and the conservatives sometimes think I am left or I am a maverick or God knows what. And I must say I couldn't care less. I don't think that the real questions of this century will get any kind of illumination by this kind of thing.[3]

This answer – especially the last sentence – provides a clue to why Arendt is so relevant for us as an independent thinker. There is a growing recognition of just how right she is – how positioning oneself among "contemporary possibilities" and ideologies is *not* the way in which the questions posed by this century will get any kind of illumination. Arendt is one of the very few thinkers of the twentieth century who articulated a positive understanding of public freedom – freedom involving speaking, acting, and debating with one's peers – that is completely free from any authoritarian overtones. Her analyses of plurality, action, natality, power, and the clash of opinions in the public debate among political equals provide fresh sources for the urgent task of rethinking what politics means today. And what is so refreshing and thought-provoking about her reflections is that they break the well-worn molds of "liberalism," "conservatism," "communitarianism," "Marxism," and so forth – indeed, most of the standard contemporary "positions."

There are now also new and provocative readings of her works. Many of the issues that have been in the foreground of "modern/ postmodern" debates are anticipated in her writings. She is a persistent critic of the logocentric tradition in philosophy that suppresses and denigrates contingency and plurality. She argues that ever since Plato (especially as a result of Plato's reaction to Socrates' trial), philosophers – with very few exceptions – explicitly or implicitly sought to impose their alien standards of truth upon the human realm of politics in which there is an irreducible conflict of opinions. The tradition of so-called political philosophy, when unmasked, is a tradition that really sought to refashion politics in the rationalistic image of philosophy. She is anti-foundationalist in the sense that she does not think that there are any firm, fixed foundations upon which to base our thinking. Arendt's critique of foundationalism and Archimedean metaphors is not meant as a contribution to academic debates about epistemology. Rather, it is the political and moral consequences of trying to think and judge without banisters (*Denken ohne Geländer*) that most concern her. She is critical of the obsessive concern with subjectivity and the self that has dominated so much of modern thinking since Descartes. The primary problem of the modern age is not *self*-alienation but *world*-alienation – the loss of a common world shared by a plurality of individuals who see it from different perspectives.[4] She is critical of all those tendencies in modern society which foster normalization. She ruthlessly exposes what she takes to be false ideas of autonomy and sovereignty. She is a relentless critic of all those grand narratives that presuppose historical necessity and inevitability. She shares Nietzsche's suspicion that underlying the demand for social equality (which she sharply distinguishes from political equality) is an infectious *ressentiment*. Like Nietzsche, she warns about the nihilistic, leveling consequences of this social *ressentiment*. She admires Nietzsche's attempt to shatter false idols, and thinks that Nietzsche brilliantly exposes how shabby morality and values have become in our time.

This is not to say that Arendt is a postmodernist or post-structuralist *avant la lettre*, even though some of her new interpreters want to claim her as a postmodern thinker. Arendt resists this classification, just as she resists all classifications. On the contrary, it is precisely because she shares so much with so-called postmodern and post-structuralist thinkers that we can appreciate her relevance as a critic of the excesses of these intellectual "positions." One of the weakest and least satisfactory aspects of these postmodern positions has been their failure to guide or illuminate political action. A key reason why so many thinkers who have been affected by postmodern currents are attracted to Arendt is because she shows the possibility of developing an understanding of politics that builds on some of the insights of post-structuralism. Arendt is also important as a counter-voice to recent postmodern excesses because she defends a concrete, historical, situated humanism which avoids the pitfalls of abstract humanism. She certainly does not join the anti-humanist bandwagon.

There have also been significant developments in feminist interpretations of Arendt – pro and con. Arendt herself never had much sympathy with the women's movement. She is an easy target for feminists who see her as celebrating masculine agonistic virtues and reifying an objectionable public/private dichotomy that reinforces the traditional image of women as belonging exclusively to the household. One might even label this the standard feminist critique of Arendt – one which, unfortunately, has prevailed. But recently there have been more subtle feminist readings of her work in which there is an appropriation of her notion of the "conscious pariah" as an exemplar of the situation of women who refuse to accept or assimilate to prevailing social relationships. There have been those who have argued that Arendt's conception of politics and public spaces provides the basis for rethinking the possibility of a feminist politics. A vital current in recent feminist readings of Arendt is the view that her thinking provides critical resources which can potentially illuminate and contribute to feminist concerns.[5]

From still another perspective, there have been a variety of studies that have focused on the complex relationships with the philosophers who influenced Arendt's thinking. Arendt never thought of herself as a professional philosopher. She even declared: "I do not belong to the circle of philosophers" (*EU*, 1). Yet she was appropriating insights and themes – in imaginative and novel ways – from the philosophic tradition. Aristotle, Heidegger, and Kant were always sources of inspiration.[6] But we are also coming to appreciate the importance of her intellectual encounters with Socrates, Plato, St Augustine, Kierkegaard, Nietzsche, and Jaspers.

There is also another dimension of her life and writings which has been coming into the foreground of discussion, and which is radically transforming our understanding of Arendt. For someone who insisted that all her thinking was grounded in "personal experiences," too little attention – at least until recently – has been paid to Arendt's own historical situatedness and the events that provoked her thinking. There are reasons for this neglect. Not only was the public/private distinction central in her writings; she was also a fiercely private person. Except for a small circle of friends, not much was known about Arendt during her lifetime.

It was only in 1982, when Elisabeth Young-Bruehl published her comprehensive and perceptive biography, that there was the opportunity to come to know something of the details of Arendt's life story. Young-Bruehl was among the first to have access to Arendt's extensive correspondence, family documents, unpublished manuscripts, lectures, and class notes. She also had the opportunity to interview many persons who knew Arendt. In addition to the many details and events of Arendt's life that Young-Bruehl reveals (including her affair with Heidegger when she went to Marburg as an 18-year-old university student), the moving story that Young-Bruehl tells is one in which Arendt's Jewishness and her concern with the fate of the Jewish people in the modern age stand at the very center of her being. Young-Bruehl's biography provides a historical context for an intelligent reading of Arendt's Jewish and Zionist writings, which were collected and published with an excellent introduction by Ron H. Feldman in 1978. Feldman gathered together Arendt's most important articles on Jewish and Zionist issues, many of which had appeared in obscure Jewish periodicals.[7] In part because of the furor over *Eichmann in Jerusalem* and the hostility of the American Jewish community toward Arendt, these writings have been barely known and rarely discussed. Young-Bruehl and Feldman make us aware of the fact that in the 20-year period prior to the publication of *The Origins of Totalitarianism*, Arendt not only worked almost exclusively for various Jewish and Zionist organizations in Paris and New York, but that most of her writings dealt with various aspects of the Jewish question. They both show that Arendt's better-known later writings were themselves influenced by her Jewish concerns. There have always been a few commentators, like Leon Botstein (also a former student of Arendt), who have emphasized this aspect of Arendt's life and work.

In 1990 Dagmar Barnouw published her book *Visible Spaces: Hannah Arendt and the German-Jewish Experience*, in which she approaches Arendt from the perspective of Arendt's own participation and response to "a German–Jewish history that ended in genocide" (p. ix). Barnouw sensitively seeks to portray what was distinctive about this German-Jewish experience. Although she disagrees with some of Young-Bruehl's interpretations, her own study supports Ann Lane's judgment that "Arendt's self-consciousness as a thinker, writer, and actor involved her Jewish heritage. Until that fact is understood, most judgments of her will be off the mark."[8] Barnouw, like Young-Bruehl, makes extensive use of Arendt's prolific correspondence. One of the richest sources of information about Arendt is her correspondence with her mentor and friend Karl Jaspers. This correspondence extends from 1926 (when Arendt was Jaspers's student in Heidelberg) to 1969, when Jaspers died. Published in Germany in 1985 and translated into English in a beautifully edited volume in 1992, this correspondence reads almost like an epistolary novel. It ranges from daily concerns about how to cook the bacon that Arendt sent to Gertrude and Karl Jaspers in care packages after the Second World War to long philosophical discussions of Plato and Kant. A leitmotif runs through this correspondence. Arendt and Jaspers return again and again to questions about Germany, the Nazis, and the Jews. This correspondence, together with the recently published correspondence between Hannah Arendt and Mary McCarthy, provides an important source for Arendt's most intimate and personal reflections. The literature situating Arendt's thinking in its historical context, a literature that shows the complexity and centrality of Arendt's response to the Jewish question, continues to grow. Jeffrey C. Isaac's recent comparative study, *Arendt, Camus, and Modern Rebellion* explores how these two "major political intellectuals of their generation . . . offer penetrating insight into the problem of rebellion and community in the modern world."[9] And in making this comparison, he assigns a prominent place to Arendt's Jewish and Zionist writings.

Finally, I want to mention Margaret Canovan's recent impressive study, *Hannah Arendt: A Reinterpretation of Her Political Thought*. In 1974 Canovan wrote the first book-length introduction to Arendt's political thought. It was based entirely on Arendt's published writings. In her new book – her reinterpretation – Canovan has made extensive and judicious use of Arendt's unpublished manuscripts which are now in the Library of Congress. Canovan argues persuasively – and shows in detail – "that responses to the most dramatic events of her time lie at the very centre of Arendt's thought," and that "virtually the entire agenda of Arendt's political thought was set by her reflections on the political catastrophes of the mid-century."[10] She argues that Arendt's major works "rise like islands out of a partly submerged continent of thought, some of it recorded in obscure articles, some of it only in unpublished writings," and that *The Origins of Totalitarianism* is the central text for understanding Arendt. She provides a new interpretation of what Arendt means by totalitarianism. By drawing upon Arendt's unpublished writings, she also provides a new context for reading *The Human Condition*. Canovan herself does not focus primarily on Arendt's Jewish writings, most of which appeared prior to the publication of *The Origins of Totalitarianism*. But Arendt herself makes it clear that her struggle to comprehend the almost incomprehensible eruption of totalitarianism (especially Nazi totalitarianism) was motivated by the desire to understand "the outrageous fact that so small (and, in world politics, so unimportant) a phenomenon as the Jewish question and antisemitism could become the catalytic agent for first, the Nazi movement, then a world war, and finally the establishment of death factories" (*OT*₃, viii).

I have mentioned a few of the landmarks that help to situate Hannah Arendt as a thinker who must be understood as responding to what she took to be the unprecedented experiences and events of her time – events which called into question all traditional political and moral categories and standards, events which brought the Jews into the very storm center of twentieth-century world politics. Despite the growing literature seeking to understand the continuity and complex relationships between her life story and her published works, there is still a strong tendency to separate Arendt's Jewish concerns from the rest of her thought. There are apparently good reasons for making such a distinction. If one focuses on *The Human Condition, On Revolution, Between Past and Future, Men in Dark Times, Crises of the Republic*, or the posthumously published *The Life of the Mind* and *Lectures on Kant's Political Philosophy*, then it certainly seems that her Jewish concerns are quite marginal. Furthermore, most of Arendt's explicit writings on Jewish issues appeared in the 1940s before she even published *The Origins of Totalitarianism*.

Yet I want to argue that such a split between Arendt's Jewish concerns and the rest of her work is untenable. I hope to show how her confrontation with the Jewish question (in its complex and varied aspects) shaped many of the fundamental issues that preoccupied her throughout her life. Approaching Arendt's thinking from this perspective provides a more nuanced reading and interpretation of her entire corpus. The thesis I intend to defend is neither merely biographical nor reductionistic. I am not simply claiming that Arendt's experience as a German-born Jewess who was forced to flee from Germany and who subsequently sought to comprehend the events leading up to the destruction of European Jewry provided the occasion for her more general reflections about politics, action, and the life of the mind. Nor do I think that Arendt's confrontation with the Jewish question is somehow a key for understanding the full range of her intellectual concerns. Such a reductionist interpretation fails to do justice to the education (Bildung) of secular German Jews of her generation who felt at home in the philosophical, literary, and cultural history of the Western tradition. The distinctive feature of Arendt's own thinking is the way in which pluralistic and diverse thought-trains interweave with each other, but are always grounded in personal experiences and specific events.[11] I intend to show that approaching Arendt from the point of view of her understanding and response to the Jewish question and the political forms of anti-Semitism that arose in the nineteenth and twentieth centuries is, to use her own language, an essential *perspective* for gaining an understanding of the most characteristic themes in her thinking. To use one of her favorite metaphors, we can say that her confrontation with the Jewish question was the catalytic agent for crystallizing her thinking. In this respect I am arguing for a much stronger conceptual connection between her writings about the Jewish question and the rest of her thought than is typically acknowledged.

I begin my study with an exploration of Arendt's important distinction between the Jewish parvenu and the Jewish pariah, a distinction that she appropriated from the French-Jewish thinker Bernard Lazare, and which she employed in telling the life story of Rahel Varnhagen. It is this distinction that provides a conceptual grid for exploring the failures of German-Jewish assimilation – assimilation understood as a personal project of becoming assimilated to "good" (Gentile) society. What Arendt admires about Rahel Varnhagen is that, despite her parvenu tendencies and aspirations, she finally rebels against becoming a parvenu. She affirms herself as a rebel; she affirms herself as a pariah. When writing this book, Arendt became aware of the important distinction between society and politics, "the social" and "the political," a distinction that is central to all her work. Her distinction between the parvenu and the pariah – and especially her appropriation of Lazare's conception of the "conscious pariah" – led her to recover "the hidden tradition" of the Jew as pariah.

Soon after Arendt fled from Germany in 1933, she began exploring the recent history and varieties of political anti-Semitism. In reflecting on the modern history of the Jewish people, she came to the conclusion that the reason why European Jewry was so completely unprepared for what happened to them in the twentieth century was because as a people they lacked political experience. Arendt argued that Jewish emancipation could only be achieved by political action if the Jewish people would fight for their rights *as Jews*. Arendt's first thinking about the character, tensions, and demise of the nation-state is from the perspective of the Jewish question. After the French Revolution, with its Declaration of the Rights of Man, all human beings (including Jews) were presumably entitled to the rights of citizens. But it was only in the context of a nation that political rights could be guaranteed, and it was questioned (especially by anti-Semites) whether the Jews really belonged to the European nation-states. The political anti-Semitism of the nation-state was ultimately replaced by a much more virulent form of supranational political anti-Semitism in the last decades of the nineteenth century. It was this supranational political anti-Semitism that ultimately became such a lethal weapon in Nazi ideology and policy.

Although Arendt insisted on the distinction between society and politics, and emphasized the importance of political responsibility and action by the Jewish people, she was initially quite vague about the *meaning* of politics. In embarking on her own political education, beginning in the 1930s, Arendt concerned herself with the *meaning* of politics – a quest which was originally stimulated by her desire to understand the failures and possibilities of a Jewish politics. I argue that there is a strong radical populist strand in her thinking about politics. She advocated a politics "from below" in which the Jewish people would organize themselves and fight for their rights *as* Jews in alliance with other oppressed groups. There is a direct continuity between her earliest summons to the Jewish people to fight for their political rights and her later attempt to recover "the lost treasure" of the revolutionary spirit. I follow the stages in Arendt's quest for the *meaning* of politics, showing how her own experiences and reflections on statelessness led her to the claim that the most fundamental right is the "right to have rights," the "right to belong to a political community," the very right which the Nazis denied to the Jews. It is in this context that we can appreciate Arendt's deep skepticism about the type of abstract humanism and defense of abstract rights which claimed that all human beings possess inalienable rights even outside a viable political community. Arendt's most profound insights into what constitutes authentic politics and how it is essential for leading a human life arose only when she confronted the full horror of totalitarian domination and terror. It is by "dwelling on horrors" of the concentration camps, the most consequential institution of totalitarian regimes, that Arendt can provide a brilliant analysis of these institutions which were the laboratories for testing the hypothesis that "everything is possible" – including the radical transformation of human nature. She analyzes how the ultimate aim of totalitarianism is to destroy human plurality, natality, spontaneity, and individuality, the conditions that are constitutive of our humanity and the basis for all action and politics. Virtually all the elements of her understanding of action, freedom, public spaces, and politics which are thematized in *The Human Condition* and *On Revolution* are implicit and emerge from her study of Nazi totalitarianism.

It was Arendt's concern with Jewish politics that initially attracted her to Zionism – and was also responsible for her break with Zionism. Zionists were the only group who shared her conviction that Jews must assume political responsibility and engage in political action. But Arendt criticized and was disappointed by the revisionist tendencies in Zionist ideology and politics. She favored the idea of a Jewish homeland based upon Arab–Jewish cooperation, but strongly objected to a Jewish *sovereign* state. Arendt's general criticism of the nation-state and the idea of national sovereignty was sharpened in her debates with her fellow Zionists. It was also in the context of these debates that Arendt came to appreciate the irreducibility and necessity for multiple perspectives and the clash of opinions (*doxoi*) in political communities. She thought of herself as a member of the "loyal opposition," not as an anti-Zionist.

One of Arendt's most original and central ideas is "the council system." It is in a federation of councils – islands of freedom – that she saw the possibility of an alternative to the nineteenth-century nation-

state and twentieth-century totalitarianism. A primary reason why
Arendt was so enthusiastic about the abortive 12-day 1956 Hungarian
revolution was because there was the appearance, once again, of the
spontaneous arising of councils. The persistent rise (and disappearance) of these councils is what she called "the innermost story of the
modern age." The councils were the manifestation of the revolutionary spirit in the modern age – the treasure that has made its brief
appearance and then been lost again. But it is rarely noted that
Arendt's earliest thinking about the council system occurred in the
context of her thinking about the political structure of a Jewish
homeland in which there would be joint Arab–Jewish local councils –
a political structure which she proposed as an alternative to a Jewish
nation-state. During one of the few periods in her life when she
engaged in direct political action, she joined with Judah Magnes and
his group (*Ihud*) to advocate a binational state of Arabs and Jews in
Palestine.

In 1945, Arendt wrote that "the problem of evil will be the
fundamental question of post-war intellectual life in Europe."[12]
Although few intellectuals in Europe (or anywhere else) became
preoccupied by this question, it did indeed become "the fundamental
question" for Arendt. It first arose in her "dwelling on horrors" – the
horrors of the death camps and the final solution. It was in this
context that she first began to reflect on the meaning of absolute or
radical evil. I seek to clarify what she meant (and did *not* mean) by
radical evil, and how radical evil is related to the willful hubristic
attempt to make human beings superfluous. I argue that her
understanding of radical evil is *compatible* with her later concept of the
banality of evil.

Finally, I turn to the book that provoked so much heated
controversy, *Eichmann in Jerusalem*. I focus on the issues that caused the
greatest scandal: her discussion of the *Judenräte* (the Jewish councils
appointed by the Nazis during the Second World War which had the
task of carrying out Nazi directives) and the precise meaning of her
claims about the banality of evil. I pursue her various attempts to
clarify what she means by the banality of evil and her justification for
employing this concept. The "factual phenomenon" of the banality
of evil which she claimed to have witnessed at the Eichmann trial
was one of the main sources for her study of the life of the mind.
She argued that it was Eichmann's inability to think and to judge
that constitute the basis for understanding how he could perform

"monstrous deeds" without "monstrous motives." I explore some of the problems in her claim that it is such a failure to think and to judge that is the key for understanding the banality of evil.

Throughout this study my primary objective has been to understand what Arendt is thinking, saying, and doing – and why. I want to show not only how central the Jewish question (in its multiple aspects) is for understanding Arendt, but how approaching her work from this perspective provides a corrective to those interpretations which ignore or downplay this aspect of her life and work. Understanding, as Arendt herself argues, is not incompatible with judging and criticizing. On the contrary, understanding itself requires critical judgment. Consequently, although my primary stance is that of a sympathetic dialogical partner, I have not hesitated to indicate some of the key places where I find her thinking incomplete, inadequate, or unsatisfactory.

Toward the end of her life Arendt said: "I would like to say that everything I did and everything I wrote – all that is tentative. I think that all thinking . . . has the earmark of being tentative" (*RPW*, 338). Arendt was not simply being modest. Tentativeness is, according to Arendt, the most distinctive and quintessential characteristic of all genuine thinking. Arendt exemplifies what she admires in Socrates: the capacity to provoke thinking by infecting others with the perplexities which she felt herself.[13] Throughout this study I have attempted to share in her own perplexities, to think *with* Arendt, and sometimes *against* Arendt.

1

The Conscious Pariah as Rebel and Independent Thinker

Hannah Arendt's lack of interest in Judaism and Jewish issues during her youth is now well documented. She tells us:

> I come from an old Königsberg family. Nevertheless, the word "Jew" never came up when I was a small child. I first met up with it through anti-Semitic remarks – they are not worth repeating – from children on the street. After that I was, so to speak, "enlightened." . . . as a child – a somewhat older child then – I knew that I looked Jewish. I looked different from other children. I was very conscious of that. But not in a way that made me feel inferior, that was just how it was. . . . [My mother] would never have baptized me! I think she would have boxed my ears right and left if she had ever found out that I had denied being a Jew. It was unthinkable, so to speak. Out of the question![1]

Arendt grew up in the social and cultural environment that had been shaped by a century of Jewish-German assimilation and "emancipation," in which many enlightened secular Jews, like her parents, no longer felt it necessary to deny their Jewish background or consider baptism in order to participate fully in German cultural life. It was all too easy to believe that there was no serious conflict between being a Jew and being a German. There was even a strong conviction among some prominent German Jews that there was a special affinity between Judaism and German culture. Arendt did experience occasional incidents of anti-Semitism, but at an early age her mother taught her to defend herself.

Even though her rebellious adolescence coincided with the growth of the German Zionist movement, which attracted many of her fellow Jews (including Hans Jonas, Walter Benjamin, and Gershom Scholem), Arendt was indifferent toward Zionism. Her paternal grandfather, Max Arendt, was typical of those enlightened German Jews who were hostile to Zionism and offended by any suggestion that cast doubt on their German loyalty. In Hannah Arendt's coming of age, it was German poetry, language, and philosophy that captured her imagination. Being a Jewess, as she stated in her famous exchange with Gershom Scholem concerning her book *Eichmann in Jerusalem*, was "one of the indisputable factual data of my life" – but without much significance or meaning.[2] In the same letter she says: "I was interested neither in history nor in politics when I was young. If I can be said to 'have come from anywhere,' it is from the tradition of German philosophy" (*JP*, 245–6). This statement, made in 1964, is consistent with what she wrote to her mentor and friend Karl Jaspers in 1933. "For me, Germany means my mother tongue, philosophy, and literature."[3] By the time Arendt was in her early twenties she had studied with several of Germany's outstanding philosophers and theologians, including Heidegger, Husserl, Jaspers, Guardini, and Bultmann. It was only during her student years in Heidelberg, where she had gone to write her dissertation on St Augustine with Jaspers, that we discover the first glimmerings of a slight but casual interest in Zionism. In 1926, more out of loyalty to Hans Jonas than because of any intrinsic interest, she attended a lecture by Kurt Blumenfeld, who was a leading spokesperson for the Zionist movement in Germany. Elisabeth Young-Bruehl shrewdly remarks that Blumenfeld's lecture "did not convert Hannah Arendt to Zionism, but it did convert her to Kurt Blumenfeld" who became a lifelong friend (*YB*, 71).[4] During this period of her life – the early 1920s – Arendt was intellectually and, perhaps even more important, emotionally remote from Jewish and Zionist concerns. She found "the so-called Jewish question boring" (*C*, 197). She was much more passionately concerned with the subtleties of Christian thinking, and was fascinated by Kierkegaard and St Augustine. She had come under the spell of the young Heidegger, who was the source of so much intellectual excitement in Germany.[5]

There is always a danger of reading history backwards, of being subtly influenced by what we now know was already happening in Germany during this time – the ominous growth of National Socialism and its virulent anti-Semitism, which Jaspers compared to a "fungal disease that spreads and eats up everything in its path" (*C*, 273). But if we are to understand the radical transformation that was shortly to occur in Arendt's life, we need to be sensitive to the German cultural ambience – the prevailing *Stimmung* (mood) – as she experienced it. One of the tragically ironical contradictions of secular German-Jewish cultural life at this time is that one could easily believe there were simply no serious barriers, no limits to participation in, and appropriations of, German culture. Paradoxically, the German university *appeared* to be more enlightened, more open, more receptive to secular Jews than universities in any other European country – or even in the United States. There is no evidence that Arendt experienced any serious discrimination in pursuing her university studies – either as a woman or as a Jew. No one questioned the appropriateness of a young Jewess writing about the concept of Christian love in St Augustine. Arendt moved freely among her Jewish and Gentile peers. She was respected, praised, and encouraged by her teachers. Although always a bit shy, she was admired for her intelligence, wit, and flair. She enjoyed being the brilliant, attractive, independent, slightly flirtatious Jewess. Unlike Rahel Varnhagen, about whom she was soon to write, Arendt never felt that being born a Jewess was a source of "shame," "misery," or "misfortune." She was never tempted to become a parvenu, and always had a disdain and contempt for what she later called the "exceptional," or "privileged," Jew. Arendt may have been naive – as she later judged herself to be (*C*, 197) – but it is not difficult to understand why "the Jewish question" seemed so boring to her especially in comparison to the intellectual excitement that was being generated by Heidegger, Husserl, and Jaspers.

Kurt Blumenfeld introduced Arendt to the writings of Bernard Lazare, who became one of her heroes.[6] Not only was Lazare an important figure for Arendt in her own Jewish political education; she even identified with his eventual marginalization and isolation from his fellow Jews. Lazare's conception of the Jews as a pariah people, and specifically his portrait of the "conscious pariah" who rebels and transforms the outcast status thrust upon the Jew into a challenge to fight for one's rights, fired Arendt's imagination. The conscious pariah is to be sharply distinguished from the Jewish parvenu, who desperately seeks to escape his pariah status and to be accepted by, and assimilated to, a society that treats the Jew as an outcast. It is this distinction between the conscious pariah as a rebel and the parvenu as a "social climber" who tries to escape her pariah status by fraud and self-deception that provided Arendt with the conceptual grid for telling the life story of Rahel Varnhagen. This became the means for exploring what Arendt took to be the ultimate failure of the project of German-Jewish assimilation and so-called emancipation – a project that became possible only in the modern age, in light of the Enlightenment legacy. We will see how this distinction between the conscious pariah and the parvenu is intimately intertwined with Arendt's first gropings toward formulating the distinction between society and politics – or "the social" and "the political" as she later described it. This is one of the most fundamental distinctions in her political thinking (even though it was to undergo several transformations in the course of her development).

"Society" in her biography of Rahel Varnhagen primarily refers to "high society," "good society," "aristocratic society" – the type of society to which one belongs, or from which one is excluded, by birth.[7] This is quite different from the understanding found in *The Human Condition*, where the "social" is identified with the distinctively modern form of bureaucratic housekeeping that threatens to engulf and destroy the dignity and autonomy of politics. It is also different from what Arendt means by "The Social Question" – the question of mass poverty that plays such a prominent role in her analysis of the differences between the American and French revolutions.[8]

There is, nevertheless, a single strand running through these different uses and meanings of "society" and "the social." Arendt consistently viewed the aspiration to find one's identity in society, or to restrict and reduce all public categories to social categories, as a threat to genuine politics, freedom, and human dignity. Her first reflections upon this threat were worked out in her critique of the project of German-Jewish assimilation whereby the parvenu seeks to become a member of "good society." We will also see how this distinction between the parvenu and the pariah is related to Arendt's complex and ambivalent attitude toward modernity, the Enlightenment legacy, and classical liberalism. Although the Enlightenment brought into the foreground the question of political rights, these were understood to be the "Rights of Man" – the rights of abstract human beings. There was no place for the recognition of the rights of Jews *as*

Jews. So, paradoxically, "emancipation" as shaped by the Enlightenment came to mean emancipation *from* one's Jewishness (i.e. Jewish suicide, not emancipation of the Jews as Jews). When Arendt did turn her attention to the Jewish question, of how we are to understand the modern age so as to grasp why there has been so much resistance and intolerance to recognizing the Jews as Jews, this issue became central. She came to see this failure to recognize the Jews *as Jews* as directly related to the rise of Nazi totalitarianism. "The comity of European peoples went to pieces when, and because, it allowed its weakest member to be excluded and persecuted."[9]

We will also explore how Arendt's self-understanding of being a conscious pariah among a pariah people – accepting the challenge and *responsibility* of being an outsider even among one's own people – is related to her self-understanding as an independent thinker. But in order to see how these motifs were beginning to take shape, we need to turn to her biography of Varnhagen, which she started writing in 1929 for her *Habilitationschrift* (the second dissertation required to pursue a German university career), and completed in the mid-1930s when she was living as a stateless person in Paris. She did not publish the book until 1957, and its American edition appeared only in 1974, the year before her death.

It was almost by accident that Arendt decided to write a "biography" of Rahel Varnhagen. After completing her dissertation, *Der Liebesbegriff bei Augustin*, she turned her attention to one of her great intellectual loves, the origins of German Romanticism. She then discovered the fascinating correspondence of Rahel Varnhagen, whom she found to be an "original, unspoiled, and unconventional intelligence, combined with an absorbing interest in people and a truly passionate nature" (*OT*$_3$, 59) – a description that is perfectly apt for Arendt herself. Rahel (as she affectionately came to be known by those who read her intimate letters) was born in 1771, and was known for her famous garret salon in Berlin, which attracted some of the most diverse and talented members of German society. She was also the originator of what came to be known as the "Goethe cult." Her extensive correspondence, edited by her husband (who was 14 years younger than her), provided an extraordinarily detailed, perceptive, and intimate portrayal of her life and times, her circle of friends, her anxieties, hopes, loves, and despair. Arendt argued that the idealized portrait of Rahel that emerged from Karl August Varnhagen's selectively edited volumes of her letters was a distortion and falsification of Rahel. He deliberately obscured Rahel's struggle with her Jewish identity, and even disguised references in her letters to her Jewish friends.[10] Arendt was especially intrigued by the way in which Rahel spent so much of her adult life trying to escape what she took to be the "misfortune," "shame," and "misery" of her life – having been born a Jewess, and how she sought to become assimilated to a society that never really accepted the Jew as a Jew. Rahel was filled with contradictory and ambivalent impulses, at once trying to play the role of the parvenu and rebelling against giving up her pariah status as an outsider.[11] Rahel's life story thereby becomes a vehicle for exploring the double binds of secular Jews during this early stage of German-Jewish assimilation. Arendt was not only ambivalent about Rahel; she was also ambivalent about her *study* of Rahel's life. When she finally agreed to its publication in 1957, she wrote in her preface:

> It was never my intention to write a book *about* Rahel; about her personality, which might lend itself to various interpretations according to the psychological standards and categories that the author introduces from outside; . . . What interested me solely was to narrate the story of Rahel's life as she herself might have told it. (*RH*, xv)

Arendt was always suspicious of – and even hostile to – psychological (and psychoanalytic) "standards and categories." She felt that these were essentially reductionistic and misleading. Ironically, one of the virtues of her otherwise abstract biography is her psychological insight into Rahel's personality – especially her sensitivity in dealing with Rahel's disappointed loves. Arendt does not really "narrate the story of Rahel's life as she herself might have told it," but rather as Arendt thinks she *should* have told it.[12]

Arendt's focus on Rahel's struggle with her Jewish identity is dramatically illustrated by the way she begins her book. She cites the words that Rahel's husband reports her to have said on her deathbed.

> "What a history! – A fugitive from Egypt and Palestine, here I am and find help, love, fostering in you people. With real rapture I think of these origins of mine and this whole nexus of destiny, through which the oldest memories of the human race stand side by side with the latest developments. The greatest distances in time and space are bridged. The thing which all my life seemed to me the greatest shame, which was the misery and misfortune of my life – having been born a Jewess – this I should on no account now wish to have missed." (*RH*, 3)

Arendt strikingly comments: "It had taken sixty-three years to come to terms with a problem which had its beginning seventeen hundred years before her birth, which underwent a crucial upheaval during her life, and which one hundred years after her death – she died on March 7, 1833 – was slated to come to an end" (*RH*, 3).

As Arendt narrates her story of Rahel's life, it is at the very moment when she came closest to achieving her goal of being accepted by society – when she married a Gentile, was baptized, and even changed her name from Rahel Levin to Antoine Friederike Varnhagen – that she rebelled and affirmed herself as a pariah Jewess.

> As a Jew Rahel had always stood outside, had been a pariah, and discovered at last, most unwillingly and unhappily, that entrance into society was possible only at the price of lying, of a far more generalized lie than simply hypocrisy. She discovered that it was necessary for the parvenu – but for him alone – to sacrifice every natural impulse, to conceal all truth, to misuse all love, not only to suppress all passion, but worse still, to convert it into a means for social climbing. (*RH*, 208)

We tend to think of assimilation as a process whereby an individual merges or blends into a group. It can be passive or active. But this is not what Arendt meant by assimilation, and it was not what she sought to identify in the German-Jewish context. Rather, assimilation was *aggressively* active, requiring the sacrifice of "every natural impulse" and the suppression of passion. Its "price – as Rahel came to realize – was lying to oneself and forced self-deception." The logic of such assimilation required assimilating and incorporating society's anti-Semitism!

> No assimilation could be achieved merely by surrendering one's past but ignoring the alien past. In a society on the whole hostile to the Jews – and that situation obtained in all countries in which Jews lived, down to the twentieth century – it is possible to assimilate only by assimilating to anti-Semitism also. If one wishes to be a normal person precisely like everybody else, there is scarcely any alternative to exchanging old prejudices for new ones. If that is not done, one involuntarily becomes a rebel – "But I am a rebel after all!" – and remains a Jew. And if one really assimilates, taking all the consequences of denial of one's own origin and cutting oneself off from those who have not or have not yet done it, one becomes a scoundrel. (*RH*, 224)

Arendt never abandoned this harsh judgment: the parvenu who fails to affirm herself as a pariah Jew "becomes a scoundrel." This judgment appears in the final chapter of *Rahel Varnhagen*, entitled "One Does Not Escape Jewishness." This was one of the chapters written in the mid-1930s when Arendt was living in exile in Paris. Between the time she started writing her biography and when she completed it, Arendt felt that she herself had been "bashed on the head by history." When she fled Germany in 1933, after having been arrested and interrogated on account of some library work she was doing for her Zionist friends about German anti-Semitism, she abandoned her biography of Rahel and her academic pursuits.[13] Reflecting on this period of her life, she wrote: "I realized what I then expressed time and again in the sentence: If one is attacked as a Jew, one must defend oneself as a Jew. Not as a German, not as a world-citizen, not as an upholder of the Rights of Man" (*EU*, 11–12). Arendt quite clearly and assertively affirmed herself as a Jewish pariah. She sought to accept the challenge and responsibility of being a member of the Jewish people.

> What can I specifically do as a Jew? . . . it was now my clear intention to work with an organization. For the first time. To work with the Zionists. They were the only ones who were ready. It would have been pointless to join those who had assimilated. Besides, I never really had anything to do with them. Even before this time I had concerned myself with the Jewish question. The book on Rahel Varnhagen was finished when I left Germany [sic]. The problem of the Jews plays a role in it. I wrote it with the idea, "I want to understand." I wasn't discussing my personal problems as a Jew. But now, belonging to Judaism had become my own problem, and my problem was political. Purely political! I wanted to go into practical work, exclusively and only Jewish work. With this in mind I then looked for work in France. (*EU*, 12)

Not only in France, but also in the United States. For the next 20 years Arendt worked almost exclusively for Zionist and Jewish organizations in Paris and New York. Her declaration that her personal problem was political indicates one of the main reasons why she was dissatisfied with her unpublished biography of Varnhagen. The entire issue of Jewish-German assimilation was abruptly and violently shattered in 1933. Arendt, who was undergoing her own political education, was critical of her political naiveté when writing her biography. Politics scarcely played any role in her analysis of

Rahel and her Jewish contemporaries. Early in the biography, Arendt does say – almost in passing – that

> A political struggle for equal rights might have taken the place of the personal struggle [for assimilation]. But that was wholly unknown to this generation of Jews whose representatives even offered to accept mass baptism. . . . Jews did not even want to be emancipated as a whole; all they wanted was to escape from Jewishness, as individuals if possible. (*RH*, 7)

The question of politics was not only "wholly unknown to this generation of Jews"; it played scarcely any role in Arendt's analysis of Rahel and her times.

The precise meaning of politics was still quite inchoate and programmatic for Arendt during the 1930s and 1940s. Her own quest to understand the meaning of politics began with her confrontation with the Jewish question, in particular with the failure of the Jewish people to assume political responsibility. Initially, Arendt emphasized the need for the Jewish people to fight for their political rights as a people in alliance with other oppressed peoples. But even here she was vague about what this meant and how it was to be achieved. At the very moment when she was being educated in politics, the rise of Nazi totalitarianism was posing a serious threat to the very possibility of any effective political action. In her grappling with the structure and dynamics of Nazi totalitarianism, Arendt refined her own understanding of politics. The point I want to emphasize here is that Arendt's original interest in politics arose in her struggle with the Jewish question. Her critique of Jewish-German assimilation led her to the conviction that the only proper "solution" to the Jewish question in the modern age was a political one, requiring a political response by the Jews themselves. Her early distinction between social assimilation and political emancipation shaped even her mature understanding of politics. But Arendt also argued that throughout their history, the Jewish people had avoided political action.

In 1952, after Arendt had published *The Origins of Totalitarianism*, she sent Karl Jaspers the manuscript of her Varnhagen biography in order to solicit his opinion about its publication. The exchange between them is extraordinarily revealing, not only because of Jaspers's perceptive and penetrating criticisms, but also because of Arendt's own retrospective evaluation of her manuscript.

Jaspers and Arendt first corresponded about the book in 1930 when she started working on it, and she sent him a preliminary lecture outlining how she planned to deal with Rahel's struggle with her Jewish identity. Jaspers expressed his doubts about this way of telling Rahel's life story (as he did again in 1952). He wrote:

> You objectify "Jewish existence" existentially – and in doing so perhaps cut existential thinking off at the roots. The concept of being-thrown-back-on-oneself can no longer be taken altogether seriously if it is *grounded* in terms of the fate of the Jews instead of being rooted in itself. (*C*, 10)

Arendt, who was 24 at the time, defended herself thus:

> I was not trying to "ground" Rahel's existence in terms of Jewishness – or at least I was not conscious of doing so. This lecture is only a *preliminary* work meant to show that on the foundation of being Jewish a certain possibility of existence *can* arise that I have tentatively and for the time being called fatefulness. (*C*, 11)

Although this exchange is heavily laden with the existential idiom shared at the time by Jaspers and his student, the point of Jaspers's reservations is clear. He was uneasy about the central place that Arendt gave to Rahel's struggle with her Jewishness in narrating her life story. Jaspers reiterated this criticism again in 1952, and even related his criticism to Arendt's own confrontation with her Jewish identity.

After praising the manuscript as "powerful and significant" and as containing "pages of extraordinary profundity," he launches into a sharp critique. He writes that "this work still seems to me to be your own working through of the basic questions of Jewish existence, and in it you use Rahel's reality as a guide to help you achieve clarity and liberation for yourself." He speaks of the "peculiar mood of the whole work," as if "Rahel [has] wakened neither your interest nor your love." "No *picture of Rahel* herself emerges but only, so to speak, a picture of the events that chose this individual as their vehicle" (*C*, 192).

> I think it likely that you could do Rahel greater justice today, mainly because you would see her not just in the context of the Jewish question but, rather, in keeping with Rahel's own intentions and reality, as a human being in whose life the Jewish problem played a very large role but by no means the only one. (*C*, 192)

Jaspers thinks not only that Arendt's view of Rahel is "loveless," but that Arendt judges isolated actions too harshly and moralistically. "Your book can make one feel that if a person is a Jew he cannot really live his life to the full" (*C*, 194).

The frankness of Jaspers's critique was written in the spirit of trust that Arendt and Jaspers so valued in their friendship. She responded in the same open, honest manner. Before taking up Jaspers's specific criticisms, she says that in view of his reaction she has decided not to publish the book.[14]

> It's my view that many of the things I say in the book should have been said publicly before 1933 (perhaps as late as 1938). They could have been said, at any rate, and they would not only have done no harm but might even have done some good. I think, too, that at some time, perhaps when this generation of German Jews, which will not be followed by any more, is dead, it will be possible to say these things again. (*C*, 197)

Jaspers expressed his apprehension that "your book in its present form is a bonanza for anti-Semites" (*C*, 195–6). Arendt was not concerned about this.

> I am afraid that people of goodwill will see a connection, which does not in fact exist, between these things and the eradication of the Jews. All this was capable of fostering social hatred of the Jews and did foster it, just as it fostered, on the other side, a specifically German breed of Zionism. The truly totalitarian phenomenon – and genuine political anti-Semitism before it – had hardly anything to do with all this. And precisely that is what I did not know when I wrote this book. It was written from the perspective of a Zionist critique of assimilation, which I had adopted as my own and which I still consider basically justified today. *But that critique was as politically naive as what it was criticizing.* (*C*, 197, emphasis added)

This comment is important for several reasons. Arendt draws a sharp distinction between "*social* hatred of the Jews" and "*political* anti-Semitism." This is not a distinction she makes explicitly in her biography. It became central for her when she sought to comprehend the "origins" of Nazi totalitarianism. She remained skeptical about the possibility of ever eliminating social discrimination and social hatred of the Jews. But such discrimination becomes dangerous only when it is used for political oppression and extermination.[15] When Arendt wrote her book, she did not make any systematic distinction between social and political anti-Semitism. Retrospectively, she emphasizes that Rahel, like most secular German Jews, understood anti-Semitism primarily as a social phenomenon – the exclusion of Jews from society. From this perspective, emancipation meant emancipation from one's Jewishness and acceptance by society. This was conceived to be not a collective project of Jews, but rather a personal, individual project that required distancing oneself from the Jewish people and becoming the "privileged," or "exceptional," Jew. Rahel and her Jewish contemporaries, like so many generations of Jews before her (and like most German Jews after her), were politically naive. This naiveté was all the more blinding in that the very historical conditions that determined the context and problematic of social assimilation also provided the opportunity to claim political rights for the Jews as Jews. But European Jewry never fully grasped this possibility or assumed political responsibility for its own destiny. Arendt speaks of her own critique of assimilation as "politically naive" because, when writing the book, she herself did not fully grasp the meaning of, and difference between, *social assimilation* and *political emancipation*. The above passage also helps us to understand what initially attracted Arendt to Zionism when she fled Germany for France. Arendt never subscribed to what she called "Zionist ideology" (or any other ideology). She was certainly not moved by any religious appeals for the return to Zion. Nor did she share the emotional pull and enthusiasm of so many secular Zionists. Zionism was the only serious movement that appreciated the need for a political solution to the Jewish question. Yet Arendt was also ambivalent about Zionism, because she had serious reservations about Zionist politics. These doubts and reservations were to become increasingly manifest.

Arendt says that she wrote her book from "the perspective of a Zionist critique of assimilation"; but it is more accurate to say that she was working out her own distinctive critique of German-Jewish assimilation. Assimilation is a social phenomenon that obscures political realities. It also hides the need for a political response to the injustices that the Jewish people have suffered.

In direct response to what seems to be Jaspers's most devastating criticism, she declares:

You're absolutely right when you say this book "can make one feel that if a person is a Jew he cannot really live his life to the full." And that is of course a central point. I still believe today that under the conditions of social assimilation and political emancipation the Jews could not "live." Rahel's life seems to me a proof of that precisely because she tried out everything on herself without attempting to spare herself anything and without a trace of dishonesty. What always intrigued me about her was the phenomenon of life striking her like "rain pouring down on someone without an umbrella." That's why, it seems to me, her life illustrates everything with such clarity. And that's also what made her so insufferable. (*C*, 198)

Arendt is reaffirming a central thesis of her book. For in this context, "political emancipation" means "legal" emancipation – granting rights to Jews as (abstract) individuals, not as Jews. Arendt objected not only to the notion of abstract human rights, but also to the abstract conception of humanity. In her 1959 lecture "On Humanity in Dark Times: Thoughts about Lessing," which she delivered when she was awarded the Lessing Prize by the city of Hamburg, she stated:

I so explicitly stress my membership in the group of Jews expelled from Germany at a relatively early age because I wish to anticipate certain misunderstandings which can arise only too easily when one speaks of humanity. In this connection I cannot gloss over the fact that for many years I considered the only adequate reply to the question, Who are you? to be: A Jew. That answer alone took into account the reality of persecution. As for the statement with which Nathan the Wise (in effect, though not in actual wording) countered the command: "Step closer, Jew" – the statement: I am a man – I would have considered as nothing but a grotesque and dangerous evasion of reality. (*MD*, 17–18)

Only gradually was Arendt herself coming to the realization that such legal emancipation is not genuine political emancipation. To say, then, that under conditions of social assimilation and political (i.e. legal) emancipation, the Jews cannot "live" means that they cannot live *as Jews*. This echoes Arendt's remark that " 'when one is attacked as a Jew, one must defend oneself as a Jew.' Not as a German, not as a world-citizen, not as an upholder of the Rights of Man." It indicates Arendt's dissatisfaction with the classical liberal tradition. The dark side of this tradition is its intolerance and hostility to recognizing the Jews as a distinctive people and not just a collection of abstract individuals with a private religion.

There is a background issue here that needs to be made explicit, for it hovers over much of Arendt's discussion of the Jewish question. It is an issue that I do not think she ever resolved adequately. What is it that characterizes a people as a people? Specifically, what is it that characterizes the Jews as Jews? What is the *normative* basis for claiming political rights and recognition of the Jews as Jews? Sometimes it seems as if Arendt simply takes the existence of the Jewish people as a historical fact and then concerns herself with the social and political questions about the history, responsibility, and destiny of that people. But this is to avoid the question of Jewish identity, not to answer it. It is not satisfactory to fall back upon the "factual" existence of the Jewish people. For, to use her own, later terminology, this does not illuminate the *meaning* of being a Jew. Arendt rarely considers the religious significance of being a Jew – what she calls "Judaism" as distinct from "Jewishness." In responding to Jaspers, who assumes "something like a more or less unbroken tradition of Judaism in which Rahel would have her place," Arendt introduces a strained, idiosyncratic, and unpersuasive distinction between "Judaism," or "Jewish substance," and "Jewishness."

> Judaism doesn't exist outside orthodoxy on the one hand or outside the Yiddish-speaking, folklore-producing Jewish people on the other. There are also people of Jewish background who are unaware of any Jewish substance in their lives in the sense of a tradition and who for certain social reasons and because they found themselves constituting a clique within society produced something like a "Jewish type." This type has nothing to do with what we understand under Judaism historically or with its genuine content. Here there is much that is positive, namely, all those things that I classify as pariah qualities and what Rahel called the "true realities of life" – "love, trees, children, music." In this type there is an extraordinary awareness of injustices; there is great generosity and a lack of prejudice; and there is – more questionably but nonetheless demonstrably present – respect for the "life of the mind." Of all these things only the last one can still be shown to have a link with originally and specifically Jewish substance. . . . The negative "Jewish" qualities have nothing to do with Judaism in this sense and all derive from parvenu stories. Rahel is "interesting" because, with utter naiveté and utterly unprejudiced, she stands right in the middle between pariah and parvenu. (*C*, 199–200)

One must be extremely cautious about placing excessive weight on a passage in a letter to a trusted friend which was never intended for publication. Nevertheless, the claims that Arendt makes here are consistent with her published writings. Her remarks are perplexing, troubling, and evasive. The distinction she makes between "Judaism," or "Jewish substance," and "Jewishness" is extremely problematic. Can one so easily separate "Judaism" from "Jewishness"? What precisely constitutes Jewishness if it is dissociated from Judaism? What is the basis for claiming that Jews are a distinctive people or nation who *ought* to be acknowledged and recognized? What is the basis for claiming rights as Jews (and not solely as individual citizens)? At times it seems that Arendt avoids the hard questions of Jewish identity. She takes the existence of the Jewish people as a "historical fact," and then concerns herself with the social and political implications of this fact.

Arendt herself was scathing in her criticism of those who merely affirmed their belief in the "Jewish people." When Arendt was in Jerusalem in 1961, attending the Eichmann trial, she had a conversation "with a prominent political personality who was defending the – in my opinion disastrous – non-separation of religion and state in Israel."[16] She reports this conversation in her letter to Gershom Scholem.

> What he said – I am not sure of the exact words anymore – ran something like this: "You will understand that, as a Socialist, I, of course, do not believe in God; I believe in the Jewish people." I found this a shocking statement and, being too shocked, I did not reply at the time. But I could have answered: the greatness of this people was once that it believed in God, and believed in Him in such a way that its trust and love towards Him was greater than its fear. And now this people believes only in itself? What good can come out of that? (*JP*, 247)

Arendt may have been genuinely shocked. But she herself does not grapple with the question of what is the substance of one's Jewish identity, what it is that constitutes the Jewish people when one no longer believes in a God "where trust and love towards Him is greater than one's fear." To assert, as Arendt does, that "I merely belong to [the Jewish people] as a matter of course, beyond dispute or argument" (*JP*, 247), is not to answer the question of Jewish identity, but to evade it.

Once Arendt positively affirmed herself as a Jew, she wanted to understand the social and political significance of being a member of the Jewish people. She had little interest in, or feeling for, the religious aspects of Judaism – except insofar as they affected political questions. This is not even the primary problem here. It is, rather, Arendt's failure to grapple seriously with the relation of "Judaism" to "Jewishness," to confront the issue of what makes the Jewish people a distinctive people or nation who have a legitimate claim to be recognized as a people.

The thinness of Arendt's understanding of Judaism and Jewishness is evidenced in her Rahel biography. It is one of the reasons why even her most sympathetic critics expressed reservations about her claim that the Jewish question was so central for Rahel. Arendt tells Rahel's story as a lifelong struggle with her Jewish identity. For most of her adult life, Rahel sought to escape the "curse" of being born a Jew. She sought to become a parvenu, yet rebelled against the lying and deceitfulness required in order to be assimilated to (Gentile) society. Rahel's triumph was her rebellion against becoming a parvenu and her affirmation of herself as a pariah. But when we closely examine what Arendt says in the final two chapters of her book, "Between Pariah and Parvenu" and "One Does Not Escape Jewishness," it becomes clear that Arendt was much more insightful about the parvenu and pariah as ideal *human* types than about the *Jewishness* of these types. She is fascinated by the pariah as outsider, the outsider who freely accepts this outsider status as a positive challenge. Even when she seeks to clarify the sense in which Rahel becomes a rebel, she stresses her identification with her non-Jewish friend Pauline Wiesel, who "exercised utter freedom in placing herself outside the pale of respectable society because her temperamental and untamable nature would submit to no conventions" (*RH*, 208). This is what attracted Rahel to Pauline, and it is what Arendt herself so admired. But it is not entirely clear what is the intrinsic relation between being "free," "rebellious," "an outsider," and being Jewish. After all, these are also characteristics of others who are stigmatized as pariahs but refuse to accept passively the status ascribed to them. To put the issue in a slightly different way, what was Rahel affirming when she declared on her deathbed that she on "no account wished to have missed" what had seemed to have been "the misery and misfortune of my life – having been born a Jewess"? Arendt has very little to say about this, and what she does say is hardly convincing. Arendt declares that Rahel "had walked down all the roads that could lead her into the alien world, and upon all these roads she had left her track, had converted them into Jewish roads, pariah roads" (*RH*,

222). But Arendt does not spell out for us what made these *Jewish* roads.

Arendt concludes her biography in what might seem a curious manner. She introduces the figure of Heinrich Heine, whom Rahel met in 1821 when she was 50 and Heine was 23. Arendt tells us that Rahel "hailed young Heine with enthusiasm and great friendship – 'only galley slaves know one another' " (*RH*, 227). Heine was a poet for whom Arendt herself had enormous affection. (She would frequently cite his poetry by heart.)

> Heine's affirmation of Jewishness, the first and last resolute affirmation which was heard from an assimilated Jew for a long time, derived from the same reasons and the same feeling for truth as Rahel's negation. Both had never been able to accept their destiny serenely; both had never attempted to hide it behind big words or boastful phrases; both had always demanded an accounting and had never gone in for "prudent silence and patiently Christian suffering" (Heine). (*RH*, 227)

According to Arendt, it was Heine who promised to be "enthusiastic for the cause of the Jews and their attainment of equality before the law." And, "with this promise spoken, Rahel could die with a peaceful heart. She left behind her an heir on whom she had much to bestow: the history of a bankruptcy and a rebellious spirit" (*RH*, 227–8). This ending to the biography is a bit forced. Heine had very little to do with Rahel's lifestory. But in suggesting that Heine was Rahel's heir, Arendt introduces a theme that was to become increasingly important for her – that there was a hidden tradition in modern Jewish history – the tradition of the Jew as pariah.

During her Paris years (1933–41) and her early years in New York, the distinction between the parvenu and the pariah became enriched and more nuanced in Arendt's thinking and writings. The parvenu as a Jewish type is not limited to the social aspirations to assimilate to society. As a type, the parvenu takes on new forms in those "privileged" Jews who always seek to accommodate themselves to existing social and political conditions – and who even inhibit genuine political action by the Jewish people. It was in Paris, where Arendt was engaged in practical work for several Zionist organizations, that she had her first encounters with wealthy Jewish philanthropists. She argued that there was a serious failure of Jewish leadership in Europe because the so-called leaders sought to avoid and even suppress

Jewish political activity. Many of these wealthy Jews exhibited parvenu tendencies. It was not so much that they sought to escape their Jewish identity as that they sought accommodation to, and acceptance by, society. Like Bernard Lazare, Arendt was disdainful of this privileged wealthy strata of Jews who were constantly tempted by parvenu aspirations. Her own experiences in Paris, and her study of the Dreyfus affair and its legacy, convinced her of the soundness of Lazare's observation that the real obstacle in the path of his people's emancipation was not primarily anti-Semitism itself. It was "the demoralization of a people made up of the poor and downtrodden, who live on the alms of their wealthy brethren, a people revolted only by persecution from without but not by oppression from within, revolutionaries in the society of others but not in their own."[17] Later we will explore how Arendt sided with Lazare in his dispute with Herzl concerning Jewish politics and the future of Zionism. Like Lazare, Arendt "did not share Herzl's idea that politics must be conducted from above" (*DA*, 239). Unlike Herzl, who even declared that "it is anti-semites who will be our staunchest friends, and the antisemitic countries which will be our allies" (*DA*, 238, n. 157), Lazare advocated (without any success) "not an escape from antisemitism but a mobilization of the people against its foes." "The consequence of this attitude was that he did not look around for more or less antisemitic protectors but for real comrades-in-arms, whom he hoped to find among all the oppressed groups of contemporary Europe" (*DA*, 238). Arendt was drawn to Lazare's portrait of the conscious pariah who seeks to fight for the political justice and equality of the Jewish people. In her Rahel biography, it was the pariah as outsider and rebel that she portrays, but she does not explicitly explore the political significance of the *conscious pariah*. During her Paris and early New York years, when she was undergoing her own political education, this aspect of her thinking became dominant.

There is still a prevailing bias among many of Arendt's critics and defenders that her understanding of politics was based primarily on her (idealized) account of the Greek *polis* and the Roman *res publica*. This is understandable if one focuses primarily on *The Human Condition*. But one should not forget that *The Human Condition* was published in 1958, when Arendt was 52. Her political education had begun 25 years earlier, and her primary concern had been to understand Jewish politics – or, rather, the failures of Jewish politics.

It was her reflections on this phenomenon that initially led her to advocate a politics from below, a politics that emerges spontaneously among a people who assume responsibility for their actions. This strand in her thinking, which first emerged in her analysis of Jewish politics, persisted and oriented her thinking when she turned to analyzing the meaning of politics in *The Human Condition*. Although Arendt stressed the need for a political solution to the Jewish question, when she turned her attention to the "origins" and distinctive character of Nazi totalitarianism, she became painfully aware that the dynamic of this totalitarianism was to destroy systematically and eliminate the very possibility of the type of political action she was describing and advocating. Most of the motifs of her understanding of politics which became fully explicit in *The Human Condition* are worked out in her attempt to comprehend the events of twentieth-century totalitarianism.

When Arendt started publishing articles in English, soon after her arrival in New York, she returned to a theme that she had sketched at the very end of her (still unpublished) biography of Rahel Varnhagen – the hidden tradition of the Jewish pariah. She outlined her thesis in an article entitled, "We Refugees" (January 1943).

> Modern Jewish history, having started with court Jews and continuing with Jewish millionaires and philanthropists, is apt to forget about this other trend of Jewish tradition – the tradition of Heine, Rahel Varnhagen, Sholom Aleichem, of Bernard Lazare, Franz Kafka or even Charlie Chaplin. It is the tradition of a minority of Jews who have not wanted to become upstarts, who preferred the status of "conscious pariah." All vaunted Jewish qualities – the "Jewish heart," humanity, humor, disinterested intelligence – are pariah qualities. All Jewish shortcomings – tactlessness, political stupidity, inferiority complexes and money-grubbing – are characteristics of upstarts. (*JP*, 65–6)

Arendt explored this hidden tradition in greater depth in an article that summarized her thinking about the parvenu and the Jewish pariah.[18] Once again she condemned those Jews who falsely believe that Jewish emancipation is "a permit to ape the gentiles or an opportunity to play the *parvenu*." Jewish emancipation requires "an admission of Jews *as Jews* to the ranks of humanity" (*JP*, 68).

In characterizing this tradition of the Jewish pariah, she writes:

In their own position as social outcasts such men reflect the political status of their entire people. It is therefore not surprising that out of their personal experience Jewish poets, writers and artists should have been able to evolve the concept of the pariah as a human type – a concept of supreme importance for the evaluation of mankind in our day and one which had exerted upon the gentile world an influence in strange contrast to the spiritual and political ineffectiveness which has been the fate of these men among their own brethren. (*JP*, 68)

The distinction between "the social" and "the political" is employed here to characterize the Jews as a pariah people. But now the nuances of the pariah as a human type emerge more sharply. Arendt is primarily concerned with types of *response* and strategies of *resistance* to the outcast status of the Jews as a pariah people. She highlights how pariahs reflect "the political status of their entire people" and analyzes four exemplars of this tradition, each of which "expresses an alternative portrayal of the Jewish people."

Our first type will be Heinrich Heine's *schlemihl* and "lord of dreams" (*Traumweltherrscher*); our second, Bernard Lazare's "conscious pariah"; our third, Charlie Chaplin's grotesque portrayal of the suspect; and our fourth, Franz Kafka's poetic vision of the fate of the man of goodwill. Between these four types there is a significant connection – a link which in fact unites all genuine concepts and sound ideas when once they achieve historical actuality. (*JP*, 69)

Let me first sketch the first and third types, the "schlemihl" and the "suspect," before turning to Lazare's "conscious pariah" and Kafka's "man of goodwill." The observations Arendt makes about the latter two types are especially relevant for comprehending both her own self-understanding as a pariah among a pariah people and her central preoccupations with both politics and independent thinking.

Arendt admired Heine for his irony, his gift for mockery, his exuberance and simple *joie de vivre*, "which one finds everywhere in children and in common people – that passion which makes them revel in tales and romances" (*JP*, 71). Innocence is the hallmark of the schlemihl.[19] But it is of such innocence that a people's poet, its "lord of dreams," is born. It is Heine's sense of "natural freedom" that is so attractive, a freedom expressed in his "cheerful insouciance" and his refusal to become cynical or bitter. It is this spontaneous sense of freedom that Arendt took to be a common link among the various forms of the pariah as a "human type."

It is this aloofness of the pariah from all the works of man that Heine regards as the essence of freedom. It is this aloofness that accounts for the divine laughter and the absence of bitterness in his verses. He was the first Jew to whom freedom meant more than mere "liberation from the house of bondage" and in whom it was combined, in equal measure, with the traditional Jewish passion for justice. To Heine, freedom had little to do with liberation from a just or unjust yoke. (*JP*, 72)

Arendt here anticipates a distinction that was to become one of the major distinctions of her political thinking and her critical analysis of modernity. It is the distinction between liberty and freedom. Liberty for Arendt is always liberty *from* – from bondage, from oppression, from poverty, from biological necessity. But liberty is not to be confused or identified with the positive tangible freedom that comes into existence only when human beings act together and create the public spaces in which genuine politics flourishes. Jewish emancipation is not to be reduced to, or identified with, "liberation from the house of bondage." Such liberation is a necessary condition only (and not a sufficient condition) for the emergence of public political freedom. This is the thesis that she developed in *The Human Condition* and *On Revolution*. According to Arendt, one of the great disasters of modernity is the tendency to confuse liberty with freedom. But her first intimations of this confusion arose in her attempt to understand Jewish emancipation. Heine's joyful sense of "natural freedom" is not yet a fully articulated concept of political freedom – but it has political significance.

Just because [Heine] refused to give up his allegiance to a people of pariahs and schlemihls, just because he remained consistently attached to them, he takes his place among the most uncompromising of Europe's fighters for freedom – of which, alas, Germany has produced so few. (*JP*, 75)

Heine also mocked the illusion that "Jews could exist as 'pure human beings' outside the range of peoples and nations": "He simply ignored the condition which had characterized emancipation everywhere in Europe – namely, that the Jew might only become a man when he ceased to be a Jew. Because he held this position he was able to do what so few of his contemporaries could – to speak the language of a free man and sing the songs of a natural one" (*JP*, 75).

It is clear why Arendt so admired Heine and assigned him such a prominent place in the tradition of the Jew as pariah. It is his sense of independence, his refusal to be intimidated by dogmas and conventions, that she so thoroughly admired. "It was Heine's achievement to recognize in the figure of the *schlemihl* the essential kinship of the pariah to the poet – both alike excluded from society and never quite at home in this world – and to illustrate by this analogy the position of the Jew in the world of European culture" (*JP*, 76). Arendt praises Heine because he never lost touch with his own people, and he refused to give up his allegiance to a people of pariahs and schlemihls. Arendt even claims that Heine is the "only outstanding example of a really happy assimilation in the entire history of that process." "He is the only German Jew who could truthfully describe himself as both a German and a Jew." He "put into practice that true blending of cultures of which others merely talked" (*JP*, 74). Unlike the typical German-Jewish assimilationists who zealously avoided any reference to their own Jewishness, Heine celebrated the "homespun Judaism of everyday life."

When Arendt sketches the figure of Charlie Chaplin's "suspect," she reiterates a thesis that we have already encountered, one which was becoming dominant in her analysis of the history of the Jewish people – their lack of political sense, insight and activity:

> While lack of political sense and persistence in the obsolete system of making charity the basis of national unity have prevented the Jewish people from taking a positive part in the political life of our day, these very qualities, translated into dramatic forms, have inspired one of the most singular products of modern art – the films of Charlie Chaplin. . . . In his very first film, Chaplin portrayed the chronic plight of the little man who is incessantly harried and hectored by the guardians of law and order – the representatives of society. (*JP*, 79)[20]

The pariah as "suspect" is also a schlemihl, but not the visionary type portrayed by Heine. Chaplin's world is one "from which neither nature nor art can provide an escape and against whose slings and arrows the only armor is one's wits or the kindness and humanity of casual acquaintances" (*JP*, 79). Arendt draws a parallel between the pariah as suspect and the refugee as a "stateless person" who is always under suspicion no matter what he does.

> Long before the refugee was to become, in the guise of the "stateless," the living symbol of the pariah, long before men and women were to be

forced in their thousands to depend for their bare existence on their wits or the chance kindness of others, Chaplin's own childhood had taught him two things. On the one hand, it had taught him the traditional Jewish fear of the "cop" – that seeming incarnation of a hostile world; but on the other, it had taught him the time-honored Jewish truth that, other things being equal, the human ingenuity of a David can sometimes outmatch the animal strength of a Goliath. (*JP*, 79–80)

The weapons of the schlemihl and the suspect are wit, humor, ingenuity, insouciance. These are the weapons by which these exemplars of the pariah seek to thwart and neutralize a hostile world. Both types reflect the condition of the Jews as pariah people; both mock the world of parvenus and the society to which they seek to be assimilated: thus both have potential political significance, although there are also differences between the suspect and the schlemihl.

Basically, the impudence of Chaplin's suspect is of the same kind as charms us so much in Heine's *schlemihl*; but no longer is it carefree and unperturbed, no longer the divine effrontery of the poet who consorts with heavenly things and can therefore afford to thumb noses at earthly society. On the contrary, it is a worried, careworn impudence – the kind so familiar to generations of Jews, the effrontery of the poor "little Yid" who does not recognize the class order of the world because he sees in it neither order nor justice for himself. (*JP*, 81)

Arendt was able to write with such insight and sensitivity about Heine and Chaplin because she could so easily identify with traits of the pariah types she portrayed. She herself exhibited the independence, the sense of "natural freedom," of Heine's "lord of dreams." She had also spent many years living as a stateless person who is never quite at home in the world and is always under suspicion by the "representatives of society." But for Arendt, it was Lazare's great achievement to make fully explicit the political significance of the Jew as pariah. The Jew as pariah must become the "conscious pariah."

[H]e knew where the solution lay: in contrast to his unemancipated brethren who accept their pariah status automatically and unconsciously, the emancipated Jew must awake to an awareness of his position and, conscious of it, become a rebel against it – the champion of an oppressed people. His fight for freedom is part and parcel of that which all the down-trodden of Europe must needs wage to achieve national and social liberation. (*JP*, 76)

Lazare insisted upon the need "to rouse the Jewish pariah to fight against the Jewish parvenu." The Jew must abandon his "double slavery" – "dependence, on the one hand, upon the hostile elements of his environment and, on the other, on his own 'highly-placed brethren' who are somehow in league with them" (*JP*, 77). Long before the grotesque turn that this was to take with the Nazis, Lazare saw clearly how the enemies of the Jews used Jews themselves to control and oppress the Jewish people.

> His experience of French politics had taught him that whenever the enemy seeks control, he makes a point of using some oppressed element of the population as his lackeys and henchmen, rewarding them with special privileges, as a kind of sop. (*JP*, 77)

Arendt could scarcely have anticipated the furor she would create when she made an analogous point about the infamous Jewish councils that were created by the Nazis in order to control, organize, and carry out Nazi orders. She also shared Lazare's judgment about the failures of those wealthy Jews who had assumed roles of leadership in the Jewish community. Although Arendt is writing about Lazare, she could just as well be speaking in her own voice:

> As soon as the pariah enters the arena of politics, and translates his status into political terms, he becomes perforce a rebel. Lazare's idea was, therefore, that the Jew should come out openly as the representative of the pariah, "since it is the duty of every human being to resist oppression." He demanded, that is, that the pariah relinquish once for all the prerogative of the *schlemihl*, cut loose from the world of fancy and illusion, renounce the comfortable protection of nature, and come to grips with the world of men and women. In other words, he wanted him to feel that he was himself responsible for what society had done to him. He wanted him to stop seeking release in an attitude of superior indifference or in lofty and rarefied cogitation about the nature of man *per se*. However much the Jewish pariah might be, from the historical viewpoint, the product of an unjust dispensation ... politically speaking, every pariah who refused to be a rebel was partly responsible for his own position and therewith for the blot on mankind which it represented. (*JP*, 77)

These are strong words, but they express Arendt's deepest commitments. According to Arendt, Lazare's failure to arouse his fellow Jews was not primarily because of the organized opposition of wealthy parvenu Jews, but because the "pariah simply refused to become a rebel."

The theme that emerges here was to become one of the dominant and most misunderstood themes in Arendt's political thinking. Initially it is shocking – and even scandalous – to assert that the Jew as pariah is "to feel that he was responsible for what society had done to him." This sounds as if she is blaming the victims for their sufferings. This is *not* what Arendt means. She is not echoing what anti-Semites have always alleged: that the Jews themselves are responsible for the attacks upon them. But neither does she think it sufficient to view the Jews as "innocent victims." It is not moral responsibility or guilt that is her concern here, but *political* responsibility. The central issue for Arendt is how the Jews *have* responded and how they *can* (and ought to) respond when they are treated as outcasts and denied their political rights. Arendt rejects any and all forms of historical determinism or arguments from necessity claiming that one's *response* as a Jew is determined by forces beyond one's control. There is a blending of philosophical and political insights. Even in the darkest of times, the question of one's response and responsibility can and must be raised. There is the possibility to initiate, to begin, to act. This is what Arendt later called "natality" (and what totalitarian regimes sought to eradicate). Long before she analyzed these capacities in *The Human Condition*, she discerned how they were fundamental for the problem (and failure) of Jewish politics in the modern age. The Jews must become aware of their political responsibility. They must break with, and defy, the tradition of passive sufferers in order to become responsible political actors. They must become rebels who do not accommodate themselves to anti-Semitism but who fight for their political rights as Jews. They must even fight against those Jewish parvenus who inhibit genuine, risky political action. They must join with their fellow Jews and form alliances with other oppressed peoples in their fight for justice. They must frankly recognize the self-deceitful and self-defeating character of assimilation as a form of Jewish suicide. They must defend themselves as Jews when attacked as Jews.

Arendt's reflections on the need for a radical Jewish politics came sharply into focus at the very time when such a politics no longer seemed to be a real historical possibility. Toward the end of her analysis of the hidden tradition of the Jew as pariah, with an allusion to the "political realities" of 1944, she openly wonders whether the life of the pariah (or the parvenu) makes sense any longer in light of the mass murder and extermination of European Jewry.

> Today the bottom has dropped out of the old ideology. The pariah Jew and the *parvenu* Jew are in the same boat, rowing desperately in the same angry sea. Both are branded with the same mark; both alike are outlaws. Today the truth has come home: there is no protection in heaven or earth against bare murder, and a man can be driven at any moment from the streets and broad places once open to all. At long last, it has become clear that the "senseless freedom" of the individual merely paves the way for the senseless suffering of his entire people. (*JP*, 90)

Arendt comes close to expressing her despair about the fate of the pariah and the parvenu in the face of the senseless suffering of her people. But this is not quite her final word. She does not flinch from trying to comprehend the full horror of what was happening to her people. She never abandons the promise and hope grounded in human natality, the human capacity to begin anew. She expresses this many times, perhaps most eloquently in her concluding remarks of *The Origins of Totalitarianism*, where she cites one of her favorite passages from Augustine.

> But there remains also the truth that every end in history necessarily contains a new beginning; this beginning is the promise, the only "message" which the end can ever produce. Beginning, before it becomes a historical event, is the supreme capacity of man; politically, it is identical with man's freedom. *Initium ut esset homo creatus est* – "that a beginning be made man was created" said Augustine. This beginning is guaranteed by each new birth; it is indeed every man. (*OT₃*, 478–9)

Arendt explores a fourth variation of the Jew as pariah. This is what she calls Kafka's "man of good will." For Arendt, as for many other European Jews of her generation, Kafka is the poet/novelist who had an uncanny sense of the desperate predicament of the twentieth-century reality for European Jewry. In her analysis of Kafka's early story *Description of a Fight* and his novel *The Castle*, Arendt enriches her portrait of the Jew as pariah.

Earlier I indicated that in the Rahel biography, society – the society to which Rahel desperately seeks to belong when she is tempted by her aspirations – is "high society," those vestiges of aristocratic society to which one is born or from which one is excluded by birth. But there are other strands involved in Arendt's reflections on society. Arendt thought that Kafka's understanding of the meaning of society in the twentieth century was far more penetrating than that of many sociologists. Her own analysis of society and the social was significantly influenced by Kafka's dark vision. Commenting on *Description of a Fight*, she writes:

> Society, we are told, is composed of "nobodies" – "I did wrong to nobody, nobody did wrong to me; but nobody will help me, nothing but nobodies," – and has therefore no real existence. Nevertheless, even the pariah, who is excluded from it, cannot account himself lucky, since society keeps up the pretense that it is somebody and he nobody, that it is "real" and he "unreal." (*JP*, 82)

The greatest injury that society inflicts on the pariah is to make him doubt his own existence; "to reduce him in his own eyes to the status of a nonentity." Kafka was able to capture this sense of society as composed of "nobodies" which nevertheless has the power to make the outsider doubt his own reality. What Kafka portrayed imaginatively was to become all too grotesquely real when the Nazis treated the Jews as if they were "nobodies" – superfluous and unreal. With Kafka's "twentieth-century sense of reality" neither nature nor art can any longer provide an escape for the despised pariah Jew who is "dismissed by contemporary society as a nobody."[21]

> Neither the freedom of the *schlemihl* and poet nor the innocence of the suspect nor the escape into nature and art, but thinking is the new weapon – the only one with which, in Kafka's opinion, the pariah is endowed at birth in his vital struggle against society. (*JP*, 83)

Arendt does not pause to explain what she means by *thinking*, although, in passing, she notes that it is "the use of this contemplative faculty as an instrument of self-preservation that characterizes Kafka's conception of the pariah." This motif of thinking as a weapon of the pariah surfaces again and again in her writings. It is only in the posthumously published *The Life of the Mind* that she explicitly thematizes the meaning of thinking as one of the primary faculties of that life. But at crucial stages in her writings she touches on the vital significance of thinking. She begins *The Human Condition* by telling us:

"what I propose, therefore, is very simple: it is nothing more than to think what we are doing" (*HC*, 5). Even though she does not focus on thinking in her examination of the *vita activa*, she concludes her book with the tantalizing remark that "if no other test but the experience of being active, no other measure but the extent of sheer activity were to be applied to the various activities within the *vita activa*, it might well be that thinking as such would surpass them all" (*HC*, 325). In her preface to *Between Past and Future*, where she gives one of the most illuminating accounts of her own "exercises in political thinking," she once again does this by interpreting a parable of Kafka to show how thinking arises in the gap between past and future. Thinking for Kafka (and Arendt) is "the most vital and liveliest part of reality" (*BPF*, 10).

Independent thinking is vital for the Jew as pariah because, in a world where action, politics, and public freedom are threatened, where twentieth-century totalitarianism sets out to destroy the human conditions required for political freedom, the only "weapon" left to the pariah is her thinking. Furthermore, Arendt's own self-understanding of her "activity" is that of an independent thinker, who engages what Lessing called *Selbstdenken*.

One of the strands that runs through Arendt's characterization of the different types of pariah is the sense of freedom, and this is also true of the pariah as an independent thinker. Arendt tells us that thinking is another "mode of moving in the world of freedom."

> Of all the specific liberties which may come into our minds when we hear the word "freedom," freedom of movement is historically the oldest and also the most elementary. . . . Freedom of movement is also the indispensable condition for action, and it is in action that men primarily experience freedom in the world. When men are deprived of the public space – which is constituted by acting together and then fills of its own accord with the events and stories that develop into history – they retreat into their freedom of thought. (*MD*, 9)

Later we will consider in greater detail what Arendt means by thinking, especially in regard to "the problem of evil." She is seeking to describe a "new kind of thinking that needs no pillars and props, no standards and traditions to move freely without crutches over unfamiliar terrain" (*MD*, 10). Always risky, such thinking requires courage. It is what Arendt called "thinking without a banister" (*Denken ohne Geländer*) (*RPW*, 336). This metaphor epitomizes what she means by the kind of thinking that she sought to practice – the independent thinking of a Jewish pariah.

For all Arendt's insight into the meaning of politics, public space, power, and the freedom that comes into being when human beings act together, she never thought of herself primarily as a political actor. On the contrary, she thought that her outsider pariah status provided her with an "advantage to look at something from the outside." In 1972, at a symposium dedicated to her work in which she participated, when pressed to clarify her stance on the relation of thinking to (political) acting, she responded:

> You see, with the political business I had a certain advantage. I, by nature, am not an actor. If I tell you that I never was either a socialist or a communist – which was absolutely a matter of course for my whole generation, so that I hardly know anybody who never committed themselves – you can see that I never felt the need to commit myself. Until finally, *schliesslich schlug mir [einer mit einem] Hammer auf den Kopf und ich fiel mir auf*: finally somebody beat me over the head and, you can say, this awakened me to the realities. But still, I had this advantage to look at something from outside. And even in myself from outside. (*RPW*, 306)

It is the pariah, then, precisely because of her status as an outsider, who has the freedom to be the independent thinker, a thinker not bound by dogmas and ideologies.

There is another aspect of Kafka's portrayal of the Jew as a pariah that Arendt highlights. In *The Castle*, the hero, K., is "plainly a Jew" not because he is characterized as having Jewish traits but, rather, because he is involved "in situations and perplexities distinctive of Jewish life." K. is "a stranger who can never be brought in line because he belongs neither to the common people nor to its rulers." He is continually charged with being superfluous, "unwanted and in everyone's way" (*JP*, 84).

Arendt sees K. as illustrating "the entire dilemma of the modern would-be assimilationist." It is Kafka who depicts "the real drama of assimilation, not its distorted counterpart." For K. does not seek to identify himself with the protection of the rulers; rather, he chooses "the alternative way – the way of good will." Kafka portrays "the average small-time Jew who really wants no more than his rights as a human being: home, work, family and citizenship" (*JP*, 85). But to seek to become "indistinguishable" from his Gentile neighbors, the

Jew has to behave as if he were utterly alone, to part company with others who are like him. So the hero of Kafka's novel tries to do what the whole world wants him to do – to renounce all his Jewish traits in order to become "individual" like everyone else! Kafka's genius is that he shows us graphically how this "experiment" works out.

> In Kafka's treatment, however, this renunciation assumes a significance for the whole problem of mankind, and not merely for the Jewish question. K., in his effort to become "indistinguishable," is interested only in universals, in things common to all mankind. His desires are directed only towards those things to which all men have a natural right. He is, in a word, the typical man of good will. (*JP*, 85)

But K. fails miserably. The more he tries to be one of the villagers, the more suspicious they become of him. He becomes increasingly isolated.

> The very fight he had put up to obtain the few basic things which society owes to men, had opened the eyes of the villagers, or at least of some of them. His story, his behavior, had taught them both that human rights are worth fighting for and that the rule of the castle is not divine law and, consequently, can be attacked. (*JP*, 88)

This is the moral that Arendt draws from Kafka's novel. For K. finally comes to understand "that the realization of his designs, the achievement of basic human rights – the right to work, to be useful, the right to found a home and become a member of society – are in no way dependent on complete assimilation to one's *milieu*, on being 'indistinguishable' " (*JP*, 87). K.'s struggle seems fruitless, and remains undecided until he dies; "he gets exhausted." But Arendt does not interpret K.'s life as a complete failure. For even if one's efforts are doomed to failure, nevertheless, "human rights are worth fighting for." We must not be seduced by the illusion that the rule of the castle is divine law, and that it cannot be attacked. Arendt claims that it was Kafka's perception of the truth that "a true human life cannot be led by people who feel themselves detached from the basic and simple laws of humanity" that made Kafka a Zionist.

> In Zionism he saw a means of abolishing the "abnormal" position of the Jews, an instrument whereby they might become "a people like other peoples." Perhaps the last of Europe's great poets, he could scarcely have wished to become a nationalist. Indeed, his whole genius,

his whole expression of the modern spirit, lay precisely in the fact that what he sought was to be a human being, a normal member of human society. It was not his fault that this society had ceased to be human, and that, trapped within its meshes, those of its members who were really men of goodwill were forced to function within it as something exceptional and abnormal – saints or madmen. (*JP*, 89)

Throughout Arendt's analysis of the hidden tradition of the Jew as pariah, there is a tension that she emphasizes constantly. The conscious pariah accepts the responsibility and challenge of being the outcast and the outsider. The pariah is a rebel and an independent thinker who rejects the type of assimilation that requires her to lose her identity and to become indistinguishable from other "abstract individuals." The Jew as a pariah knows that it is only within the framework of a people that one can live a fully human life. So, for all the freedom and independence of the pariah, her identity is bound up with being a member of her people – the Jewish people. What is emerging here is a distinctive type of humanism which is sharply critical of the very idea of an abstract universal human nature and the abstract individual and abstract human rights. Arendt saw that the most dangerous tendencies of the modern age were those that furthered this sort of abstractness and anonymity which suppresses differences. And she knew all too well how this drive toward empty universality can boomerang and explode into barbaric forms of "tribal nationalism," which grows out of an atmosphere of rootlessness.[22] The Jews as a people must resist all those tendencies that encourage them to commit suicide as a people.

> *For only within the framework of a people can a man live as a man among men, without exhausting himself. And only when a people lives and functions in consort with other peoples can it contribute to the establishment upon earth of a commonly conditioned and commonly controlled humanity.* (*JP*, 90) (emphasis added)

The great failure of the European nations during the nineteenth and twentieth centuries was the failure to learn this lesson. And the great failure of the Jews themselves was their inability to assume political responsibility, to fight for their rights as Jews, so that they might become a people living and functioning "in consort with other peoples." But assuming responsibility requires understanding political realities. Arendt's most persistent passion was to understand. When she dealt with the problem of the Jews in *Rahel Varnhagen*, she "wrote it with the idea, 'I want to understand' " (*EU*, 12). But in order to understand the tragedy of the Jewish people in the twentieth century, she needed to probe the distinctive character and origins of European political anti-Semitism. Even before Arendt fled Germany in 1933, she had begun to investigate what was distinctive and so lethal about the new varieties of anti-Semitism. Despite her turn to practical work during her years in Paris, she continued her exploration of the origins and disastrous consequences of the political anti-Semitism that erupted in the last decades of the nineteenth century.

2

Anti-Semitism as a Political Ideology

For an ideology differs from a single opinion in that it claims to possess either the key to history, or the solution of all "riddles of the universe," or the intimate knowledge of the hidden universal laws which are supposed to rule nature and man.

OT_3

In 1942, a year after Arendt arrived in New York, she published her first major article in English, "From the Dreyfus Affair to France Today."[1] She concluded the article, which was based upon research that she had begun in Paris, and subsequently revised and incorporated into *The Origins of Totalitarianism*, with a brief comparison of Lazare and Herzl. Both had witnessed the Dreyfus trial, and both were profoundly transformed by the experience. The Dreyfus affair "kindled the flame of political Zionism" (*DA*, 235). It was especially important for Arendt because it was a "prelude to Nazism," and clearly revealed a "subterranean stream of European history." The significance of the Dreyfus affair became fully manifest only in the "final crystallizing catastrophe" of Nazi totalitarianism (*OT₃*, xv).

Arendt's sympathies, as I have already indicated, were clearly with Lazare's call for a Jewish politics "from below," where the Jewish people would ally themselves with other oppressed European peoples in order to fight for their political emancipation, rather than with Herzl's presumably "more realistic" demand to work with the recognized Great Powers in order to achieve Zionist objectives. She knew, of course, that Herzl's views dominated twentieth-century Zionism whereas Lazare had become a pariah among his own people, dying in poverty and obscurity. Before contrasting the political positions of Herzl and Lazare, Arendt describes what they had in common.

Both men were turned into Jews by antisemitism. Neither concealed the fact. Both realized just because they were so "assimilated" that normal life was possible for them only on the condition that emancipation should not remain a dead letter, while they saw that in reality the Jew had become the pariah of the modern world. Both stood outside the religious tradition of Judaism and neither wished to return to it. Both were removed, as intellectuals, from those narrow and parochial Jewish cliques which had somehow grown up within the framework of gentile society. . . . When they were drawn back Judaism could no longer mean to them a religion, yet to neither could it mean a half-hearted adherence to one of many cliques. For them their Jewish origin had a political and national significance. They could find no place for themselves in Jewry unless the Jewish people was a nation. In their subsequent careers both men came into serious conflict with the forces which then controlled Jewish politics, namely, the philanthropists. In these conflicts . . . both were to learn that the Jewish people was threatened not only by the antisemites from without but also by the influence of its own "benefactors" from within. (*DA*, 236–7)

What Arendt says here about Herzl and Lazare, she might have written about herself. She too was "turned into" a Jew by anti-Semitism – although in radically different historical circumstances. When Arendt was awakened to the political realities of anti-Semitism, she affirmed her identity as a Jew. It was not Judaism as a religion that attracted her – and certainly not "those narrow and parochial Jewish cliques" which she always detested. For her, too, her Jewish origin had primarily a political significance.

To say that Arendt was "turned into" a Jew by anti-Semitism is *not* to say that she accepted the thesis that the Jew is the "creation" of the anti-Semite – that it is anti-Semitism that defines Jewish identity and even accounts for the historical persistence of the Jewish people. On the contrary, she categorically rejects this "existentialist" interpretation of the Jew as someone who is defined and regarded as a Jew by others (anti-Semites).

[E]ven a cursory knowledge of Jewish history, whose central concern since the Babylonian exile has always been the survival of the people against the overwhelming odds of dispersion, should be enough to dispel the latest myth in these matters, a myth that has become somewhat fashionable in intellectual circles after Sartre's "existentialist" interpretation of *the* Jew as someone who is regarded and defined as a Jew by others. (OT_3, xv)[2]

Arendt strongly objected to the suggestion of a symbiotic relation between the anti-Semite and the Jew because of its pernicious consequences. To claim that the Jew is someone who is defined as a Jew by others is to present the mirror image of what the Jewish parvenu so desperately wants to believe. In the parvenu's self-deceptive struggle to be accepted by the society that rejects him, he secretly hopes that others will no longer regard him as a Jew. If social anti-Semitism were to disappear (or at least no longer be directed against "exceptional Jews" like himself), then he would finally be free from experiencing the "shame" of being a Jew!

There is another consequence of this "existentialist" interpretation which Arendt finds even more dangerous. If Jewish identity is really dependent on anti-Semitism, then those Jews who are concerned to preserve Jewish identity will, overtly or covertly, be complicit in preserving anti-Semitism. Arendt was always sharply critical of those who were tempted by the idea that the anti-Semites were the secret allies of the Zionists. This is the strain in Herzl's thinking which, despite his other achievements, she singled out for her sharpest criticism. "Antisemitism far from being a mysterious guarantee of the survival of the Jewish people has been clearly revealed as a threat of its extermination" (OT_3, 8). Later we shall see that this is one of the primary reasons for her break with Zionism. She objected to the Zionists' "open acceptance of anti-Semitism as a 'fact,' and therefore a 'realistic' willingness not only to do business with the foes of the Jewish people but also to take propaganda advantage of anti-Jewish hostility" (*JP*, 135). Arendt consistently affirmed that "From the 'disgrace' of being a Jew there is but one escape – to fight for the honor of the Jewish people as a whole" (*JP*, 121). And for her, such a fight meant a political fight for the right of the Jewish people to live as Jews.

Arendt's focus on the new phenomenon of political anti-Semitism in the late nineteenth century helps to clarify what might otherwise seem to be a perplexing and idiosyncratic claim. She begins her discussion of anti-Semitism in *The Origins of Totalitarianism* by declaring:

Anti-Semitism, a secular nineteenth-century ideology – which in name, though not in argument, was unknown before the 1870s – and religious Jew-hatred, inspired by the mutually hostile antagonism of two conflicting creeds, are obviously not the same; and even the extent to which the former derives its arguments and emotional appeal from the latter is open to question. (*OT*₃, xi)

The claim that anti-Semitism "was unknown before the 1870s," if taken out of context, might seem like a perverse assertion. But Arendt is *not* speaking of "anti-Semitism" as a general term designating the varieties of religious Jew-hatred that have existed throughout history. Rather, she wants to underscore what she takes to be a new and distinctively nineteenth-century phenomenon – the emergence of a secular political ideology, an ideology that arose within the context of modern nation-states with their mass political parties and movements. What at first seemed to be only a marginal phenomenon turned out to be a powerful political weapon that was successfully employed to galvanize the masses. It is this new form and use of anti-Semitism as a *political ideology* that became so virulent and central for twentieth-century Nazi totalitarianism.

But why does Arendt begin her study of the origins of totalitarianism with an analysis of nineteenth-century political anti-Semitism? Unlike those historians and political analysts who claim that anti-Semitism was only a pretext of the Nazis "for winning the masses or an interesting device of demagogy," Arendt claims that Nazi ideology centered on anti-Semitism and that it "consistently and uncompromisingly, aimed at the persecution and finally the extermination of the Jews" (*OT*₃, 3).

In the original preface to *The Origins of Totalitarianism*, after stating that "comprehension, in short, means the unpremeditated, attentive facing up to, and resisting of reality – whatever it may be," she writes:

> In this sense, it must be possible to face and understand the outrageous fact that so small (and, in world politics so unimportant) a phenomenon as the Jewish question and antisemitism could become the catalytic agent for first, the Nazi movement, then a world war, and finally the establishment of death factories. (*OT*₃, viii)

Arendt frequently reiterates (albeit with subtle significant variations) her belief that the Jewish question was the catalytic agent for the most horrendous events of the twentieth century. In the opening chapter of *The Origins of Totalitarianism*, "Antisemitism as an Outrage of Common Sense," she wrote:

> There is hardly an aspect of contemporary history more irritating and mystifying than the fact that of all the great unsolved political questions

of our century, it should have been this seemingly small and unimportant Jewish problem that had the dubious honor of setting the
whole infernal machine in motion. Such discrepancies between cause
and effect outrage our common sense. (*OT*₃, 3)

When Arendt wrote a new preface in 1968 for the separate publication
"Antisemitism," she was even more emphatic.

Twentieth century political developments have driven the Jewish
people into the storm center of events; the Jewish question and
antisemitism, relatively unimportant phenomena in terms of world
politics, became the catalytic agent first for the rise of the Nazi
movement and the establishment of the organizational structure of the
Third Reich, in which every citizen had to prove that he was *not* a Jew,
then for a world war of unparalleled ferocity, and finally for the
emergence of the unprecedented crime of genocide in the midst of
Occidental civilization. That this called not only for lamentation and
denunciation but for comprehension seemed to me obvious. This book
is an attempt at understanding what at first and even second glance
appeared simply outrageous. (*OT*₃, xiv)

We can see how radically Arendt had changed from the days when
she found "the Jewish question" boring. She had come to believe that
it was "the catalytic agent" that had thrust the Jewish people into the
storm center of twentieth-century world-political events.

But what precisely does this mean? What is Arendt affirming when
she tells us that the Jewish question and anti-Semitism set "the whole
infernal machine in motion?" This question goes to the very heart of
what she was doing in *The Origins of Totalitarianism*. Furthermore, we
will see how deeply Arendt's thinking about the Jewish question and
anti-Semitism shaped her understanding of history and politics.

Arendt, to the frustration of many of her readers, rarely engaged in
methodological reflections on her work. In an age when methodology
has become an obsession, Arendt's remarks about her "method" are
casual, metaphoric, and frequently confusing.[3] Nowhere is this more
of a problem than in the diverse types of study that constitute *The
Origins of Totalitarianism*.[4] At first, and even second, glance, the book
reads more like a series of fragments than a sustained narrative or
argument. When it was published, Eric Voegelin criticized Arendt for
her lack of a consistent methodological orientation. In her reply, she
gives one of the clearest statements about her approach, which is

especially relevant for understanding how she examines political anti-Semitism. She writes that she has attempted

> to discover the chief elements of totalitarianism and to analyze them in historical terms, tracing these elements back in history as far as I deemed proper and necessary. That is, I did not write a history of antisemitism or of imperialism, but analyzed the element of Jew-hatred and the element of expansion insofar as these elements were still clearly visible and played a decisive role in the totalitarian phenomenon itself. The book, therefore, does not really deal with "origins" of totalitarianism . . . but gives a historical account of the elements which crystallized into totalitarianism.[5]

The metaphor of "crystallization" is central. If "origins" is taken to mean historical causes, then she is explicitly denying that she is attempting to specify the causes of totalitarianism. Her stance is even more radical. "Causality," she tells us, "is an altogether alien and falsifying category in the historical sciences. Not only does the actual meaning of every event always transcend any number of past 'causes' which we may assign to it . . . this past itself comes into being only with the event itself. . . . The event illuminates its own past; it can never be deduced from it."[6] This is one of Arendt's most basic convictions concerning history – the radical contingency of history. She was relentlessly critical of all modern appeals to historical causal necessity or inevitability – whether the inevitability of "progress" or that of "decline." The belief in "historical necessity" or "historical inevitability" is a fiction – a dangerous fiction – which became all too respectable in the nineteenth century. This fiction was intertwined with the rise of ideologies that claimed to provide "the key to history." This belief in historical inevitability takes on a grotesque form in totalitarian ideologies, where appeal to supranatural or suprahistorical laws of development is paradoxically juxtaposed with the extreme hubris of the triumph of the will.[7]

Retrospectively, from the vantage point of the "unprecedented event" of totalitarianism, we can tell the story of those subterranean historical elements that crystallized into totalitarianism. But we must be vigilant against the fallacy of sliding from such a retrospective account (the type of account of totalitarianism that Arendt seeks to provide) into the fictitious belief of the historical inevitability of totalitarianism. The reason why Arendt is so insistent on this point is that although she did believe that there were subterranean trends in modernity that came together and crystallized into the horrible event of totalitarianism, she did *not* believe – and strongly opposed – the thesis that totalitarianism was the historically inevitable outcome of forces and trends set in motion in the modern age. Speaking of totalitarianism, Arendt says: "Whenever an event occurs that is great enough to illuminate its own past, history comes into being. Only then does the chaotic maze of the past happenings emerge as a story which can be told, because it has a beginning and an end" (*EU*, 319). This is the perspective from which Arendt examines political anti-Semitism, as well as other elements, that were crystallized into twentieth-century totalitarian movements.[8]

These reflections on the radical contingency of history indicate an even more basic reason why Arendt consistently opposed all appeals to historical necessity or inevitability which tempt us to think that what *has* happened *must* have happened. Here, too, her understanding of the Jewish question and anti-Semitism shaped her more general understanding of both history and politics. For, according to Arendt, the "philosophy of history" – at least those versions which make explicit or implicit appeal to historical necessity – is the deadly enemy of genuine politics. "The *raison d'être* of politics is freedom" (*BPF*, 10), and indeed the very possibility of politics is freedom, where there is the spontaneity of a "new beginning." "Beginning . . . is the supreme capacity of man; politically, it is identical with man's freedom" (*OT₃*, 479).[9] Throughout her writings Arendt stresses the opposition and incompatibility of necessity and freedom. In her critiques of Enlightenment theories of historical progress and in her quarrels with Hegel and Marx, she constantly returns to rooting out any appeal to historical necessity. She challenges the claim that freedom itself emerges from historical necessity. In this context I want to emphasize that Arendt's reflections on history and politics were never merely "theoretical." They had their deepest roots in her own experiences and response to twentieth-century events. They arose in her attempt to confront the Jewish question, especially the response (or the failure of a political response by the Jewish people) to the growth of political anti-Semitism. It is from this perspective that her reflections on modern history and politics first arose. Furthermore, the traces of Arendt's struggle with the Jewish question are evident in her more general analyses of politics, freedom, action, and the need to create public spaces in which the conflict of opinions among one's peers can be expressed and debated. This, of course, is not to deny the extent to which Arendt's understanding of politics was shaped by her appropriation of the civic republican tradition. Indeed, this provides her with a model of what a Jewish politics might become. In her analysis of the Dreyfus affair, she boldly declares:

> There was only one basis on which Dreyfus could or should have been saved. The intrigues of a corrupt Parliament, the dry rot of a collapsing society and the clergy's lust for power should have been met squarely with the stern Jacobin concept of the nation based upon human rights, – that republican view of communal life which asserts that by infringing on the rights of one you infringe on the rights of all. (*DA*, 217)

Arendt wrote this at approximately the same time that she started writing occasional articles for the New York German-Jewish weekly *Aufbau*. The first was entitled "Die jüdische Armee – der Beginn einer jüdische Politik?" (The Jewish Army – The Beginning of a Jewish Politics?).[10] She argued that such an army was needed so that the Jewish people could fight the Nazis *as* Jews (not solely as citizens of the allied nations), and in order to develop the type of solidarity required for a Jewish politics wherein the Jewish people would take their own political initiative. In this sense there might yet be a "beginning of a Jewish politics."

Earlier I cited Arendt's remark that when she fled Germany in 1933, her Jewishness had become her problem: "[A]nd my problem was political. Purely political! I wanted to go into practical work, exclusively and only Jewish work." Initially this meant working for various Jewish and Zionist organizations in Paris and later in New York. But it is from this time that one can also date Arendt's quest for the *meaning* of politics.

Arendt came to recognize that in writing *The Origins of Totalitarianism*, she was writing a *political* book. When the second edition appeared in 1958, she used the occasion to reflect on the book and to clarify her intentions:

> What does bother me is that the title suggests, however faintly, a belief in historical causality which I did not hold when I wrote the book and in which I believe even less today. . . . While I was writing the book, these intentions presented themselves to me in the form of an ever recurring image: I felt as though I dealt with a crystallized structure which I had to break up into its constituent elements in order to destroy it. This image bothered me a great deal, for I thought it an impossible

task to write history, not in order to save and conserve and render fit for remembrance, but on the contrary, in order to destroy. Finally, it dawned upon me that I was not engaged in writing a historical book, even though large parts of it clearly contain historical analyses, but a political book, in which whatever there was of past history not only was seen from the vantage-point of the present, but would not have become visible at all without the light which the event, the emergence of totalitarianism, shed on it. In other words, the "origins" in the first and second part of the book are not causes that inevitably lead to certain effects; rather, they became origins only after the event had taken place.[11]

The above claims reinforce Arendt's understanding of both history and politics. The historical emergence of political anti-Semitism was not a "cause" that inevitably led to the emergence of totalitarianism. More generally, there are no historical causes (or set of such causes) that *necessitated* what happened. This also means that prior to the crystallized structure of the event of totalitarianism there was the real *political* possibility of preventing its emergence. We will also see that *The Origins of Totalitarianism* is a "political book" in another sense. Oxymoronically, Arendt came to understand totalitarianism as a "political movement" that seeks to destroy and eliminate the very possibility of politics. Virtually all the features that became integral to Arendt's understanding of politics, public space, action, and freedom are anticipated in *The Origins of Totalitarianism*. In this sense, it is a significant development in her quest for the *meaning* of politics, a quest that was originally provoked by her reflections on the necessity for, and failures of, a Jewish politics.

We need to probe what Arendt means by "political antisemitism" and the failure of the Jewish people to respond adequately to this new ideology. But in order to do so, we must consider why Arendt so adamantly rejects the two prevailing theories of anti-Semitism: scapegoat theories and doctrines of "eternal antisemitism." She criticizes scapegoat theories for several reasons. They uphold "the perfect innocence of the victim, an innocence which insinuates not only that no evil was done but nothing at all was done which might possibly have a connection with the issue at stake" (*OT₃*, 5). Consequently, it becomes an unhistorical mystery why some individual, group, or people is singled out as the scapegoat. Not only are scapegoat theories unhistorical; they are pseudo-historical. For although they purport to offer a historical explanation of events, they fail to explain anything. Even if one grants that there is a social-psychological need to blame someone for one's real or imagined misfortunes, the historical question is why this *particular* group is singled out for blame. To make her point emphatically, Arendt reports a joke that was told after the First World War. "An antisemite claimed that the Jews had caused the war; the reply was: Yes, the Jews and the bicyclists. Why the bicyclists? asks the one. Why the Jews? asks the other" (*OT₃*, 5).

Scapegoat theories are caught on the horns of a dilemma. Either they explain a historical occurrence by appealing to what is unhistorical – "One needs a scapegoat to blame" – thereby failing to account for what demands explanation – namely, why this *particular* scapegoat? Or they slip back into ordinary historical accounts which undermine the explanatory force of claiming that a scapegoat is required.

> Whenever . . . its adherents painstakingly try to explain why a specific scapegoat was so well suited to his role, they show that they have left the theory behind and have got themselves involved in the usual historical research – where nothing is ever discovered except that history is made by many groups and that for certain reasons one group was singled out. (*OT₃*, 5)

Arendt is even more scathing in her criticism of the double-edged notion of "eternal antisemitism": that is, that Jew-hatred is a permanent phenomenon in the sense that Jews have always been (and always will be) hated and persecuted. She objects to this doctrine regardless of whether it is invoked by anti-Semites, unbiased historians, or even by Jews themselves. Taken to its logical conclusion, this makes anti-Semitism a normal, permanent condition of history. "If it is true that mankind has insisted on murdering Jews for more than two thousand years, then Jew-killing is a normal, and even human, occupation and Jew hatred is justified beyond the need of argument" (*OT₃*, 7).

There is common ground to Arendt's rejection of both scapegoat theories of anti-Semitism and the doctrine of eternal anti-Semitism. Both types of theory turn away from confronting how modern Jewish history has been entwined with modern European history; they divert us from understanding the specific historical ways in which the Jewish people responded to the concrete situations in which they found themselves. They turn us away from honestly confronting the question of the Jews' "share of responsibility."

> The so-called scapegoat . . . does not simply cease to be coresponsible because it became the victim of the world's injustice and cruelty. (OT_3, 6)

> [J]ust as antisemites understandably desire to escape responsibility for their deeds, so Jews, attacked and on the defensive, even more understandably do not wish under any circumstances to discuss their share of responsibility. (OT_3, 7)

> It is quite remarkable that the only two doctrines which at least attempt to explain the political significance of the antisemitic movement deny all specific Jewish responsibility and refuse to discuss matters in specific historical terms. (OT_3, 8)

Arendt is raising the explosive issue of the responsibility (or, more accurately, co-responsibility) of the Jewish people for what happened to them. We must be careful not to misinterpret what she is claiming. For the issue is not one of blame, guilt, or even *moral* responsibility. It is, rather, a question of political responsibility: of how the Jews have (and have not) responded to the concrete political situations in which they have found themselves. The Jewish people are not merely passive sufferers and victims, although certainly they have been oppressed, persecuted, and murdered throughout history. The Jewish people, like any other historical people, are not merely the sufferers of history; they are also agents who have responded in different ways. A historical account of political anti-Semitism must seek not only to identify and properly characterize this phenomenon, but also to examine how the Jews responded to it.

Arendt argues that it was the lack of any significant political experience and a failure to accept their share of responsibility that left European Jewry so unprepared and defenseless when political anti-Semitism erupted in the anti-Semitic pan-Germanic and pan-Slavic movements of the late nineteenth century. She makes the following striking claim about Jewish history:

> Jewish history offers the extraordinary spectacle of a people, unique in this respect, which began its history with a well-defined concept of history and an almost conscious resolution to achieve a well-circumscribed plan on earth and then, without giving up this concept,

avoided all political action for two thousand years. The result was the political history of the Jewish people became even more dependent upon the unforeseen, accidental factors than the history of other nations, so that the Jews stumbled from one role to the other and accepted responsibility for none. (*OT*$_3$, 8)

This is an extremely provocative claim. One may want to accuse Arendt, as her friend and mentor Karl Jaspers once did, of exaggeration in making such a sweeping generalization. But we can appreciate the rhetorical force of her exaggeration.[12] Arendt firmly believed that in the modern age the only viable solution to the Jewish question was a political one. Social assimilation was incompatible with Jewish emancipation. She wanted the Jewish people to recognize and assume their political responsibility, in order to fight for their rights *as Jews* – to join together with others in the fight against political anti-Semitism. Initially, Arendt was extremely vague about what this meant in the concrete historical situation in which European Jewry found itself. Even during the darkest period of the Second World War, she called for the formation of a Jewish army as a "beginning of a Jewish politics." This call, this summons to assume political responsibility, became a generalized theme in all her writing. She protested against the growth in the modern age of social bureaucracy and administrative housekeeping which led to the submergence of genuine political action. I fully agree with Margaret Canovan when she says that the most urgent aspect of Arendt's reevaluation of politics is "her message about our responsibility for politics: our duty to be citizens, looking after the world and taking responsibility for what is done in our name."[13] This is the message that Arendt first addressed to her fellow Jews.

Arendt qualifies her sweeping generalization of how the Jewish people avoided political action for two thousand years. She tells us that "during the twenty centuries of their Diaspora the Jews made only two attempts to change their condition by direct political action."[14] The first was the seventeenth-century Sabbatai Zevi movement; the second, twentieth-century Zionism. I want to consider what Arendt says about the seventeenth-century Sabbatian movement, because it reveals a great deal about her understanding of Jewish history, and especially about her early gropings to understand the meaning of politics. (Later I will explore her complex, ambivalent relationship with Zionism.)

The Sabbatai Zevi (Sabbatian) movement was "the mystic-political movement for the salvation of Jewry which terminated the Jewish Middle Ages and brought about a catastrophe whose consequences determined Jewish attitudes and basic convictions for over two centuries thereafter" (*JP*, 166–7). Sabbatai Zevi was the self-appointed Messiah who was to lead the Jews back to Palestine. The movement that formed around him, in which the "prophet" Nathan of Gaza played a major role, aroused Jewish communities throughout the entire Diaspora. In the prior history of the Diaspora, there was no other event that generated as much popular enthusiasm among the disparate Jewish communities throughout the world. The catastrophe occurred as a result of Sabbatai Zevi's apostasy, when he publicly converted to Islam. Arendt summarizes her understanding of this mystic-political movement, its glory and its catastrophic aftermath, when she writes:

> In preparing as they did to follow Sabbatai Zevi, the self-appointed "Messiah," back to Palestine in the mid-1600s, the Jews assumed that their ultimate hope of a Messianic millennium was about to be realized. Until Sabbatai Zevi's time they had been able to conduct their communal affairs by means of a politics that existed in the realm of imagination alone – the memory of a far-off past and the hope of a far-off future. With the Sabbatai Zevi movement these centuries-old memories and hopes culminated in a single exalted moment. Its catastrophical aftermath brought to a close – probably forever – the period in which religion alone could provide the Jews with a firm framework within which to satisfy their political, spiritual and everyday needs. (*JP*, 167)

The basis for Arendt's interpretation of the Sabbatian movement is the path-breaking research of the great twentieth-century scholar of Jewish mysticism, Gershom Scholem. In 1948, Arendt wrote a laudatory review of Scholem's classic, *Major Trends in Jewish Mysticism.* Arendt, unlike Scholem, was fascinated not by the religious significance of this mystical tradition, but by its political significance. Scholem, Arendt claims, "changes the whole picture of Jewish history."[15] He challenges the dominant view that "in sharp contrast to all other nations, the Jews were not history-makers but history-sufferers" (*JP*, 96). Arendt felt that Scholem was an ally in her own attempt to make a similar point – at least to show that the Jewish people could be "history-makers." According to Arendt, Scholem showed the power of Jewish Kabbalistic thought in preparing for, and leading the Jews to, political action. For in Kabbalistic teachings, there is an emphasis on the role of "human participation in the drama of the world."

> [T]he school of Isaac Luria was bolder than all predecessors when it dared to give a new interpretation of the exile existence of the people: "Formerly (the Diaspora) had been regarded either as a punishment for Israel's sins or as a test of Israel's faith. Now it still is all this, but intrinsically it is a mission: its purpose is to uplift the fallen sparks from all their various locations." For the first time, the role of the "protagonist in the drama of the world" was defined in terms which applied to every Jew. (*JP*, 103)

This "myth of exile" could serve two conflicting purposes:

> Through its mystical interpretation of exile as action instead of suffering, it could rouse the people to hasten the coming of the Messiah and lead to "an explosive manifestation of all those forces to which it owed its rise and its success" in the Sabbatian movement. But after the decline of this movement, it served equally well the needs of the disillusioned people who, having lost the Messianic hope, wanted a new, more general justification of exile, of their inactive existence and mere survival. (*JP*, 103)

For one "exalted" moment, "Jewish mysticism alone was able to bring about a great political movement and translate itself directly into real popular action" (*JP*, 104). This is the aspect of Scholem's research that captured Arendt's imagination. Whereas Scholem was interested in Sabbatianism primarily as a religious movement inspired by Kabbalistic teachings, which (in serendipitous ways) shaped subsequent Jewish religious life, Arendt focuses on (and tends to exaggerate) the translation of the mystical teachings into "real popular action." For it was such popular action that Arendt found missing from so much of Jewish history. The same impulses that attracted her to Lazare's summons for a popular Jewish politics from below attracted her to Scholem's interpretation of Jewish mysticism as tending toward action and realization.

Consequently, the Sabbatian movement was at once an exalted moment in Jewish history of "real popular action" and one of its greatest catastrophes.

> The catastrophe of this victory of mystical thought was greater for the Jewish people than all the other persecutions had been, if we are to

measure it by the only available yardstick, its far-reaching influence upon the future of the people. From now on, the Jewish body politic was dead and the people retired from the public scene of history. (*JP*, 104–5)

This is Arendt's jeremiad, her tale of woe of the Jewish people. Her reading of Jewish history is one in which, except for the brief period when the Sabbatian movement became "a great political movement," the Jewish people failed to assume political responsibility and take political initiative. The real catastrophe of the Sabbatian movement was that Jews subsequently used it to *justify* their withdrawal from "the public scene of history." This reinforced the disastrous belief that they were not, and could not be, history-makers, but only history-sufferers – that they were "invariably the innocent victims of a hostile and sometimes brutal environment." What gives so much poignancy to Arendt's jeremiad is that it is because of this withdrawal, this refusal to assume any political responsibility for their destiny, that the Jews were left so unprepared for the growth of political anti-Semitism in the late nineteenth century.

This reading of Jewish history also shows why Arendt (despite her ambivalence) was initially so attracted to Zionism – at least from the time she fled Germany in 1933. Zionists read Jewish history in a similar way. They too summoned the Jewish people to become history-makers, to no longer assume the role of innocent victims, or history-sufferers. Arendt's ambivalence about, and eventual break with, the Zionists was not over the critical need for political action. It was about what *type* of political action was appropriate for the Jewish people.

Arendt's interpretation of the Sabbatian movement as a political movement is revealing for several reasons. She never really explains in any detail in what sense Sabbatianism was a *political* movement, rather than a mass religious movement. One might argue that what she calls a "catastrophe" was a consequence of its being so un-political. There was certainly no political organization of Sabbatians; nor were there any clear political objectives. As a messianic movement, it was completely out of touch with seventeenth-century political realities. Ironically, Arendt, who was so critical of European Jewry in the nineteenth and twentieth centuries for its failure to grasp existing "political realities," fails to see an analogous failure in the Sabbatians. Following Scholem, she highlights the Kabbalistic inspiration that stresses "human participation in the drama of the world" and "the doctrine of Tikkun (Luranic Kabbalah)" which "raised every Jew to the rank of a protagonist in the great process of restitution in a manner never heard of before" (*JP*, 102). But even if we grant this, even if we grant that there was a widespread "popular movement," it still needs to be explained in what sense this popular movement was a political movement. Arendt, in her enthusiasm for Scholem's discovery that "Jewish mysticism had tended toward action and realization," glosses over these difficulties.

Nevertheless, we learn something extremely important about Arendt's deepest convictions concerning politics from the way she interprets the Sabbatian movement. We might call this the populist or radical strand in her political thinking – populist in the sense that the type of politics she favored and sought to defend is one in which spontaneous collective action arises from a people who create their own public spaces, in which speech and deeds make their appearance. Arendt has frequently been accused of being elitist in her understanding of politics. And the accusation is valid insofar as she did not think that everyone should or would engage in the rigors of political action. Politics, she thought, was always for the few – the few who had the courage to join in agonistic debate with their peers; but this type of elitism was perfectly compatible with the populism that she advocated when human beings begin something new and create those spaces in which tangible worldly freedom appears. Arendt's critique of European Jewry's failure to face political realities and to engage in political action, her attraction to Lazare's summons for a politics "from below," her skepticism regarding Jewish leaders and philanthropists who were nervous about engaging in a Jewish politics, her call in the early 1940s for the formation of a Jewish army to fight Nazi totalitarianism, and her reading of the glory (and catastrophe) of the Sabbatian movement were all motivated by this radical populist strain in her thinking – a strain that emerged in her own confrontation with the Jewish question and the disastrous consequences of political anti-Semitism.

According to Arendt, Jewish history, with the exception of the Sabbatian messianic movement and the birth of modern Zionism, offers the extraordinary spectacle of a people who avoided all political action for two thousand years. The real catastrophe of the Sabbatian movement was not the disillusionment, despair, and confusion that occurred in the wake of Sabbatai Zevi's apostasy. It was, Arendt claims, the fact that the Jewish people withdrew from the public scene of history, "and now offered a religious justification for this withdrawal. The Jewish body politic was dead." From the seventeenth century on (until the birth of modern Zionism), European Jewry did not engage in any significant political activity. Arendt's basic thesis is that something radically new emerged in the nineteenth century which must be carefully distinguished from all previous forms of Jew-hatred. Following her own injunction to analyze anti-Semitism in its historical context (and not appeal to misleading scapegoat theories or doctrines of eternal anti-Semitism), she argues that modern political anti-Semitism can be understood only in its relation to the rise and decline of the nation-state. She also maintains that it is essential to distinguish social anti-Semitism from political anti-Semitism. Social anti-Semitism arose in the modern age, when Jews aspired to assimilate to "society." By her own admission, it is only when she was completing *Rahel Varnhagen*, in Paris, that she became aware of the full significance of the distinction between social anti-Semitism and political anti-Semitism. During her Paris years, Arendt began a more systematic inquiry into the varieties and development of political anti-Semitism in European nation-states. Much of her thinking, especially concerning French anti-Semitism, was summarized in "From the Dreyfus Affair to France Today." The Dreyfus affair, she wrote,

> brings into the open all other elements of nineteenth-century antisemitism in its ideological and political aspects; it is the culmination of the antisemitism which grew out of the special conditions of the nation-state. Yet its violent form foreshadowed future developments, so that the main actors of the Affair sometimes seem to be staging a huge dress rehearsal for a performance that had to be put off for more than three decades. It drew together all the open or subterranean, political or social sources which had brought the Jewish question into a predominant position in the nineteenth century; its premature outburst, on the other hand, kept it within the framework of a typical nineteenth-century ideology which, although it survived all French governments and political crises, never quite fitted into twentieth-century political conditions. (*OT*$_3$, 45)

When Arendt says that the Dreyfus affair "never quite fitted into twentieth-century conditions," she is alluding to a distinction that became central for her thinking – a distinction between *two* types of political anti-Semitism. In a letter to Jaspers (Aug. 17, 1946) Arendt summarizes this distinction.

> I distinguish in modern times between two kinds of anti-Semitism. First comes anti-Semitism in the nation-state (beginning with the Wars of Liberation in Germany, ending with the Dreyfus affair in France), which came about because the Jews emerged as a group particularly useful to the state and receiving special protection from it. As a consequence of that, every group in the population that came into conflict with the state became anti-Semitic. Then comes the anti-Semitism of the imperial age (which began in the 1880s). This latter form was, from the outset, international in its organization. (*C*, 55)[16]

It is this second type of international, or supranational, anti-Semitism, which seemed quite marginal when it was manifested in the pan-Germanic and pan-Slavic parties, that was eventually to prove far more dangerous. Let us first consider her account of how anti-Semitism developed in the context of the rise and decline of the nation-state.

Arendt distinguishes four stages in her "schematic outline of the simultaneous rise and decline of the European nation-state and European Jewry" (*OT₃*, 14).[17] (1) The first stage begins in the seventeenth and eighteenth centuries, when the nation-states develop under the tutelage of absolute monarchs. Here we find the emergence of a group of wealthy "court Jews," who helped to finance state affairs and handled the financial affairs of their princes. These "court Jews," unlike their poorer coreligionists, were granted special privileges and protections. (2) After the French Revolution, a larger amount of credit and capital was needed than could be supplied by individual court Jews. But the "combined wealth of the wealthier strata of Western and Central European Jewry . . . could suffice to meet the new enlarged governmental needs." So in this second stage special privileges were granted to a larger group of wealthy Jews who had international connections, although most Jews were still excluded from these privileges and from those "rights" which were presumably the rights of all men. (3) This stage came to an end with the transformation of nation-states into imperialistic nations. Imperialism "undermined the very foundations of the nation-state." During the rapid rise of imperialism, wealthy Jews lost their exclusive position in state business "to imperialistic-minded business." So with the rise and spread of imperialism, Jewish wealth became less and less significant in supporting state functions. But as the real financial influence of wealthy Jews declined, political anti-Semitism increased. Jewish financiers had been useful to the state precisely because they posed no serious political threat to those in power. But when different social groups and classes came into conflict with the state, the Jews were blamed as the power behind the power. (4) With the eventual triumph of imperialism and the disintegration of nation-states, wealthy Jews became atomized into a herd of individuals. "In an imperialist age, Jewish wealth had become insignificant; to a Europe with no sense of balance of power between its nations and of inter-European solidarity, the non-national, inter-European Jewish element became an object of universal hatred because of its useless wealth, and of contempt because of its lack of power" (*OT*₃, 15).

When Arendt speaks of "Antisemitism as an Outrage to Common Sense," she wants to highlight the seeming paradox – the outrage – that political anti-Semitism in Europe reached its climax at a time when Jews were rapidly losing any public power or influence. She tells us that "When Hitler came to power, the German banks were already almost *judenrein*. . . . German Jewry as a whole, after a long steady growth in social status and numbers, was declining so rapidly that statisticians predicted its disappearance in a few decades" (*OT*₃, 4).

Arendt's approach to, and understanding of, the development of the nation-state was shaped by her concern with the Jewish question. Approaching the nation-state from this perspective made her specially sensitive to the "secret conflict" – the unstable contradiction – between *state* and *nation*. This conflict, present at the very birth of the modern nation-state, had profound consequences for the fate of European Jewry.

> The secret conflict between state and nation came to light at the very birth of the modern nation-state, when the French Revolution combined the declaration of the Rights of Man with the demand for national sovereignty. The same essential rights were at once claimed as the inalienable heritage of all human beings *and* as the specific heritage of specific nations, the same nation was at once declared to be subject to laws, which supposedly would flow from the Rights of Man *and* sovereign, that is, bound by no universal law and acknowledging nothing superior to itself. The practical outcome of this contradiction was that from then on human rights were protected and enforced only as national rights and that the very institution of a state, whose

supreme task was to protect and guarantee man his rights as man, as citizen and as national, lost its legal, rational appearance and could be interpreted by the romantics as the nebulous representative of a "national soul" which through the very fact of its existence was supposed to be beyond or above the law. National sovereignty, accordingly, lost its original connotation of freedom of the people and was being surrounded by a pseudomystical aura of lawless arbitrariness. (*OT*$_3$, 230)

The Jews were caught in the middle of this "secret conflict," a conflict that played itself out in the course of the nineteenth century. As human beings and members of a state, they presumably deserved to be protected by the Rights of Man, the presumed "inalienable heritage of all human beings." But did they really belong to the *nation* that was to guarantee these rights? As a separate people, with their own religious beliefs, strange customs, and rituals, they did not really belong to the nation – or so the anti-Semites claimed. They were a foreign element, even if they had lived in a national territory for generations. With the growth of the mystique of "national sovereignty" which transcended any effective claim to universal human rights, the Jews were to be excluded from the "national soul." For all its violence, this form of political anti-Semitism did not call for the complete extermination of the Jewish people, even when the terrifying slogan "Death to the Jews" was shouted during the Dreyfus affair. The anti-Semitism that was identified with the nation-state called for the purification of the nation, the expulsion of the foreign, Jewish element from the "national soul."

But, according to Arendt, the epoch of competing, independent nation-states and a European balance of power came to an end with the triumph of imperialism and the unlimited hunger for expansion. With the rapid extension of imperialistic projects, fostered by racist thinking, a new form of international or supranational anti-Semitism arose in the political ideologies of the pan-Germanic and pan-Slavic parties and movements.

Race-thinking was not a German invention. Race-thinking and racism as an ideology which had strong appeal to the masses "emerged simultaneously in all Western countries during the nineteenth century" (*OT*$_3$, 158). Racism, which cut across all national boundaries, "whether defined by geographical, linguistic, traditional, or any other standards," became the main ideological weapon of imperialist politics. The constellation of imperialist politics, racism, and the eruption of a supranational form of political anti-Semitism was the beginning of what would ultimately become the "final solution," the systematic extermination of the Jewish people: "Hitlerism exercised its strong international and inter-European appeal during the thirties because racism, although a state doctrine only in Germany, had been a powerful trend in public opinion everywhere" (OT_3, 158). In a statement that today sounds almost prophetic, Arendt warned:

> Racism may indeed carry out the doom of the Western world and, for that matter, of the whole of human civilization. When Russians have become Slavs, when Frenchmen have assumed the role of commanders of a *force noire*, when Englishmen have turned into "white men," as already for a disastrous spell all Germans became Aryans, then this change will itself signify the end of Western man. For no matter what learned scientists may say, race is, politically speaking, not the beginning of humanity but its end, not the origin of peoples but their decay, not the natural birth of man but its natural death. (OT_3, 157)

In distinguishing political anti-Semitism in the nation-state from the anti-Semitism that arose with imperialism, Arendt stresses how the pan-movements – pan-Germanism and pan-Slavism – were essentially anti-nation-state international movements. When the so-called "logic" of this form of anti-Semitism became fully manifest, it called not for the elimination of the Jews in order to purify a "national soul," but rather for the extermination of the Jews from the human race. What seemed originally to be a marginal movement on the fringes of political reality was to take on a hyper-reality in the Nazi movement. Arendt insists that it is a mistake to think that the Nazis were nationalists. "Their nationalist propaganda was directed toward their fellow-travelers and not their convinced members." Their approach to politics was essentially supranational.

> The Nazis had a genuine and never revoked contempt for the narrowness of nationalism, the provincialism of the nation-state, and they repeated time and time again that their "movement," international in scope . . . was more important to them than any state, which would necessarily be bound to a specific territory. And not only the Nazis, but fifty years of antisemitic history, stand as evidence against the identification of antisemitism with nationalism. The first antisemitic parties in the last decades of the nineteenth century were also the first that banded together internationally. From the very beginning, they called inter-

national congresses and were concerned with a co-ordination of international, or at least inter-European, activities. (*OT*₃, 3–4)

Arendt distinguishes a newer, much uglier form of nationalism – "tribal nationalism" – from the older form of nationalism characteristic of the nation-state. It is this tribal nationalism that provides a clue as to how anti-Semitism became the central component of a new type of political ideology. According to Arendt, tribal nationalism became the driving force behind continental imperialism.[18]

> The clue to the sudden emergence of antisemitism as the center of a whole outlook on life and the world – as distinguished from its mere political role in France during the Dreyfus Affair . . . lies in the nature of tribal nationalism rather than in political facts and circumstances. The true significance of the pan-movements' antisemitism is that hatred of the Jews was, for the first time, severed from all actual experience concerning the Jewish people, political, social, or economic, and followed only the peculiar logic of an ideology. (*OT*₃, 229)

Politically speaking, tribal nationalism feeds upon an "atmosphere of rootlessness," and insists that its own people are surrounded by a "world of enemies." It claims that its people, its *Volk*, is unique, individual, incompatible with others – and threatened by all outsiders. Supranational political anti-Semitism wedded to this new tribal nationalism proved to be an extremely powerful political weapon in organizing the "mob." It created a "new kind of nationalist feeling whose violence proved an excellent motor to set mob masses in motion and quite adequate to replace the older national patriotism as an emotional center" (*OT*₃, 226).

Tribal nationalism, hostility to the nation-state, racist imperialism, and a supranational anti-Semitism were all anticipated in the pan-Germanic and pan-Slavic movements that originated in the last decades of the nineteenth century. This is why Arendt declares that "Nazism and Bolshevism owe more to Pan-Germanism and Pan-Slavism (respectively) than to any other ideology or political movement" (*OT*₃, 222). It was Georg von Schoenerer, founder of the Austrian pan-Germanic movement, who declared that "we Pan-Germans regard antisemitism as the mainstay of our national ideology." But there was a time lag between the formulation of the pan-movements' ideology and its serious political application.

It . . . was Hitler who, shrewder than Schoenerer his spiritual father, knew how to use the hierarchical principle of racism, how to exploit the antisemitic assertion of the existence of a "worst" people in order properly to organize the "best" and all the conquered and oppressed in between, how to generalize the superiority complex of the pan-movements so that each people, with the necessary exception of the Jews, could look down upon one that was even worse off than itself. (OT_3, 241)

According to Arendt, the Jews became the main target of the political racist ideologies of the pan-movements because of the clash between the respective claims to chosenness.

But what drove the Jews into the center of these racial ideologies more than anything else was the even more obvious fact that the pan-movements' claim to chosenness could clash seriously only with the Jewish claim. It did not matter that the Jewish concept had nothing in common with the tribal theories about the divine origin of one's own people. The mob was not much concerned with such niceties of historical correctness and was hardly aware of the difference between a Jewish mission in history to achieve the establishment of mankind and its own "mission" to dominate all other peoples on earth. (OT_3, 240)

Consequently, there was a deep envy, a *ressentiment* against the Jews which had nothing to do with Jewish deeds and misdeeds. Hatred of Jews became the mainstay of the ideology of the pan-movements. Tribal nationalism is the "precise perversion of a religion which made God choose one nation." Arendt tells us:

The hatred of the racists against the Jews sprang from a superstitious apprehension that it actually might be the Jews, and not themselves, whom God had chosen, to whom success was granted by divine providence. There was an element of feeble-minded resentment against a people who, it was feared, had received a rationally incomprehensible guarantee that they would emerge eventually, and in spite of appearances, as the final victors in world history. (OT_3, 242)

The doctrine of being "the chosen people" was radically perverted. "Chosenness was no longer the myth for an ultimate realization of the ideal of a common humanity – but for its final destruction" (OT_3, 243).

Let us step back and – once again – reflect on Arendt's appropriation of the metaphor of crystallization. Arendt was searching not for causes or origins of totalitarianism, but rather for those subterranean tendencies and elements that erupted and crystallized contingently into the unprecedented phenomenon of totalitarianism. Seyla Benhabib notes that Arendt, like Walter Benjamin, wants "to break the chain of narrative continuity, to shatter chronology as the natural structure of narrative, to stress fragmentariness, historical dead ends, failures and ruptures."[19] Lisa J. Disch suggests that Arendt may also have had Kant in mind in her use of the metaphor of crystallization. "In *Third Critique*, Kant introduces 'crystallization' as a metaphor for contingency. . . . Crystallization describes the formation of objects that come into being not by a gradual, evolutionary process but suddenly and unpredictably 'by a *shooting together*, i.e. by a sudden solidification, not by a gradual transition . . . but all at once by a *saltus*, which transition is also called *crystallization*'."[20] Once such an event as totalitarianism has crystallized, then we can try to trace its history backward: "Whenever an event occurs that is great enough to illuminate its own past, history comes into being."

Like Benjamin, Arendt was brushing "against history." She wanted to write about totalitarianism in a way that would help to destroy it. She maintained that although writing history generally seeks "to save and conserve and render fit for remembrance," what she wanted to do was to break up and destroy the "crystalline structure" of totalitarianism. She came to recognize that *The Origins of Totalitarianism* was essentially a "political book," one whose primary intent was to enable us to comprehend and destroy "the structure of totalitarian movements and domination itself."

What Arendt discovered is that in order to grasp how the Jewish question and anti-Semitism "could become the catalytic agent for, first, the Nazi movement, then a world war, and finally the establishment of death factories," one needed to understand how the modern history of the Jews, anti-Semitism, and the Jewish question were intertwined with the more general history of modern Europe. Anti-Semitism (in its social and political forms) could be understood only in the larger context of the origins and disintegration of the modern nation-state. One must understand why, at the very moment when Jews were losing their public influence, the ideology of political anti-Semitism triumphed, and see how with the triumph of imperialism and racist thinking a new form of supranational anti-Semitism emerged. One must analyze how anti-

Semitism was transformed from an *opinion* into an *ideology* that "claims to possess either the key to history, or the solution for all the 'riddles of the universe,' or the intimate knowledge of the hidden universal laws which are supposed to rule nature and man." One must understand why and how this supranational political anti-Semitism became such a powerful weapon in organizing rootless, atomized masses.

Although Arendt insisted that the only solution to the Jewish question was a political one, a point that she reiterated over and over again from the time she fled Germany, she did not spell out what in her view would constitute an adequate political response. She wanted the Jewish people (primarily European Jewry) to assume their share of responsibility, to take political initiative. But, except in the most general terms, she did not indicate what this might involve. Despite her insistence that European Jewry was oblivious to the growth of political anti-Semitism in the nineteenth century, she never addressed forthrightly the issue of what sort of Jewish political action was viable – *when* and by *whom*. The rhetoric of calling for Jews to fight for their rights as Jews might be uplifting, but of a thinker who chided her people for being naive and ignorant about "political realities" one might expect at least an attempt to indicate how the Jewish people might have acted politically in the historical circumstances in which they found themselves. Otherwise, Arendt herself is open to the criticism that she levels at her fellow Jews – that of ignoring "political realities."

I have suggested that we can read *The Origins of Totalitarianism* as an all-important stage in Arendt's quest for the meaning of politics. We have already seen the importance of what I have called her populist strain – her conviction that authentic politics emerges from the collective action of a people who assume their share of political responsibility and are willing to risk political initiative. Furthermore, we have seen that when Arendt first introduces the sharp distinction between a social response to discrimination and a political response to the ideological uses of political anti-Semitism, her primary emphasis is on the need for Jews to fight for their (political) *rights* as Jews. But, thus far, there has been very little concrete specification about what this might mean, and how she construes the concept of rights. One of the most remarkable and illuminating chapters of *The Origins of Totalitarianism* is "The Decline of the Nation-State and the End of the Rights of Man." In this chapter we discover what Arendt means by rights, and what she takes to be our most fundamental right.

3

Statelessness and the Right to Have Rights

I do not believe that there is any thought process possible without personal experience. Every thought is an afterthought [*Nachdenken*], that is, a reflection on some matter or event.

EU

In 1964 Hannah Arendt was asked: "Is there a definite event in your memory that dates your turn to the political?" Without hesitating, she answered: "I would say February 27, 1933, the burning of the Reichstag, and the illegal arrests that followed during the same night." From that moment on, she "felt responsible." "That is, I was no longer of the opinion that one can simply be a bystander" (*EU*, 4–5). In the following months Arendt helped others to escape from Germany. She also aided her Zionist friends. It was this activity that led to the incident which compelled her to flee from Germany. The Zionists wanted to document anti-Semitic statements, which were not well known outside Germany. Because she was not explicitly identified with the Zionists, Arendt was the ideal person to conduct this research in the Prussian State Library. She readily agreed to help, even though the Nazis considered this to be "horror propaganda." She was subsequently apprehended, arrested, and interrogated for eight days. This is her account of what happened:

> Yes. I was found out. I was very lucky. I got out after eight days because I made friends with the official who arrested me. He was a charming fellow! He'd been promoted from the criminal police to a political division. He had no idea what to do. What was he supposed to do? He kept saying to me, "Ordinarily I have someone there in front of me, and I just check the file, and I know what's going on. But what

shall I do with you?" . . . Unfortunately, I had to lie to him. I couldn't let the organization be exposed. I told him tall tales, and he kept saying, "I got you in here. I shall get you out again. Don't get a lawyer! Jews don't have any money now. Save your money!" Meanwhile the organization had gotten me a lawyer. . . . And I sent this lawyer away. Because this man who arrested me had such an open, decent face. I relied on him and thought that here was a much better chance than with some lawyer who himself was afraid. (*EU*, 5–6)

As soon as she was released, she quickly prepared to leave Germany – without any legal travel documents. After a farewell drunken party with her friends, she and her mother crossed the Czech border in the middle of the night. From that night until 18 years later, when she became a naturalized United States citizen, she lived the precarious existence of a stateless person – or, more accurately, a stateless *nonperson*. She traveled from Prague to Geneva, and finally to Paris, where many Jews who had fled Germany gathered. Most of Arendt's fellow émigré Jews in Paris lived a Kafkaesque existence, moving from cheap hotel to cheap hotel, trying to find some means to support themselves. As illegal immigrants, they could not get *cartes d'identité*. But without proper documents, they could not get work. Arendt was one of the lucky ones, for she managed to find work with a variety of Jewish organizations. She was hired as director of Youth Aliyah, the Zionist organization that arranged for the emigration of Jewish children to Palestine. In the late 1930s the situation of Jewish refugees in Paris deteriorated rapidly. The organizers of Youth Aliyah decided to move their headquarters from Paris to London, so Arendt was left unemployed. In 1938, however, she was hired by the Jewish Agency to help Jewish refugees in Paris.

In May 1940, "enemy aliens" (primarily German Jews) were ordered to report to be transported to internment camps. Elisabeth Young-Bruehl vividly describes what happened.

On 5 May 1940, announcements issued by the *Gouverneur Général* of Paris appeared in all the newspapers: all men between the ages of 17 and 55 and unmarried or childless married women who had come from Germany, the Saar, or Danzig, were to report for transport to either *prestataire* or internment camps. The men were to appear on 14 May at the Stadion Buffalo and the women on 15 May at the Vélodrome d'Hiver, an enormous glass-roofed sports palladium. The dreadful orders were banally specific: the "enemy aliens" were to carry food sufficient for two days, their own utensils, and sacks or suitcases "weighing no more than 30 kilos." Thus equipped, the refugees were ready to become what Hannah Arendt sarcastically referred to as "the new kind of human being created by contemporary history," the kind that "are put into concentration camps by their foes and into internment camps by their friends." (*YB*, 152)[1]

These orders meant that Arendt was separated from her second husband, Heinrich Blücher, and from her mother, who was over 55, and therefore allowed to stay in Paris. (Arendt had married Günther Stern in 1929, but they had separated a few years later. In 1936 she met Blücher in Paris. They were married in January 1940 after they had both obtained divorces from their former spouses.) After a chaotic week at the Vélodrome, the women were shipped to Gurs. This was the lowest point of despair for Arendt. For no one knew what would happen next, and there was good reason to fear the worst.

> At the camp of Gurs . . . where I had the opportunity of spending some time, I heard only once about suicide, and that was the suggestion of a collective action, apparently a kind of protest in order to vex the French. When some of us remarked that we had been shipped there *"pour crever"* [to be done in] in any case, the general mood turned suddenly into a violent courage of life. The general opinion held that one had to be abnormally asocial and unconcerned about general events if one was still able to interpret the whole accident as personal and individual bad luck and, accordingly, ended one's life personally and individually. But the same people, as soon as they returned to their own individual lives, being faced with seemingly individual problems, changed once more to this insane optimism which is next door to despair. (*JP*, 59)

Arendt's good luck continued. It is little wonder that the goddess *Fortuna* played such an important role in Arendt's thinking. Arendt managed to escape from the internment camp at Gurs. In 1962 she described her escape.

> A few weeks after our arrival in the camp . . . France was defeated and all communications broke down. In the resulting chaos we succeeded in getting hold of liberation papers with which we were able to leave the camp. There existed no French underground at the time. . . . None of us could "describe" what lay in store for those who remained behind. All that we could do was to tell them what we expected would happen – the camp would be handed over to the victorious Germans. (About 200

women of a total of 7,000 left.) . . . It was a unique chance, but it meant that one had to leave with nothing but a toothbrush since there existed no means of transportation. (*YB*, 155)

In 1942 and 1943, most of those who remained behind in Gurs and managed to survive its atrocious conditions were shipped to extermination camps. It was Adolf Eichmann who was responsible for sending these women to their death. Arendt did not discover this until after the Second World War was over. But a remark she made when she was preparing to attend the Eichmann trial (20 years after her escape from Gurs) has a poignant significance: "to attend this trial is somehow, I feel, an obligation I owe my past" (*YB*, 329).

One of the reasons why so few women were prepared to risk escaping from Gurs was because there was no place to go – no place where Jews could be safe. There was no French underground at the time to help, and no public transportation that they could safely use. Arendt managed, by hitchhiking and walking, to make her way to Montauban, which had become a center for ex-internee "enemy aliens." It was where her German friend Lotta Sempell Klenbort had temporarily rented a house. Arendt then tried to find out what had happened to Heinrich. By another fortuitous event, she ran into him on the streets of Montauban. The internment camp to which he had been sent had been evacuated when the Germans marched on Paris, and he had made his way to Montauban. During the next months Hannah and Heinrich lived a furtive life, avoiding all contact with the French police, and began the frustrating process of trying to secure visas to escape from Europe to the United States. This required several "illegal" trips to Marseilles, where they sometimes met their good friend, Walter Benjamin. Unlike Benjamin, who committed suicide on the night he was turned back from the French–Spanish border, Hannah and Heinrich not only managed to secure visas, but were able to cross the border and travel to Lisbon. After a wait of three months, they sailed for New York. Hannah and Heinrich were carrying with them Walter Benjamin's "Theses on the Philosophy of History" (which he had entrusted to them the last time they saw him in Marseilles). During their three-month wait in Lisbon, they discussed intensely the meaning of Benjamin's theses. The famous ninth thesis had special significance for them.

A Klee painting named "Angelus Novus" shows an angel looking as though he is about to move away from something he is fixedly contemplating. His eyes are staring, his mouth is open, his wings are spread. This is how one pictures the angel of history. His face is turned toward the past. Where we perceive a chain of events, he sees one single catastrophe which keeps piling wreckage upon wreckage and hurls it in front of his feet. The angel would like to stay, awaken the dead, and make whole what has been smashed. But a storm is blowing from Paradise; it has got caught in his wings with such violence that the angel can no longer close them. This storm irresistibly propels him into the future to which his back is turned, while the pile of debris before him grows skyward. This storm is what we call progress.[2]

I have told this story of Arendt's flight from Germany, from France, and finally from Europe for several reasons. Retrospectively, it is all too easy to imagine what might have happened to her, what her life story might have been, had she been interrogated in Germany by a less sympathetic German official, had she not escaped from Gurs, had she not been lucky enough to secure a visa to enter the United States, had she not managed to make her way to Lisbon. These events meant the difference between life and death. It was these personal experiences that impressed upon her so deeply the radical contingency of events – a sense of contingency that influenced and pervaded all her thinking. Furthermore, it was her experiences as a stateless Jew and an "enemy alien" that marked her understanding of the frightening terrors of twentieth-century bureaucracy. It was not the rationality of bureaucracy that she emphasized, but its sheer irrationality. It was not Max Weber but Franz Kafka who grasped and portrayed the nightmarish quality of what bureaucracy was to become in the twentieth century.

The reader of Kafka's stories is very likely to pass through a stage during which he will be inclined to think of Kafka's nightmare world as a trivial though, perhaps, psychologically interesting forecast of a world to come. But this world actually has come to pass. The generation of the forties and especially those who have the doubtful advantage of having lived under the most terrible regime history has so far produced know that the terror of Kafka adequately represents the true nature of the thing called bureaucracy – the replacing of government by administration and of laws by arbitrary decrees. We know that Kafka's construction was not a mere nightmare. . . . Kafka's so-called prophecies were but a sober analysis of underlying structures which today have come into the open. (*EU*, 73–4)

Arendt's experiences as a wandering, stateless Jew also shaped her insight into the hidden tradition of the Jewish pariah. Like Chaplin's "suspect," Arendt learned that survival meant relying on one's wits. She also had good reason to be suspicious of the police – the cop – "that seeming incarnation of a hostile world" (*JP*, 80). To survive and resist succumbing to despair and suicide, one needed a sense of that "natural freedom" and joy in living that she so admired in Heine. But this wasn't enough. One needed to resist the temptation to accommodate oneself to anti-Semitism or to turn away from "political realities." In a world in which even the possibility of any political activity was becoming increasingly remote, one needed to remember the moral of the story of Kafka's K.: "that human rights are worth fighting for and that the rule of the castle is not divine law" (*JP*, 88). One needed to remember that "*thinking* is the new weapon."

In "We Refugees," Arendt captures the pathos, anxiety, false optimism, despair, absurdity, and even the humor of the stateless Jew. She tells us: "In the first place, we don't like to be called 'refugees'. We ourselves call each other 'newcomers' or 'immigrants'. A refugee used to be a person driven to seek refuge because of some act committed or some political opinion held. . . . With us the meaning of the term 'refugee' has changed. Now 'refugees' are those of us who have been so unfortunate as to arrive in a new country without means and have to be helped by Refugee Committees" (*JP*, 55).

Arendt graphically describes what happens when one loses home, occupation, family, and the everyday life-world of one's language. Mocking the absurdities of the aspiration to adjust and assimilate, she tells the story of the German Jew who, having just arrived in France, organizes "one of those societies of adjustment in which German Jews asserted to each other that they were already Frenchmen. In his first speech he said: 'We have been good Germans in Germany and therefore we shall be good Frenchmen in France.' The public applauded enthusiastically and nobody laughed; we were happy to have learnt how to prove our loyalty" (*JP*, 64). There is something desperate about this false optimism, this eagerness to assimilate to new surroundings, whereby one slips into the "insane desire to be changed, not to be Jews." "Under the cover of our 'optimism' you can easily detect the hopeless sadness of assimilationists" (*JP*, 63).

With sarcastic irony, Arendt relates how assimilation did not mean simply adjustment to a new country, mores, and language, but took on a "deep" philosophical significance.

We had scholars write philosophical dissertations on the predestined harmony between Jews and Frenchmen, Jews and Germans, Jews and Hungarians, Jews and . . . . Our so frequently suspected loyalty of today has a long history. It is the history of a hundred and fifty years of assimilated Jewry who performed an unprecedented feat: though proving all the time their non-Jewishness, they succeeded in remaining Jews all the same. (*JP*, 64)

Arendt's phenomenological description of the mentality of being a Jewish refugee, which ranges from playful humor to the pathos of despair, has a deadly serious point. For she poignantly highlights the plight of the stateless human being – the nonperson – who has no legitimate legal or political status. This is a problem with which she continued to struggle throughout her life. It is one of the sources of her critique of that strain in the Enlightenment legacy and in classical liberalism that stresses the importance of the abstract human being and his alleged "inalienable rights."

In the closing paragraphs of "We Refugees," after sketching the dilemmas and plight of Jewish refugees, she writes:

But before you cast the first stone at us, remember that being a Jew does not give any legal status in this world. If we should start telling the truth that we are nothing but Jews, it would mean we expose ourselves to the fate of human beings who, unprotected by any specific law or political convention, are nothing but human beings. I can hardly imagine an attitude more dangerous, since we actually live in a world in which human beings as such have ceased to exist for quite a while; since society has discovered discrimination as the great social weapon by which one may kill men without any bloodshed; since passports or birth certificates, and sometimes even income receipts, are no longer formal papers but matters of social distinction. (*JP*, 65)

To be a stateless person means that one is "unprotected by any specific law or political convention." This is the situation that Arendt thinks is so potentially dangerous and sinister. With the event of Nazi totalitarianism, one discovered how talk of inalienable human rights was hollow.

One need only remember the extreme case of the Nazis, who insisted that all Jews of non-German nationality "should be deprived of their citizenship either prior to, or, at the latest, on the day of deportation (for German Jews such a decree was not needed, because in the Third

Reich there existed a law according to which all Jews who had left the territory – including, of course, those deported to a Polish camp – automatically lost their citizenship) in order to realize the true implications of statelessness. (OT_3, 280)

Reading what Arendt wrote in 1951 has the hyper-real quality of a commentary on our contemporary world situation. Arendt's experiences as a stateless Jew provided her with a sharp insight into the ominous paradoxes and instability that happen when masses of refugees and stateless persons are "created" by political eruptions. She considered the sudden emergence of new stateless masses to be one of the most intractable problems of the twentieth century – a problem that outlasted totalitarian regimes. The danger of this new mass phenomenon of statelessness was one of the issues she had in mind when, toward the conclusion of *The Origins of Totalitarianism*, she wrote that "totalitarian solutions may well survive the fall of totalitarian regimes in the form of strong temptations which will come up whenever it seems impossible to alleviate political, social, or economic misery in a manner worthy of man" (OT_3, 459).

Earlier I mentioned the conflict between *state* and *nation* that came to light at the birth of the modern nation-state: the conflict between the declaration of the *universal* Rights of Man and the demand for territorial national sovereignty.[3] "The Declaration of the Rights of Man at the end of the eighteenth century was a turning point in history. It meant nothing more nor less than that from then on, Man, and not God's command or the customs of history, should be the source of law" (OT_3, 290). These rights were understood to be inalienable, ahistorical, universal rights which were to be upheld even against the sovereignty of the state. But how were the rights to be guaranteed and protected? Man, presumably, "appeared as the only sovereign in matters of law as the people was proclaimed the only sovereign in matters of government."

> In other words, man had hardly appeared as a completely emancipated, completely isolated being who carried his dignity within himself without reference to some larger encompassing order, when he disappeared again into a member of a people. From the beginning the paradox involved in the declaration of inalienable human rights was that it reckoned with an "abstract" human being who seemed to exist nowhere. (OT_3, 291)

As long as the nineteenth-century fiction that all Europeans were members of a nation and belonged to "the family of nations" existed, the unstable tension between the declaration of universal rights (according to which all human beings – or, at least, all white, propertied males – had "inalienable" rights) and the declaration of territorial national sovereignty (whereby one belongs to a culturally identifiable nation which secures and protects these rights) could be ignored. But with the undermining of the nation-state, with the growth and spread of imperialism, and especially with the explosion of the First World War, which set off a chain reaction of unintended consequences, this fiction completely collapsed, and the nation-state, the alleged protector of human rights, disintegrated.

> The full implication of [the] identification of the rights of man with the rights of peoples in the European nation-state system came to light only when a growing number of people and peoples suddenly appeared whose elementary rights were as little safeguarded by the ordinary functioning of nation-states in the middle of Europe as they would have been in the heart of Africa. The Rights of Man, after all, had been defined as "inalienable" because they were supposed to be independent of all governments; but it turned out that the moment human beings lacked their own government and had to fall back upon their minimum rights, no authority was left to protect them and no institution was willing to guarantee them. (OT_3, 291–2)

The explosion of 1914, with its severe consequences of instability, "shattered the façade of Europe's political system" of nation-states. And this instability was exacerbated by the Versailles treaty, in which it was disastrously assumed that one could establish new artificial nation-states and protect "minorities" with special minority "Peace treaties."

> The treaties lumped together many peoples in single states, called some of them "state people" and entrusted them with the government, silently assumed that others (such as Slovaks in Czechoslovakia, or the Croats and Slovenes in Yugoslavia) were equal partners in the government, which of course they were not, and with equal arbitrariness created out of a remnant a third group of nationalities called "minorities," thereby adding to the many burdens of the new states the trouble of observing special regulations for part of the population. (OT_3, 270)

This was a "preposterous solution," and representatives of "great nations knew only too well that minorities within nation-states must sooner or later be either assimilated or liquidated" (*OT*₃, 273). It was this radically unstable, dangerous state of affairs that destroyed the precarious balance between nation and state.

> With the emergence of the minorities in Eastern and Southern Europe and with the stateless people driven into Central and Western Europe, a completely new element of disintegration was introduced into postwar [First World War] Europe. Denationalization became a powerful weapon of totalitarian politics, and the constitutional inability of European nation-states to guarantee human rights, to those who had lost nationally guaranteed rights, made it possible for the persecuting governments to impose their standard of values even upon their opponents. Those whom the persecutor had singled out as scum of the earth – Jews, Trotskyites, etc. – actually were received as scum of the earth everywhere; those whom persecution had called undesirable became *indésirables* of Europe. (*OT*₃, 269)

What Hannah Arendt wrote almost 50 years ago is no less true – and perhaps even more so now.

> Much more stubborn in fact and much more far-reaching in consequence had been statelessness, the newest mass phenomenon in contemporary history, and the existence of an ever-growing new people comprised of stateless persons, the most symptomatic group in contemporary politics. Their existence can hardly be blamed on one factor alone, but if we consider the different groups among the stateless it appears that every political event since the end of the First World War inevitably added a new category to those who lived outside the pale of law. (*OT*₃, 276–7)

Long before the large-scale use of "denationalization" by totalitarian regimes, whereby innocent groups of people who had lived for generations within a national territory were stripped of all rights, it was becoming obvious that appeals to the Rights of Man were politically impotent, unenforceable, and subject to endless debates about how they were to be defined.

> The Rights of Man, supposedly inalienable, proved to be unenforceable – even in countries whose constitutions were based upon them – whenever people appeared who were no longer citizens of any sovereign state. To this fact, disturbing enough in itself, one must add the confusion created by the many recent attempts to frame a new bill of

human rights, which have demonstrated that no one seems able to define with any assurance what those general human rights, as distinguished from the rights of citizens, really are. Although everyone seems to agree that the plight of these people consists precisely in their loss of the Rights of Man, no one seems to know which rights they lost when they lost these human rights. (OT_3, 293)

Statelessness is a problem that has affected millions during the twentieth century, before and after the rise and fall of totalitarian regimes. But during the 1930s and 1940s it was especially acute for European Jews. For it was European Jewry that found itself to be in the "abnormal position" of suddenly being "outside the pale of society and nation" (OT_3, 240).

> The calamity of the rightless is not that they are deprived of life, liberty, and the pursuit of happiness, or of equality before the law and freedom of opinion – formulas which were designed to solve problems *within* given communities – but that they no longer belong to any community whatsoever. Their plight is not that they are not equal before the law, but that no law exists for them; not that they are oppressed but that nobody wants even to oppress them. Only in the last stage of a rather lengthy process is their right to live threatened; only if they remain perfectly "superfluous," if nobody can be found to "claim" them, may their lives be in danger. Even the Nazis started their extermination of Jews by first depriving them of all legal status (the status of second-class citizenship) and cutting them off from the world of the living by herding them into ghettos and concentration camps; and before they set the gas chambers into motion they had carefully tested the ground and found out to their satisfaction that no country would claim these people. The point is that a condition of complete rightlessness was created before the right to live was challenged. (OT_3, 295–6)

I have been arguing that Arendt began her quest for the *meaning* of the political from the time of her turn to politics in 1933. In her struggle to comprehend the phenomenon of Nazi totalitarianism, she was deepening her sense of politics. Her personal experiences as a stateless Jew who was compelled to flee Germany, France and finally Europe provided her with a distinctive perspective for understanding action and politics. A striking stage in her quest occurs in her reflections on the significance and consequences of statelessness, of being stripped of political and legal rights. If one reads carefully her discussion entitled "The Perplexities of the Rights of Man" (OT_3, 296–302), the final section of Part II of *The Origins of Totalitarianism*, one can discern the anticipation of the major themes of her much fuller discussion of politics, action, plurality, and freedom in *The Human Condition* and *On Revolution*. It is as if Arendt's experience of, and reflection upon, statelessness taught her what politics means, and why it is so essential to be a citizen in a polity to live a fully human life. What is it about statelessness and being deprived of human rights that is so revealing?

> The fundamental deprivation of human rights is manifested first and above all in the deprivation of a *place in the world* which makes *opinions* significant and actions effective. Something much more fundamental than *freedom* and justice, which are rights of citizens, is at stake when belonging to the community into which one is born is no longer a matter of course and not belonging no longer a matter of choice, or when one is placed in a situation where, unless he commits a crime, his treatment by others does not depend on what he does or does not do. This extremity, and nothing else, is the situation of people deprived of human rights. They are deprived, not of the right to freedom, but of the right to *action*; not of the right to think whatever they please, but of the right of *opinion*. (*OT*₃, 296; emphasis added)

Every one of the italicized items becomes an essential motif in Arendt's analysis of (authentic) politics. The world of which she speaks is the common, tangible world that is created and shared by a *plurality* of human beings – human beings who become fully human only when they have a "*place* in the world." It is this place that enables human beings to have a distinctive perspective on what they share. As she tells us in *The Life of the Mind*, "Living beings, men and animals, are not just in the world, they are *of the world*, and this precisely because they are subjects and objects – perceiving and being perceived – at the same time" (*LM*, 20). To have a place in the world means that each singular individual, who is different from other individuals, has a site from which to form a distinctive opinion on a common, shared world. In *The Human Condition*, Arendt explores how *world*-alienation, not *self*-alienation, "has been the hallmark of the modern age" (*HC*, 254). And it is precisely this worldlessness, this world-alienation, that has so profoundly characterized Jewish history. When we lose our sense of – or are forcibly kept from – sharing a common world from a plurality of perspectives with our fellow human beings, we lose something of our humanity.

The fundamental deprivation that occurs when one is stripped of the right to have rights is that an individual no longer has the opportunity to act. This right is even more basic than those of freedom and justice in the sense that a presupposition of becoming a citizen (where freedom and justice are relevant) is the ability to act, to initiate, and to form opinions on a shared, common world. Opinion (*doxa*) is the very stuff of politics. It requires imagination and judgment to form, test, and debate opinions with one's peers. Opinions are not to be confused with interests or mere subjective preferences.[4]

The most basic right is "the right to have rights (and that means to live in a framework where one is judged by one's actions and opinions) and a right to belong to some kind of organized community" (*OT*₃, 296–7). The full shock of witnessing what happened when millions of people suddenly appear who have lost, and cannot regain, this "right to have rights" taught Arendt how the sudden loss of home, of one's place in the world, of one's political status, "[became] identical with expulsion from humanity altogether" (*OT*₃, 297).

> [W]hat we must call a "human right" today would have been thought of as a general characteristic of the human condition which no tyrant could take away. Its loss entails the loss of the relevance of speech (and man, since Aristotle, has been defined as a being commanding the power of speech and thought), and the loss of all human relationship (and man, again since Aristotle, has been thought of as the "political animal," that is one who by definition lives in a community), the loss, in other words, of some of the most essential characteristics of human life. . . . *Not the loss of specific rights, then, but the loss of a community willing and able to guarantee any rights whatsoever, has been the calamity which has befallen ever-increasing numbers of people. Man, it turns out, can lose all the so-called Rights of Man without losing his essential quality as man, his human dignity. Only the loss of a polity itself expels him from humanity.* (*OT*₃, 297; emphasis added)

A passage like this makes dramatically clear how wrongheaded and perverse it is to think that Arendt's reflections on action and politics have their "origin" in an idealized nostalgic picture of a Greek polis (that never existed). This misguided, but all too fashionable, view of Arendt is based on a superficial reading of *The Human Condition*. The site of Arendt's thinking, her "political exercises," is the gap between past and future. It was her attempt to come to grips with the overwhelming political fact of the twentieth century, the sudden emergence of millions of people who are excluded from political communities, from the "right to have rights," that provoked her quest for the meaning of politics.

Her statement that "only the loss of a polity itself expels [man] from humanity" epitomizes the significance of action and politics for living a *human* life. This claim echoes her concluding remarks in "The Jew as Pariah": "For only within the framework of a people can a man live as a man among men, without exhausting himself. And only when a people lives and functions in consort with other peoples can it contribute to the establishment upon earth of a commonly conditioned and commonly controlled humanity" (*JP*, 90). We can also now understand what is distinctive about Arendt's situated, humanistic orientation. There is clearly a *universal* thrust in her claim that every *single* individual has (or ought to have) the "right to have rights." But this right becomes concrete only in the life of a *particular* community. In this respect, she thought that there was a certain "pragmatic soundness" in Edmund Burke's opposition to the French Revolution's Declaration of the Rights of Man. Although she does not endorse Burke's appeal to tradition and inheritance as a source of the legitimacy of a person's rights, she does think that he perceived the "arbitrariness" of appealing to universal rights which presumably belong to us in our "abstract nakedness of being human."

> The conception of human rights, based upon the assumed existence of a human being as such, broke down at the very moment when those who professed to believe in it were for the first time confronted with people who had indeed lost all other qualities and specific relationships – except that they were still human. The world found nothing sacred in the abstract nakedness of being human. . . .
>
> The survivors of the extermination camps, the inmates of concentration and internment camps, and even the comparatively happy stateless people could see without Burke's arguments that the abstract nakedness of being nothing but human was their greatest danger. (*OT*₃, 299–300)

Arendt's remarks have relevance for recent controversies concerning liberalism and communitarianism. One of the reasons why these tangled debates can seem so abstract and "academic" is that the issues are frequently discussed without relating them to concrete political experiences, the kind of experiences that are so manifest in

Arendt's reflections. No one could accuse her of being a communitarian – or, at least, the type of communitarian who softens the irreducibility, conflict, and plurality of perspectives and opinions within communal political life. But Arendt's lifelong suspicion of liberalism is in part motivated by her own experience of what it means concretely to be treated as an abstract human being who presumably has (or ought to have) rights in her "abstract nakedness of being nothing but human." The dark underside of the Enlightenment conception of a human being as someone who possesses rights simply by virtue of being an "abstract human being" is to leave human beings completely defenseless and powerless in the face of totalitarian terror. "Rights" talk is empty and hollow unless rights are concretely embodied in, and protected by, political institutions.

There are two further, central political consequences of Arendt's reflections on the "right to have rights." The first is negative, and it is why Arendt was so critical of the concept of sovereignty. Sovereignty is not to be confused with the legitimate right of a people or a nation for self-determination. Arendt thought that the precarious balance between state and nation that existed during the nineteenth century (before the rise of imperialism) was not only upset by, but eventually led to, unrestrained claims to national sovereignty, wherein the doctrine of sovereignty was so perverted that totalitarian regimes could claim "their sovereign right of denationalization," the "right" to exclude (and ultimately to exterminate) those who did not belong to the pure nation or race.

> Theoretically, in the sphere of international law, it had always been true that sovereignty is nowhere more absolute than in matters of "emigration, naturalization, nationality and expulsion"; the point, however, is that practical consideration and the silent acknowledgment of common interests restrained national sovereignty until the rise of totalitarian regimes. One is almost tempted to measure the degree of totalitarian infection by the extent to which the concerned governments use their sovereign right of denationalization. . . . But one should bear in mind at the same time that there was hardly a country left on the Continent that did not pass between the two wars some new legislation which, even if it did not use the right extensively, was always phrased to allow for getting rid of a great number of its inhabitants at any opportune moment. (*OT*₃, 278–9)

The second important consequence of Arendt's reflections on the "right to have rights" is her analysis of equality as a *political* concept, and of the need to understand what is distinctive about political equality. She tells us:

> Equality, in contrast to all that is involved in mere existence, is not given us, but is the result of human organization insofar as it is guided by the principle of justice. We are not born equal; we become equal as members of a group on the strength of our decision to guarantee ourselves mutually equal rights.
>
> Our political life rests on the assumption that we can produce equality through organization, because man can act in and change and build a common world, together with his equals and only with his equals. (*OT*₃, 301)

This claim, that equality comes into being only when human beings organize themselves into a polity, is one of the major themes in Arendt's understanding of politics. It is already anticipated in her earliest reflections on what has been lacking in Jewish history. For, since the Babylonian exile, the Jewish people never had an opportunity to "build a common world, together with [their] equals and only with [their] equals." This theme becomes central not only in *The Human Condition*, but also in *On Revolution*.[5] It is only in and through the creation of a polity that we can confront our fellow human beings as equals – and thereby create a distinctively human life. As natural or social beings, we are *not* equal. Arendt was deeply skeptical of all those tendencies in modern life that foster a false sense of social equality and homogeneity. When this happens, society triumphs over, and obliterates, the very possibility of politics. Like Nietzsche, she was convinced that what underlies the demand for *social equality* is envy and *ressentiment*. To deny or level differences among human beings is also to deny their distinctive individuality. To achieve our full humanity, we have to acknowledge, and even celebrate, our differences. This is not only compatible with, but is a precondition for, creating *political equality*, in a political community.

Statelessness, the sudden loss of political rights – what Arendt experienced directly from the time she fled Germany until 1951, when she became a United States citizen – was the basic phenomenon that provoked her reflections (*Nachdenken*) on the meaning of politics. Without the opportunity to exercise political rights, to belong to a political community, one could not live a fully human life. But statelessness is not yet the worst. In a condition of statelessness, one can still appeal to "rights" talk, even if it is feeble and impotent. The Nazis understood well that statelessness, denationalization, systematically stripping individuals of all rights, constituted only a *first* step on the way to the "final solution" – extermination.

> In comparison with the insane end-result – concentration-camp society – the process by which men are prepared for this end, and the methods by which individuals are adapted to these conditions, are transparent and logical. The insane mass manufacture of corpses is preceded by the historically and politically intelligible preparation of living corpses. The impetus and what is more important, the silent consent to such unprecedented conditions are the products of those events which in a period of political disintegration suddenly and unexpectedly made hundreds of thousands of human beings homeless, stateless, outlawed and unwanted, while millions of human beings were made economically superfluous and socially burdensome by unemployment. This in turn could only happen because the Rights of Man, which had never been philosophically established but merely formulated, which had never been politically secured but merely proclaimed, have, in their traditional form, lost all validity. (OT_3, 447)

For Arendt, looking into "totalitarian hell," "dwelling on horrors," searching to say "what is outside the realm of human speech" (OT_3, 446), seeking to comprehend the insane world of concentration-camp society – "the most consequential institution of totalitarian rule" – led her to her most profound insights concerning the meaning of politics, our responsibility for public life, and the sense in which politics is essential for leading a human life. The ultimate end of totalitarianism is "not the transformation of the outside world or the revolutionizing transmutation of society, but the transformation of human nature itself" (OT_3, 458). And this transformation meant the destruction of the very human conditions required for action and politics – spontaneity, natality, individuality, and plurality.

4

The Descent into Hell

> The reality of concentration camps resembles nothing so much as medieval pictures of Hell.
>
> *OT*₃

When Hannah Arendt first heard about Auschwitz, she was incredulous. Even though she and Heinrich had been sent to internment camps just three years before, they, like many of their contemporaries, did not believe the first reports that the Nazis were systematically exterminating innocent people in death camps. This is how Arendt describes her initial reaction to the reports about Auschwitz:

> That was in 1943. And at first we didn't believe it – although my husband and I always said that we expected anything from that bunch. But we didn't believe this because militarily it was unnecessary and uncalled for. My husband is a former military historian, he understands something about these matters. He said don't be gullible, don't take these stories at face value. They can't go that far! And then a half-year later we believed it after all, because we had the proof. That was the real shock. Before that we said: Well, one has enemies. That is entirely natural. Why shouldn't a people have enemies? But this was something different. It was really as if an abyss had opened. . . . *This ought not to have happened.* And I don't mean just the number of victims. I mean the method, the fabrication of corpses and so on – I don't need to go into that. This should not have happened. Something happened there to which we cannot reconcile ourselves. None of us ever can. (*EU*, 13–14)

Unlike many who continued in disbelief or denial, who turned away from "dwelling on horrors" (*OT*₃, 441), Arendt sought to confront these horrors. She believed that the concentration camps were "the most consequential institution of totalitarian rule" (*OT*₃, 441). No totalitarian government can exist without terror, and no terror can be effective without concentration camps. This realization caused her to change her mind (once again) about the shape of *The Origins of Totalitarianism* – and finally enabled her to bring her book to completion. No longer was this to be an "imperialism" book, or even a book limited to the elements that crystallized into Nazi totalitarianism. The book would be about the hidden structure of totalitarianism. By 1947, she had already written most of the material included in the first two parts of the book: "Antisemitism" and "Imperialism." But in a letter to Jaspers (Sept. 4, 1947) she indicated that there had been a change in her thinking: "the third and concluding part will be devoted to the structures of totalitarian states. I have to rewrite this completely because I've only recently become aware of some important things here, especially in regard to Russia" (*C*, 98). Concentration camps are not just a Nazi phenomenon, they are the essential institution for *any* totalitarian regime.

When Arendt became aware of how important concentration camps were for the terror apparatus of totalitarian regimes, she wrote a proposal to establish a research institute to gather information and testimonies and to study concentration camps. Elisabeth Young-Bruehl describes succinctly what she did.

> When she became aware of the importance of concentration camps in the totalitarian regimes, Arendt prepared a memo for *Jewish Social Studies*, dated 10 December 1948, requesting support for a "Research Project on Concentration Camps." The project would include locating documents on the camps and preparing a bibliography, interviewing survivors, writing a history of the camps against the background of a survey of all types of detention and internment camps in use prior to the war, and evaluating all the assembled materials. A similar proposal formed part of a general project Hannah Arendt recommended to Elliot Cohen, the editor of *Commentary*. She asked whether *Commentary* would support a research institute to investigate not only the concentration camps but the entire spectrum of postwar Jewish issues as they related to worldwide political trends. (*YB*, 204)

Neither proposal was accepted. We can see how emphatically Arendt identified herself as a Jewish intellectual in 1948, when she said in her letter to Elliot Cohen: "We [Jews] lack an intelligentsia which has been grounded in history and educated through a long political tradition." She indicated her hope that such a research institute would provide Jews with the information that might prepare them for the possibility that "world political developments may well again crystallize around hostility to the Jews" (*YB*, 204–5).[1]

In 1948, Arendt also published one of her most brilliant and perceptive articles with the unembellished title "The Concentration Camps." She later reworked this article, and included it as the final section of her chapter "Totalitarianism in Power" in *The Origins of Totalitarianism.* Arendt revised this section once again for the second, enlarged 1958 edition of that book. There are subtle but significant differences in these subsequent revisions.[2] The original article and its revisions are important for four reasons. (1) Arendt's realization that concentration camps are the most consequential institution for totalitarian regimes crystallized her own thinking about "the hidden structure of totalitarianism." (2) She provides a graphic and incisive analysis of the stages in the process of total domination. (3) She completed the argument that she began in "The Decline of the Nation-State and the End of the Rights of Man." Just as Arendt's reflections on statelessness led her to articulate the meaning of politics, and why belonging to a polity is essential for our humanity, so her analysis of total domination led her to an even deeper insight into what is quintessential to living a human life. This emerges from her analysis of how the "concentration camps are the laboratories where changes in human nature are tested" (*OT*₃, 458). (4) It is here that we find the basis for Arendt's reflections on the meaning of absolute or radical evil.[3]

The phenomenon of the concentration camps, more than any other aspect of totalitarianism, seems to defy the very possibility of comprehension. Yet, understanding the role that the concentration camps play in totalitarian regimes is essential for grasping what is distinctive about the dynamics of totalitarian movements. Arendt thinks that "the horror of the concentration and extermination camps can never be fully embraced by the imagination, for the very reason that it stands outside of life and death" (*CC*, 748). Furthermore, "there are no parallels to the life of the concentration camps. All seeming parallels create confusion and distract attention from what is essential. Forced labor in prisons and penal colonies, banishment, slavery, all seem for a moment to offer comparisons, but on closer examination lead nowhere" (*OT*₁, 416).[4] All traditional categories and concepts for comprehending, understanding, or judging what happened break down. We can appreciate the poignancy of her remark in the preface to *The Origins of Totalitarianism*: "comprehension . . . [means] examining and bearing consciously the burden which our century has placed on us – neither denying its existence nor submitting meekly to its weight" (*OT₃*, viii). "The extraordinary difficulty which we have in attempting to understand the institution of the concentration camp and fit it into the record of human history is precisely the absence of . . . utilitarian criteria, an absence which is more than anything else also responsible for the curious air of unreality that surrounds this institution and everything connected with it."[5]

Arendt goes even further. Long before "Holocaust denial" became so perversely fashionable, she knew how "unreal" the concentration camps seem to be. Even the films of the living dead corpses which were taken when the camps were liberated are "just about as convincing as snapshots of mysterious substances taken at spiritualist séances" (*OT₃*, 446).

> There is a great temptation to explain away the intrinsically incredible by means of liberal rationalizations. In each one of us, there lurks such a liberal, wheedling us with the voice of common sense. We attempt to understand elements in present or recollected experience that simply surpass our powers of understanding. We attempt to classify as criminal a thing which, as we all feel, no such category was ever intended to cover. What meaning has the concept of murder when we are confronted with the mass production of corpses? We attempt to understand the behavior of concentration camp inmates and SS-men psychologically, when the very thing that must be realized is that the psyche [or character] *can* be destroyed even without the destruction of the physical man; that, indeed, psyche, character, and individuality seem under certain circumstances to express themselves only through the rapidity or slowness with which they disintegrate. (*OT₁*, 415)

In order to comprehend the institution of the concentration and extermination camps, one must first appreciate how they defy any commonsense utilitarian thinking. They are "anti-utilitarian." The "unquestioned fundamental preconceptions" of the social sciences are completely inadequate for understanding this institution.[6] Nevertheless, it is this anti-utilitarian character that provides a clue about their function.

In other words, it is not only the non-utilitarian character of the camps themselves – the senselessness of "punishing" completely innocent people, the failure to keep them in a condition so that profitable work might be extorted from them, the superfluousness of frightening a completely subdued population – which gives them their distinctive and disturbing qualities, but their anti-utilitarian function, the fact that not even the supreme emergencies of military activities were allowed to interfere with these "demographic policies." It was as though the Nazis were convinced that it was of greater importance to run extermination factories than to win the war. (*EU*, 233)

But why? To indicate just how anti-utilitarian and irrational the machinery of extermination seems to be, we might consider the example of the Hungarian Jews. By the spring and summer of 1944, it was quite clear that the Nazis were losing the war. Not only were they losing the war, but they desperately needed every resource available to defend themselves on two fronts. Yet no effort was spared to transport Hungarian Jews to extermination camps. By the fall of 1944, 400,000 Jews had been sent to their death.[7]

What, then, is the anti-utilitarian function of these camps? Part of the answer is the perverse logic of ideological racist thinking. If we "consider only the fantastic ideological claims of racism in its logical purity, then the extermination policy of the Nazis makes almost too much sense. Behind its horrors lies the same inflexible logic which is characteristic of certain systems of paranoiacs where everything follows with absolute necessity once the first insane premise is accepted" (*EU*, 233). If "pure" Aryans are a superior race which is in danger of being infected and contaminated by inferior races, then these infectious agents must be exterminated, just as vermin are exterminated. Even anti-Semitism as a political ideology is not sufficient to account for the extermination camps. "Neither the fate of European Jewry nor the establishment of death factories can be fully explained and grasped in terms of anti-Semitism. . . . Anti-Semitism only prepared the ground to make it easier to start the extermination of peoples with the Jewish people. We know now that this extermination program of Hitler's did not stop short of planning the liquidation of large sections of the German people" (*EU*, 235). Gypsies, homosexuals, Communists, mentally ill Germans, and many other "undesirable" groups were also slated for extermination.

The most essential function of the concentration camps is their role "in the larger terror apparatus." Totalitarian terror must be able to strike at any time and any place. Total terror is directed indiscriminately at the guilty and the innocent. "Terror is the essence of totalitarian domination" (OT_3, 464), and the most effective institutions for total domination are the concentration and extermination camps – those "laboratories in which the fundamental belief of totalitarianism that everything is possible is being verified" (OT_3, 437).

Arendt classifies concentration camps into three types, corresponding to three "basic Western conceptions of a life after death: Hades, Purgatory, and Hell" (OT_3, 445).

> To Hades correspond those relatively mild forms, once popular even in nontotalitarian countries, for getting undesirable elements of all sorts – refugees, stateless persons, the asocial and the unemployed – out of the way; as DP camps, which are nothing other than camps for persons who have become superfluous and bothersome, they have survived the war. (OT_3, 445)

This accurately describes Gurs, the camp where Arendt herself was interned. I suspect that she might have been scandalized, but not shocked, that 50 years after the Second World War there are an increasing number of camps corresponding to Hades.

> Purgatory is represented by the [former] Soviet Union's labor camps, where neglect is combined with chaotic forced labor. Hell in the most literal sense was embodied by those types of camp perfected by the Nazis, in which the whole of life was thoroughly and systematically organized with a view to the greatest possible torment. (OT_3, 445)[8]

What all three have in common is that "the human masses sealed off in them are treated as if they no longer existed, as if what happened to them were no longer of any interest to anybody, as if they were already dead" (OT_3, 455). "The real horror of the concentration and extermination camps lies in the fact that the inmates, even if they happen to keep alive, are more effectively cut off from the world of the living than if they had died, because terror enforces oblivion" (OT_3, 443).[9]

But precisely how did the concentration camps function in order to secure total domination? Here we come to the heart of Arendt's remarkably penetrating analysis, which I do not think has ever been surpassed. She analyzes this as a three-stage process.

(1) "The first essential step on the road to total domination is to kill the juridical person in man" (OT_3, 447). This was started by the

Nazis even before they established concentration camps. Arendt is referring to the stringent series of legal measures which, beginning in 1933, stripped Jews (and others) of their juridical rights. In the camps themselves no one had any rights. The Rights of Man which allegedly belong to every human being by virtue of being a human being become sheer fiction in a concentration camp. "The aim of an arbitrary system is to destroy the civil rights of the whole population, who ultimately become just as outlawed in their own country as the stateless and homeless. The destruction of man's rights, the killing of the juridical person in him, is a prerequisite for dominating him entirely" (OT_3, 451). But this destruction of rights is not yet "total domination."

(2) "The next decisive step in the preparation of living corpses is the murder of the moral person in man. This is done in the main by making martyrdom, for the first time in history, impossible" (OT_3, 451). The SS, who supervised the camps, corrupted all human solidarity. The Nazis were perversely brilliant in organizing the camps so that the inmates themselves were forced to become responsible for the daily routine and administration. Here one is witnessing a grotesque version of something that Lazare noted long before twentieth-century concentration camps existed: namely, how the oppressors (exterminators) of the Jews used Jews to carry out their policies. Death in the concentration camps became anonymous (making it impossible to find out whether a prisoner was alive or dead). Death was robbed of meaning, and the Nazis sought to destroy all witnesses, so that there could be no testimony.

Arendt notes that the attack "on the moral person might still have been opposed by man's conscience which tells him it is better to die a victim than to live as a bureaucrat of murder" (OT_3, 452), or, as Socrates proclaimed: it is better to suffer an injustice than to commit an injustice. But the Nazis used terror to destroy the last vestiges of conscience.

> Totalitarian terror achieved its most terrible triumph when it succeeded in cutting the moral person off from the individualist escape and in making the decisions of conscience absolutely questionable and equivocal. When a man is faced with the alternative of betraying and thus murdering his friends or of sending his wife and children, for whom he is in every sense responsible, to their death; when even suicide would mean the immediate murder of his own family – how is he to decide? The alternative is no longer between good and evil, but

between murder and murder. Who could solve the moral dilemma of the Greek mother, who was allowed by the Nazis to choose which of her three children should be killed? (*OT*₃, 452)

Arendt returned again and again to the question of conscience – what it is and how it functions. These issues become especially important in her report on the Eichmann trial and her subsequent reflections on morality and judgment. Our traditional moral and legal systems presuppose that every mature normal person is capable of exercising her moral conscience, and thereby capable of distinguishing right from wrong, regardless of what she actually does. Arendt even tells us that this is something which she never really questioned in her own upbringing. But the concentration camps – those laboratories of totalitarianism where the hypothesis that everything is possible is tested – taught us that even one's conscience can be obliterated.

(3) Killing the juridical person and the moral person – even annihilating conscience – is not yet the worst. There is a third and final step in the process of manufacturing living corpses – killing off all individuality and spontaneity.

> After murder of the moral person and annihilation of the juridical person, the destruction of the individuality is almost always successful. Conceivably some laws of mass psychology may be found to explain why millions of human beings allowed themselves to be marched unresistingly into the gas chambers, although these laws would explain nothing else but the destruction of individuality. It is more significant that those individually condemned to death very seldom attempted to take one of their executioners with them, that there were scarcely any serious revolts, and that even in the moment of liberation there were very few spontaneous massacres of SS men. *For to destroy individuality is to destroy spontaneity, man's power to begin something new out of his own resources, something that cannot be explained on the basis of reactions to environment and events.* (*OT*₃, 455; emphasis added)

I have emphasized this last sentence for several reasons. Later, when we consider Arendt's Eichmann report, we will see that several of her harshest critics claimed that she not only "blamed" the victims for what happened to them, but put forth the false romantic idea that the victims – especially the Jews – could have rebelled against their persecutors. Ironically, she always stressed the perverse effectiveness of the techniques used by the Nazis to destroy individuality and spontaneity. Unless we grasp this – unless we grasp that totalitarianism seeks to transform human nature and eliminate all spontaneity, an aim that was largely fulfilled in the concentration camps – we will never comprehend adequately the full horror of totalitarian regimes.

There is another reason for emphasizing the above sentence. Arendt's characterization of individuality and spontaneity – "man's power to begin something new" – is the very characterization of what she was later to call *natality*, the capacity to act which is the necessary condition for the exercise of human freedom.

This is how Arendt describes those in whom all individuality and spontaneity has been killed:

> Nothing then remains but ghostly marionettes with human faces, which all behave like the dog in Pavlov's experiments, which all react with perfect reliability even when going to their own death, and which do nothing but react. This is the real triumph of the system: "The triumph of the SS demands that the tortured victim allow himself to be led to the noose without protesting, that he renounce and abandon himself to the point of ceasing to affirm his identity. And it is not for nothing. It is not gratuitously, out of sheer sadism, that the SS men desire his defeat. They know that the system which succeeds in destroying its victim before he mounts the scaffold . . . is incomparably the best for keeping a whole people in slavery. In submission. Nothing is more terrible than these processions of human beings going like dummies to their death. The man who sees this says to himself: 'For them to be thus reduced, what power must be concealed in the hands of the masters,' and he turns away, full of bitterness but defeated." (*OT*₃, 455)[10]

The final goal of total domination is "the liquidation of all spontaneity" (*OT*₃, 456). All spontaneity, no matter how unpolitical and harmless it may be, is to be liquidated. "Pavlov's dog, the human specimen reduced to the most elementary reactions, the bundle of reactions that can always be liquidated and replaced by other bundles of reactions that behave in exactly the same way, is the model 'citizen' of a totalitarian state; and such a citizen can be produced only imperfectly outside of the camps" (*OT*₃, 456).

Consequently, the anti-utilitarian character of the concentration camps is only *apparent*. The truth is that concentration and extermination camps are essential for the functioning of totalitarianism.

> Without concentration camps, without the undefined fear they inspire and the very well-defined training they offer in totalitarian domination,

which can nowhere else be fully tested with all of its most radical possibilities, a totalitarian state can neither inspire its nuclear troops with fanaticism nor maintain a whole people in complete apathy. (OT_3, 456)

Total domination involves killing the juridical person, killing the moral person and obliterating conscience, and liquidating individuality and spontaneity. But there is a sense in which the very phrase "total domination" is misleading. For it suggests that total domination is domination over *human beings*. But totalitarianism does not stop with the "despotic rule over men." The "logic" of totalitarianism strives to produce a system in which men are *superfluous*.

Total power can be achieved and safeguarded only in a world of conditioned reflexes, of marionettes without the slightest trace of spontaneity. . . . As long as all men have not been made equally superfluous – and this has been accomplished only in concentration camps – the ideal of totalitarian domination has not been achieved. (OT_3, 457)

This ruthless, systematic attempt to make all human beings (victims and persecutors) – in their individuality, spontaneity, and *plurality* – superfluous is the essential clue for understanding what Arendt means by absolute or radical evil (see ch. 7).

One of the reasons why Arendt's analysis "total domination" is so important is because it brings into sharp focus her concepts of action and politics. Let me explain more fully what I mean. I have been arguing that if we want to gain an adequate understanding of Arendt's thinking about politics, we must return to those personal experiences and events which originally motivated her, and so deeply influenced the contours of her thinking. From (at least) 1933, Arendt was involved in a quest for the *meaning* of politics. In speaking of meaning, I am using the word the way Arendt used it, as the result of *thinking*. Arendt maintains a sharp distinction between meaning and truth (while acknowledging their interdependence). She came to associate meaning with the faculty that Kant called *Vernunft* and truth with *Verstand*. What is important about "meaning" as Arendt uses this word is that it has no *finality*. It requires ever new and vigilant attempts to engage in the activity of thinking. As she tells us in *The Life of the Mind*, "It is more than likely that men, if they were ever to lose that appetite for meaning we call thinking and cease to ask unanswerable questions, would lose not only the ability to produce those thought-things that we call works of art but also the capacity to ask all answerable questions upon which every civilization is founded" (*LM*, 62). By "unanswerable questions" Arendt does not mean questions not worth asking. On the contrary, she means the questions that are the most important to keep asking and trying to answer – with the full awareness that no answer can be final and definitive.[11]

Arendt's quest for the meaning of politics began with a reflection on Jewish politics – or, rather, with her judgment that there had been a lack of any significant Jewish politics in the modern age. In her attraction to the ideas of Bernard Lazare, in her understanding of the "conscious pariah," in her claim that in the modern age the only solution to the Jewish question is a political one, she envisioned a type of spontaneous politics from below in which the Jewish people would fight collectively for their rights as Jews.

We have also seen how in Arendt's reflections on statelessness (starting from her own experiences as a stateless Jew), she refined her understanding of rights. She exposed the speciousness and full danger of thinking of human beings as abstract individuals who (outside a political community) possess inalienable rights simply by virtue of being human beings. The Nazis made a mockery of this fiction. She showed how depriving human beings of rights makes them into something less than human. For it is only in a political community that rights can be exercised and protected. She argued that "the fundamental deprivation of human rights is manifested first and above all in the deprivation of a place in the world which makes opinions significant and actions effective" (*OT*₃, 296).

But it is only when Arendt took on the most difficult and challenging task of attempting to comprehend the character and role of concentration camps for totalitarian regimes that she penetrated most deeply into what is required for authentic politics – to act, to initiate, to begin spontaneously something new, to be a distinctive individual among a plurality of human beings, to have a perspective and place in a common world. For the goal of totalitarianism is to destroy the spontaneity of our humanity, to transform human beings into a species that reacts automatically to commands.[12] This is what the concentration camps set out to demonstrate as possible. This would have been the supreme "proof" that "everything is possible."

It was by descending into hell, into the abyss that had opened up, in "dwelling on horrors" of the concentration camps, that Arendt was able to see so lucidly what is fundamental and vital for action, politics, and living a human life. This is what her mentor, Karl Jaspers, would have called one of those "limit-experiences" that enable us to break through the clichés, the prejudices of common sense, and thereby discover what we would not discern otherwise – what is constitutive of our humanity.

In the 1958 revision of the section dedicated to the analysis of total domination, Arendt added a few paragraphs near the beginning of her analysis which show how keenly aware she was of the aim of this domination. She writes:

> Total domination, which strives to organize the infinite plurality and differentiation of human beings as if all humanity were just one individual, is possible only if each and every person can be reduced to a never changing identity of reactions, so that each of these bundles of reactions can be exchanged at random for any other. The problem is to fabricate something that does not exist, namely, a kind of human species resembling other animal species whose only "freedom" would consist in "preserving the species." Totalitarian domination attempts to achieve this goal both through ideological indoctrination of the elite formations and through absolute terror in the camps; and the atrocities for which the elite formations are ruthlessly used become, as it were, the practical application of the ideological indoctrination – the testing ground in which the latter must prove itself – while the appalling spectacle of the camps themselves is supposed to furnish the "theoretical" verification of the ideology.
>
> The camps are meant not only to exterminate people and degrade human beings, but also serve the ghastly experiment of eliminating, under scientifically controlled conditions, spontaneity itself as an expression of human behavior and transforming the human personality into a mere thing, into something that even animals are not; for Pavlov's dog, which, as we know, was trained to eat not when it was hungry but when a bell rang, was a perverted animal. (OT_2, 438)

Plurality, spontaneity, individuality, action, opinion, "a place in the world," freedom – these are the *major* strands of Arendt's understanding of the *meaning* of politics. This is the cluster of concepts she discovered in her probing of statelessness and the total domination of the concentration camps. Arendt returned to these strands, weaving them together in novel ways, in *The Human Condition, On Revolution*, and *The Life of the Mind.* The quest for meaning can never be complete.

Arendt began her study of totalitarianism by seeking to comprehend why the Jewish people were thrust into the storm center of twentieth-century world politics. Her "dwelling on horrors," her reflections on the total domination of the concentration camps, led her to a deep understanding of what is required to lead a fully human life – spontaneity, action, and plurality. I agree with Claude Lefort when he says:

> Arendt's reading of totalitarianism, in both its Nazi and Stalinist variants, governs the subsequent elaboration of her theory of politics. She conceptualizes politics by inverting the image of totalitarianism, and this leads her to look, not for a model of politics – the use of the term "model" would be a betrayal of her intentions – but for a reference to politics in certain privileged moments when its features are most clearly discernible: the moment of the Greek City in Antiquity and, in modern times, the moments of the American and French Revolutions. The moment of the workers' councils in Russia in 1917, and that of the Hungarian workers' councils of 1956, might also be added to the list.[13]

Lefort has it just right when he claims that Arendt's concern with "certain privileged moments" of politics "when its features are most clearly discernible" is motivated by the desire to discover reference points in order to understand the meaning of politics. It is for the sake of understanding our present condition and its *dangers* that she turns to the past. "Like a pearl diver who descends to the bottom of the sea, not to excavate the bottom and bring it to light but to pry loose the rich and the strange, the pearls and the coral in the depths of the past and to carry them to the surface" (*MD*, 205): this is the spirit in which Arendt sought to wrest those "thought fragments," those reference points, which enable us to grasp what totalitarianism so perilously endangered.

5

Zionism: Jewish Homeland
or Jewish State?

Palestine and the building of a Jewish homeland constitute today
the great hope and the great pride of Jews all over the world.
What would happen to Jews, individually and collectively, if this
hope and pride were to be extinguished in another catastrophe is
almost beyond imagining. . . . There is no Jew in the world whose
whole outlook on life and the world would not be radically
changed by such a tragedy.
"To Save the Jewish Homeland: There is Still Time" (May 1948)

In my Introduction I cited the interchange that took place between
Hans Morgenthau and Hannah Arendt when Morgenthau bluntly
asked her "What are you? Are you a conservative? Are you a liberal?
What is your position within contemporary possibilities?" In that
same interchange, Arendt went on to say the following:

I don't belong to any group. You know the only group I ever belonged
to were the Zionists. This was only because of Hitler, of course. And
this was from '33 to '43. And after that I broke. The only possibility to
fight back *as a Jew* and not as a human being – which I thought was a
great mistake, because if you are attacked as a Jew, you have got to
fight back as a Jew, you cannot say, "Excuse me, I am not a Jew; I am
a human being." This is silly. And I was surrounded by this kind of
silliness. There was no other possibility, so I went into Jewish politics –
not really politics – I went into social work and was somehow also
connected with politics. (*RPW*, 333–4)

Even this forthright reply is misleading. It sounds as if Arendt is
telling us that for a 10-year period she belonged to the Zionists "only
because of Hitler," and then broke with them. But the reality is much
more complex. Arendt tells us that when she fled from Germany
in 1933, she posed the question to herself "What can I specifically
do as a Jew? . . . it was now my clear intention to work with an

organization. For the first time. To work with the Zionists. . . . I wanted to go into practical work, exclusively and only Jewish work. With this in mind I then looked for work in France" (*EU*, 12). Although she was closely associated with various Jewish and Zionist organizations during her Paris years and her early years in New York, she never identified totally with Zionism. Her voice was always that of a dissenting critic. To fully understand her reservations, her ambivalence, and the basis for her criticisms, we must again recall something of her early history. It was not any religious, spiritual, or even deeply emotional experiences that attracted her to Zionism. Her mother, who brought her up, was "completely a-religious" (*EU*, 6). Her paternal grandfather, who was president of the liberal Jewish community, was an outspoken anti-Zionist. She never joined any German Zionist youth group. As a university student, she became friends with Hans Jonas and Kurt Blumenfeld, both of whom were committed Zionists and emigrated to Palestine, but there is no evidence that Arendt herself ever seriously considered Aliyah. When she fled Germany in 1933, her destination was Paris, not Jerusalem. She was led to Zionism after being "hit on the head" by political realities – the rise of the Nazis and the political virulence of anti-Semitism. Her own thinking compelled her to confront Zionism, because she believed that the great failure of modern European Jewry was the failure to engage in a viable Jewish politics. The Zionists were the only people who fully understood and acted on this conviction. It was politics – the need for a Jewish politics – that led her to Zionism. And it was politics – her critique of Zionist politics – that was the reason for her later break with it.

During Arendt's Paris years, as the situation for European Jews deteriorated, she still did not seriously consider "going up" to Palestine, even though she was helping children to escape to Palestine in her work with Youth Aliyah. When she made her first trip there in 1935, accompanying a group of Youth Aliyah trainees, she was most excited by her side visits to Syracuse, where she saw her first Greek temple (to which she returned many years later) and her visit to Petra in Transjordan where she viewed the famous Roman temple. These made a far more vivid and lasting impression upon her than anything she saw in Palestine.[1]

Arendt's imagination was, however, captured by the experiment of the kibbutzim. The kibbutz movement was creating a new type of Jew, a Jewish "aristocracy," but she herself was not tempted to live the life of a *chalutz* (Jewish pioneer).[2] What, then, drew Arendt to Zionism? It was her firm conviction that the modern European Jewish project of social assimilation was a complete disaster. The aspiration for Jewish emancipation had been confused with a desperate attempt to assimilate based upon hypocrisy and self-deception. European Jewry was discovering that assimilation was no protection against anti-Semitism – or extermination. If the Jews themselves were to assume responsibility for their own destiny, if they were not to be merely victims and "sufferers of history," then they must engage in political action.

It is almost as if Arendt became a Zionist as the logical conclusion of what Aristotle calls a "practical syllogism." If the only solution to the Jewish question is a political one and the only Jewish group that is prepared to engage in political action are the Zionists, then one must join the Zionists. She certainly did not feel any emotional or spiritual "call to Zion." Nor did she ever think that living in the Diaspora was incompatible with Zionism. A Zionism without a thriving Jewish life outside Palestine would become provincial. Even when she identified most closely with the Zionists, she was always bitingly critical of Zionist *ideology* (she opposed all forms of ideology).

Arendt's idiosyncratic Zionism was shaped more by Bernard Lazare than by Theodor Herzl or Chaim Weizmann. She was attracted by Lazare's rebellious *élan* – his vision of the Jewish people rising up to fight for their rights. For her, as for Lazare, "the territorial question was secondary – a mere outcome of the primary demand that 'the Jews should be emancipated as a people and in the form of a nation.' " Like Lazare, what she sought "was not an escape from antisemitism but a mobilization of the people against its foes" (*JP*, 128). Arendt consistently opposed that strand in Zionism (she traced it back to Herzl) which assumed that Zionist goals could be achieved only by working with the "great powers" and anti-Semitic governments.[3] Thus she thought that it was cynical and dangerous for Zionists to cooperate with the Nazis, as they did during the early days of the rise of the Nazis because of their "mutual" interests, the Nazis wanting to get rid of Jews and the Zionists wanting European Jews to emigrate to Palestine.

Arendt did not have any significant influence on the course of Zionist politics. At best, she was taken to be an intellectual maverick without a concrete sense of "political realities," and, at worst, a betrayer of the Zionist cause. From the perspective of the history of

Zionism, Arendt really is a minor, insignificant figure. But her concrete warnings about what might happen if the Zionists and the Jews in Palestine failed to face their problems honestly – for example, the Jewish–Arab question – have as much relevance for us today as they did when she forcefully stated them in the 1940s. What is most important about her dissenting Zionist opinions is what they reveal concerning her own thinking about politics in the twentieth century: what is wrong with the concept (and practice) of the nation-state and national sovereignty and what the political alternative to the nation-state might be.

Arendt never hesitated to express and defend her opinions in the strongest possible ("exaggerated") language. She became increasingly outspoken in her criticism of Zionist policies. She objected to the Biltmore Program that the Zionists adopted in 1942, whereby it was proposed that the Jews in Palestine (who were a minority at the time) would in their "homeland" grant the actual majority (Arabs) minority rights. She felt that for 50 years, from the time of the first Zionist Aliyah to Palestine, Zionists had ignored, obscured, and suppressed the explosive issue of Jewish–Arab relations.

Arendt's sharpest, most bitter critique of the Zionists was provoked by a resolution adopted unanimously at the October 1944 meeting of the American Zionists (and later affirmed by the World Zionist Organization). The resolution called for the establishment of a "free and democratic Jewish commonwealth . . . [which] shall embrace the whole of Palestine, undivided and undiminished." For Arendt, this was a decisive turning point in Zionist history, with the more moderate general Zionists completely capitulating to the more extreme revisionists.[4]

The article she wrote, "Zionism Reconsidered," damning this resolution and giving her own interpretation of the history and failures of the Zionist movement, was more passionate and vehement than anything else she had previously written on Jewish or Zionist issues. She used all the rhetorical means at her command: irony, sarcasm, condemnation, scorn, and blunt denunciation. Her passion arose not from "anti-Zionism" but, rather, from her anger and disappointment in the victorious forces of the international Zionist movement. The rhetoric of "Zionism Reconsidered" was so vehement that *Commentary* refused to publish it. When Arendt protested, Clement Greenberg, one of the editors, admitted that he thought it "contained too many anti-semitic implications – not in the sense that you intend them as such implications, but that the unfriendly reader might intend them as such" (cited in *YB*, 223).[5]

Arendt knew that her voice was a minority one, that her opinion was being shouted down by others, but this did not deter her. One of her favorite quotations, which she cited over and over again, virtually became a motto: *victrix causa diis placuit, sed victa Catoni* (the victorious cause pleases the gods, but the defeated one pleases Cato). This declaration took on a special meaning for Arendt, which is reflected in her thinking about republicanism and judgment.[6] Not only did the victorious cause please the gods, but historians, especially modern historians, were overwhelmingly biased toward giving weight to the victorious causes and movements of history. Much of modern history was written as the progressive development of "victorious" causes. Arendt, like Walter Benjamin, who so deeply influenced her thinking on the question of history, was critical of this bias – where history is understood to be a narrative of continuous, progressive victories.

Both Benjamin and Arendt believed that much more could be learned from those defeated causes – those causes which were forgotten, marginalized, and obliterated from most historical accounts and memory. This theme came to prominence when she sought to recover the "lost treasure" of the revolutionary spirit and those fleeting moments of tangible freedom that spontaneously arise – and so quickly disappear (and were suppressed) – in the "progressive" development of revolutions. This is the sense in which *Victrix causa diis placuit, sed victa Catoni* was the "spirit of republicanism."

She knew from direct experience what it was like to express and defend an opinion, only to be shouted down or disregarded by one's peers. Like Bernard Lazare, Arendt herself (long before *Eichmann in Jerusalem*) was becoming a pariah among her own people. She was not only disturbed by the Zionist turn to revisionism, but was alarmed by the growing pressures toward ideological conformity, a conformity that did not tolerate any dissent and suppressed conflicting opinions. In her quest for the meaning of politics, she highlighted the role of opinion (*doxa*) – specifically the plurality and conflict of opinions, which are debated in public spaces among one's peers. This, for her, was the heart of authentic politics and tangible public freedom.[7] For Arendt, the tendency toward unanimity – the displacing of different perspectives on a common world with a single "truth" of one man, one party, one ideology – was the most pernicious tendency of the modern age. This is one of the key reasons why she distinguished so categorically "the political" from "the social." For "the social" in the modern age named all those tendencies that sought to routinize human beings – to eliminate human spontaneity and plurality. Furthermore, her ongoing, friendly quarrel with philosophy revolved primarily around her defense of the irreducible plurality of opinions against the "coercion" of a single philosophical truth. Philosophers (with very few exceptions) were intolerant toward the uncertainty of *doxa*. They argued that *doxa* was to be measured, and preferably replaced, by *aletheia*. At first glance it might seem that Arendt's strong defense of the need to create public spaces in which opinions can be tested and contested is similar to classical liberal arguments for free speech. But she diverges significantly from traditional liberalism insofar as she does not justify this plurality because she believes that the clash of opinions leads to *the* truth. To hold such a view is still to measure opinion by the standard of truth. Arendt's point is that, although truth is important for the formation of opinion – and in critical situations, can be decisive – nevertheless, opinions and truth are not the same. The clash of opinions is to be judged not by the standards of truth, but by whether it leads to better-informed, better-grounded opinion.[8] The point that I want to emphasize in this context is that Arendt's defense of the plurality and clash of opinions was not merely theoretical. It was not the result solely of her reflections on the relation of philosophy and politics, or her understanding of the subterranean tendencies of the modern age. It was the result of her own "personal experiences" with Zionism and Zionist ideology. In her article "To Save the Jewish Homeland," she warned her fellow Jews:

> Unanimity of opinion is a very ominous phenomenon, and one characteristic of our modern mass age. It destroys social and personal life, which is based on the fact that we are different by nature and by conviction. To hold different opinions and to be aware that other people think differently on the same issue shields us from that god-like certainty which stops all discussion and reduces social relationships to those of an ant heap. A unanimous public opinion tends to eliminate bodily those who differ, for mass unanimity is not the result of agreement, but an expression of fanaticism and hysteria. In contrast to agreement, unanimity does not stop at certain well-defined objects, but spreads like an infection into every related issue. (*JP*, 182)

I want to examine several of the key points that Arendt makes in

"Zionism Reconsidered." For this article sums up her convictions concerning Zionism, which had been evolving over the previous decade. It clearly indicates the basic lines of her critique of Zionism. Most important, we can see how Arendt's encounter with "really existing" Zionist politics sharpened her own understanding of politics. Consequently, it will further support my central thesis that in order to understand the nuances of Arendt's political thinking, we must see how it is grounded in, and arises out of, her multifaceted encounter with the Jewish question.

Consider the dramatic and prickly critical opening of this essay:

The end result of fifty years of Zionist politics was embodied in the recent resolution of the largest and most influential section of the World Zionist Organization. American Zionists from left to right adopted unanimously, at their last annual convention held in Atlantic City in October, 1944, the demand for a "free and democratic Jewish commonwealth . . . [which] shall embrace the whole of Palestine, undivided and undiminished." This is a turning-point in Zionist history; for it means that the Revisionist program, so long bitterly repudiated, has proved finally victorious. The Atlantic City Resolution goes even a step further than the Biltmore Program (1942), in which the Jewish minority had granted minority rights to the Arab majority. This time the Arabs were simply not mentioned in the resolution, which obviously leaves them the choice between voluntary emigration or second-class citizenship. It seems to admit that only opportunist reasons had previously prevented the Zionist movement from stating its final aims. These aims now appear to be completely identical with those of the extremists as far as the future political constitution of Palestine is concerned. It is a deadly blow to those Jewish parties in Palestine itself that have tirelessly preached the necessity of an understanding between the Arab and the Jewish peoples. On the other hand, it will considerably strengthen the majority under the leadership of Ben-Gurion, which, through the pressure of many injustices in Palestine and the terrible catastrophes in Europe, have turned more than ever nationalistic. (*JP*, 131)

This opening paragraph raises the central issues that most troubled Arendt. The primary issue is "the question of which kind of political body Palestine Jewry was to form": whether Palestine was to be the site of a "Jewish homeland" or whether (as the revisionists demanded) the only viable goal of Zionist aspirations was the founding of a sovereign Jewish state. Taking a stand on this question required an honest confrontation with the Jewish–Arab conflict and the issue of majority and minority rights. Arendt claimed that through much of Zionist history in Palestine there had been a failure to face up to the complexity of the issue (in part because of the succession of Arab riots). The revisionists at least had the advantage of being brutally forthright. They boldly insisted on the creation of a Jewish nation-state encompassing the whole of "ancient" Palestine, including Transjordan. The result would be a homogeneous Jewish State from which the Arab population would be "transferred" to other Arab countries. Arendt thought that such a solution would be intolerable. It would create a new stateless people, the Palestinian Arab refugees. We should recall her sardonic remark in *The Origins of Totalitarianism*: "After the war it turned out that the Jewish question, which was considered the only insoluble one, was indeed solved – namely, by means of a colonized and then conquered territory – but this solved neither the problem of the minorities nor the stateless. On the contrary, like virtually all other events of our century, the solution of the Jewish question merely produced a new category of refugees, the Arabs, thereby increasing the number of the stateless and rightless by another 700,000 to 800,000 people" (*OT₃*, 290).

Arendt emphatically argued in "Zionism Reconsidered" – and in virtually all her writings on Palestine and Israel – that peace in the Near East required, and would only come about with, direct negotiations between Jews and Arabs. It was foolhardy and dangerous for the Jewish people to think that the "big powers," whether the British, the Americans, or the Russians, could solve the problems of Palestine. What Arendt asserted so firmly in 1950 is as true (perhaps even more so) almost 50 years later.

> Peace in the Near East is essential to the State of Israel, to the Arab people and to the Western World. Peace, as distinguished from an armistice, cannot be imposed from the outside, it can only be the result of negotiations, of mutual compromise and eventual agreement between Jews and Arabs. (*JP*, 193)

Before the founding of the State of Israel, Arendt feared (with a certain perspicacity) that if the Zionists "continue to ignore the Mediterranean peoples and watch out only for the big faraway powers," they "will appear only as their tools, the agents of foreign and hostile interests."

Jews who know their own history should be aware that such a state of affairs will inevitably lead to a new wave of Jew-hatred; the antisemitism of tomorrow will assert that Jews not only profited from the presence of the foreign big powers in that region but had actually plotted it and hence are guilty of the consequences. (*JP*, 133)

This is a charge which has been reiterated endlessly by anti-Zionists and anti-Semites.

Arendt criticized the Zionist tendency to think that the establishment of a Jewish nation-state was the only goal for a Zionist politics. The Zionists were falling into the trap of adopting the political model which Arendt thought was no longer viable. A nation-state, in the European sense of the word, meant a state governing a basically homogeneous population – that is, a population unified by common traditions, language, and shared experiences. The "logic" of the nation-state meant that minority populations were always problematic.[9] The revisionists refused to acknowledge that they wanted to do to the Palestinian Arabs precisely what the European nation-states had done to them – to make the Arabs into second-class citizens or, better, to exclude them altogether from the new state. Arendt warned about the emergence of an ugly form of Jewish nationalism. "Nationalism is bad enough when it trusts in nothing but the rude force of the nation. A nationalism that necessarily and admittedly depends upon the force of a foreign nation is certainly worse" (*JP*, 132–4).

But if the founding of a Jewish nation-state is to be rejected, what, then, is the alternative? Arendt sharply distinguishes between a Jewish *homeland* and a Jewish sovereign *state*. She identified herself with a small group of Zionists living in Palestine who have "tirelessly preached for an understanding between the Arab and the Jewish peoples." In 1925, a small group, consisting primarily of intellectuals and university professors, organized and called themselves Brit Shalom (Covenant of Peace). They advocated a binational state in which Jews and Arabs would have equal rights. They even opposed the 1917 Balfour Declaration, which was welcomed by most Zionists as epoch-making. Specifically, the members of Brit Shalom took the extremely unpopular position that Great Britain should not have "promised" Palestine to the Jews. Most of those who identified with Brit Shalom were considered not only to be naive and unrealistic, but to be betrayers of Zionism. The guiding leader of Brit Shalom, Judah Magnes, the first president of the Hebrew University, was vilified as a traitor to the Zionist cause. Brit Shalom never attracted wide support. It lost much of its modest support after the street battles between the Jews and Arabs that broke out in 1929 and during the 1930s. This was taken as confirmation by many Zionists that it was completely unrealistic to think that Jews and Arabs could live in peace together as equals within the same territory. Nevertheless in 1942, Magnes continued his efforts on behalf of Jewish-Arab reconciliation. He founded a new party Ihud, (Unity) which had the support of such outstanding figures as Martin Buber, Henretta Szold (the founder of Youth Aliyah) and Ernst Simon. Initially Arendt was critical of Magnes' pro-British leanings, although she approved of Ihud as a reaction against outworn Zionist slogans and policies. But she herself was coming very close to the binational policies advocated by Magnes. For a brief period, after the breaking out of hostilities in Palestine that led to the founding of the State of Israel, she worked closely with Magnes and his support group in America. This is one of the brief periods in Arendt's life in which she engaged in direct political action – as a member of the loyal opposition. But before exploring Arendt's active support of Magnes and Ihud, I want to consider Arendt's understanding of the history of Zionism which she elaborated in "Zionism Reconsidered."

According to Arendt, the Zionist movement had been "fathered by two typical nineteenth-century European political ideologies" – socialism and nationalism. There had been an "amalgam of these two seemingly contradictory doctrines" in those "national-revolutionary movements of small European peoples whose situation was equally one of social as of national oppression. But within the Zionist movement, such an amalgam has never been realized" (*JP*, 137–6). There had been a tension.

> The movement was split from the beginning between the social-revolutionary forces which had sprung from the East European masses and the aspiration for national emancipation as formulated by Herzl and his followers in the central European countries. The paradox of this split was that, whereas the former was actually a people's movement, caused by national oppression, the latter, created by social discrimination, became the political creed of intellectuals. (*JP*, 137)

Arendt, a German-Jewish intellectual, was herself much more sympathetic to the social-revolutionary forces of "the East European masses," because this was genuinely a people's movement. This allegiance to social-revolutionary forces is a constant theme in Arendt's thinking about the Jewish question and Zionism. It is the basis of her scathing critique of Herzl and his followers, who were fearful of these social-revolutionary forces. Herzl, she claimed, "had a blind hatred of all revolutionary movements as such" (*JP*, 171). The populist strain in Arendt's thinking comes out strongly in her narrative of what happened to Zionism. She reminds us that socialism was once "an inspiring source of the revolutionary labor movement," just as nationalism was itself a "great and revolutionary principle of the national organization of peoples" (*JP*, 140–1). Both, unfortunately, had degenerated into *ideologies* – and this too has been the fate of Zionism.

Arendt argues that it is the political history of Zionism itself that has betrayed the Zionist revolutionary élan. Her critique of "really existing" Zionism is an immanent one, reminding us of the promise of social-revolutionary Zionism.

> Sad as it must be for every believer in government of the people, by the people and for the people, the fact is that a political history of Zionism could easily pass over the genuine national revolutionary movement which sprang from the Jewish masses. The political history of Zionism must be concerned mainly with those elements that did not come of the people: it must be concerned with men who believed in government by the people as little as did Theodor Herzl whom they followed – although it is true that they all emphatically wished to do something for the people. (*JP*, 142)

Arendt's understanding of what might have happened if Zionists had been true to their *own* revolutionary origins is eloquently, albeit bitterly, expressed when she writes:

> Those who are dismayed at the spectacle of a national movement that, starting out with such an idealistic élan, sold out the very first moment to the powers-that-be – that felt no solidarity with other oppressed peoples whose cause, though historically otherwise conditioned, was essentially the same – that endeavored even in the morning-dream of freedom and justice to compromise with the most evil forces of our time by taking advantage of imperialistic interests – those who are dismayed should in fairness consider how exceptionally difficult the conditions were for the Jews who, in contrast to other peoples, did not even possess the territory from which to start their fight for freedom. The alternative to the road that Herzl marked out, and Weizmann followed through to

the bitter end, would have meant an alliance with all progressive forces in Europe; it would certainly have been to organize the Jewish people in order to negotiate on the basis of a great revolutionary movement. This would have involved great risks. The only man within the Zionist Organization known to have ever considered this way was the great French Zionist Bernard Lazare . . . and he had to resign from the Organization at the early date of 1899. From then on no responsible Zionist trusted the Jewish people for the necessary political strength of will to achieve freedom instead of being transported to freedom; thus no official Zionist leader dared to side with the revolutionary forces in Europe. (*JP*, 152)

Neither here nor in any other place did Arendt identify these "revolutionary forces." Nor did she specify which Jewish communities might have joined in such solidarity, when, where, and how. Insofar as she failed to address these issues in detail, she could be accused of being irresponsibly romantic and utopian. But Arendt was critical of those appeals to realism, and to what was to become a Zionist litany – "No Choice" – which closed off possibilities, constrained the imagination, and limited serious debate. While she might be criticized for not proposing "practical" solutions, she was *judging* what was happening to the Zionist movement and thereby recalling the promise of Zionism. She sought to turn the tables on so-called political and practical Zionists. By "political" Zionists, she meant those for whom "Zionism belongs to these nineteenth-century political movements that carried ideologies, *Weltanschauungen*, keys to history, in their portmanteaus" (*JP*, 140). Such ideologies were once "fed on the very life-blood of genuine political passions," but have undergone the "sad fate of having outlived the political conditions only to stalk together like living ghosts amid the ruins of our times" (*JP*, 140). Arendt was a bit more sympathetic to Weizmann's "practical" Zionism, which emphasized the need for practical achievements in the "upbuilding of Palestine." But she saw it as naive to think that such an upbuilding was a solution to international anti-Semitism. She criticized Weizmann's dictum that "the upbuilding of Palestine is our answer to anti-semitism." The "absurdity" of this dictum was exposed "when Rommel's army threatened Palestine Jewry with exactly the same fate as in European countries" (*JP*, 149).

Arendt was even critical of the lack of political leadership in the kibbutz movement, which she had praised so highly for its social experiments in creating "a new type of Jew." What she meant is that the kibbutzniks, although concerned with the achievements and destiny of their movement, were not sufficiently interested in Jewish or Palestinian politics that did *not* affect the kibbutz movement. "In a sense, indeed, they were too decent for politics, the best among them somehow afraid of soiling their hands with it; but they were also completely disinterested in any event in Jewish life outside Palestine which did not land thousands of Jews as new immigrants; and they were bored by any Jew who was not himself a prospective immigrant" (*JP*, 138). It was perhaps unrealistic to judge Zionism by its failure to be the avant-garde protagonists of a worldwide social-revolutionary movement of the Jewish people – but this is the perspective from which Arendt was evaluating the successes and failures of Zionism. With disappointment, Arendt wrote:

> Thus the social-revolutionary Jewish national movement, which started half a century ago with ideals so lofty that it overlooked the particular realities of the Near East and the general wickedness of the world, has ended – as do most such movements – with the unequivocal support not only of national but of chauvinist claims – not against the foes of the Jewish people but against its possible friends and present neighbors. (*JP*, 140)

"Zionism Reconsidered" was written in 1944. At the time, the Second World War was still being fought, the Nazi death camps were still functioning smoothly, Great Britain's infamous White Paper had virtually closed Palestine to Jewish immigration, and the United Nations had not yet been founded. In the few years after the surrender of Germany, events concerning Palestine developed with extra-ordinary rapidity. At the time, Arendt was completing *The Origins of Totalitarianism*, but she was preoccupied with what was happening in Palestine. On June 30, 1947, she wrote to Jaspers: "For me and many others today, it has become a matter of course that the first thing we do when we open a newspaper is to see what's going on in Palestine" (*C*, 91). On September 4, 1947, she expressed her positive attitude toward the Zionist movement and what had been accomplished in Palestine. She wrote to Jaspers:

> [The Zionists] – and not the proponents of assimilation – are the only ones who no longer believe in the idea of a chosen people. What has been done in Palestine itself is extraordinary: not merely colonization

but a serious attempt at a new social order, . . . As far as Jews as a people are concerned, an alteration of such great significance has taken place in them in recent years that we can speak of a genuine change in the so-called national character. (Whether it is permanent I can't say.) (*C*, 98)

On April 18, 1948, a month before the declaration of the founding of the State of Israel and the outbreak of full-scale hostilities in Palestine, Arendt expressed her anxiety; "But the political situation looks so bad that even we, who don't really believe a war is in the making, still sometimes feel a touch of fear" (*C*, 108).

It was on November 29, 1947, that the United Nations made one of its first major decisions – to accept the partition of Palestine and the establishment of a Jewish State. The problem that plagued the old League of Nations was also to plague the UN. It was somehow assumed that no outside force would be needed to implement this decision.

It took the Arabs less than two months to destroy this illusion and it took the United States less than three months to reverse its stand on partition, withdraw its support in the United Nations, and propose a trusteeship for Palestine. Of all the member states of the United Nations, only Soviet Russia and her satellites made it unequivocally clear that they still favored partition and the immediate proclamation of the Jewish State. (*JP*, 178)

Trusteeship was immediately and categorically rejected by both the Jewish Agency and the Arab Higher League. The Jews claimed the "moral right" to adhere to the original decision of the United Nations; the Arabs claimed the "moral right" to adhere to the League of Nations' right to self-determination, which would mean that Palestine would be ruled by the existing Arab majority with the Jews being granted "minority rights." In the meantime the Jewish Agency proclaimed the existence of the new State of Israel, regardless of any United Nations decision. With no external authority willing to impose or implement a solution and the failure of attempts to stop the fighting between Jews and Arabs, a full-fledged war seemed inevitable. It was this situation that prompted Arendt to write her plea of May 1948, "To Save the Jewish Homeland: There is Still Time." She thought that "the present desire of both peoples to fight it out at any price is nothing less than sheer irrationality" (*JP*, 179).

Arendt lamented the fact that among American Jews and Jews in

Palestine, there was an overwhelming consensus to found a new sovereign state. Zionism was no longer a partisan, controversial issue. There was "no organization and almost no individual Jew that doesn't privately or publicly support partition and the establishment of a Jewish State." With her characteristic biting irony, this is how she described the American Jewish situation:

> Jewish left-wing intellectuals who a relatively short time ago still looked down upon Zionism as an ideology for the feeble-minded, and viewed the building of a Jewish homeland as a hopeless enterprise that they, in their great wisdom, had rejected before it was ever started; Jewish business men whose interest in Jewish politics had always been determined by the all-important question of how to keep Jews out of newspaper headlines; Jewish philanthropists who had resented Palestine as a terribly expensive charity, draining off funds from other "more worthy" purposes; the readers of the Yiddish press, who for decades had been sincerely, if naively, convinced that America was the promised land – all these, from the Bronx to Park Avenue down to Greenwich Village and over to Brooklyn are united in the firm conviction that a Jewish state is needed. (*JP*, 180)

Arendt found the same unanimity among Palestinian Jews, and noted that the left-wing kibbutzim, the Hashomer Hatzair, a group which had strongly advocated a binational program, had now sacrificed this program in the face of "the 'accomplished fact' of the United Nations' decision." It is in this situation that Arendt warns us that such "unanimity of opinion is a very ominous phenomenon" (*JP*, 182).

Once again she strikes out – almost recklessly – against "the cynical and deep-rooted conviction that all Gentiles are anti-Semitic, and everybody and everything is against the Jews." She speaks of this as "plain racist chauvinism" (*JP*, 183), and claims that the general mood of Palestinian Jews is one in which "terrorism and the growth of totalitarian methods are silently tolerated and secretly applauded" (*JP*, 181).

Arendt expresses her concern about what might happen if the "Yishuv went down," if the Jews experienced another "catastrophe." "This Jewish experiment in Palestine holds out hope of solutions that will be acceptable and applicable, not only in individual cases, but also for the large mass of men everywhere whose dignity and very humanity are in our time so seriously threatened by the pressures of modern life and its unsolved problems" (*JP*, 186).

Furthermore, the very possibility of another precedent would go down with the Yishuv – "that of close cooperation between two peoples, one embodying the most advanced ways of European civilization, the other an erstwhile victim of colonial oppression and backwardness." The idea of Arab–Jewish cooperation, though never realized on any scale and today seemingly farther off than ever, is not an idealistic day dream but a sober statement of the fact that without it the whole Jewish venture in Palestine is doomed" (*JP*, 186).

We should not forget that in May 1948, despite the euphoria that resulted from the founding of the State of Israel, the fate of this newly proclaimed state surrounded by Arab enemies determined to drive the Jews into the sea was uncertain. What is most chilling, disturbing, and almost uncanny – especially when read from our present perspective – is Arendt's prognosis of what might happen even if the Jews *did* win the war.

> And even if the Jews were to win the war, its end would find the unique possibilities and the unique achievements of Zionism in Palestine destroyed. The land that would come into being would be something quite other than the dream of world Jewry, Zionist and non-Zionist. The "victorious" Jews would live surrounded by an entirely hostile Arab population, secluded inside ever-threatened borders, absorbed with physical self-defense to a degree that would submerge all other interests and activities. The growth of a Jewish culture would cease to be the concern of the whole people; social experiments would have to be discarded as impractical luxuries; political thought would center around military strategy; economic development would be determined exclusively by the needs of war. And all this would be the fate of a nation that – no matter how many immigrants it could still absorb and how far it extended its boundaries (the whole of Palestine and Transjordan is the insane Revisionist demand) – would still remain a very small people greatly outnumbered by hostile neighbors. (*JP*, 187)

Given her pessimistic portrayal of both possibilities, winning and losing, what could be done? Arendt thought that there was a "way out of this predicament," no matter how remote, desperate, and fantastic it might appear. She was never one to shy away from unpopular positions or championing a cause, even if it seemed utterly hopeless. She recommended that the United Nations

> summon up the courage in this unprecedented situation to take an unprecedented step by going to those Jewish and Arab individuals who

at present are isolated because of their records as sincere believers in Arab–Jewish cooperation, and asking them to negotiate a truce. On the Jewish side, the so called Ihud group among the Zionists, as well as certain outstanding non-Zionists, are clearly the people most eligible for this purpose. (*JP*, 189–90)

Arendt was, in effect, recommending trusteeship rather than partition as a *first* step. She acknowledged that "every single possible and practicable step is today a tentative effort whose chief aim is pacification and nothing more." But she was proposing more than a truce and a postponement of partition. She had consistently argued that the nation-state was no longer an appropriate model for founding a Jewish state (or any other new state). So the question was, what was the alternative? The question now had an urgent concreteness in light of the war that was beginning in Palestine. We find here one of the first sketches of the political alternative that was to become one of the most novel themes in Arendt's political thinking. She advocated the development of a "federated state" based upon local Arab–Jewish community councils. With explicit reference to Magnes and Ihud, Arendt writes:

> The alternative proposition of a federated state, also recently endorsed by Dr. Magnes, is *much more realistic*; despite the fact that it establishes a common government for two different peoples, it avoids the troublesome majority–minority constellation, which is insoluble by definition. A federated structure, moreover, would have to rest on *Jewish–Arab community councils*, which would mean that the Jewish–Arab conflict would be resolved on the lowest and most promising level of proximity and neighborliness. A federated state, finally, could be the natural stepping-stone for any later, federated structure in the Near East and the Mediterranean area. (*JP*, 191; emphasis added)

Given the options available at the time (May 1948), Arendt favored trusteeship rather than partition, *not* because she saw trusteeship as "an ideal" or "eternal" solution, but because it would allow time for the transition to federation. She was quite explicit that a federated state could not be *imposed* "over the heads and against the opposition of both peoples." (Arendt consistently opposed the idea that some third power, whether the United Nations or Great Britain, the United States or Soviet Russia, could be relied on to impose a solution.)

Arendt concluded her article with a forceful set of proposals – proposals which she claimed were "the only way of saving the reality of the Jewish homeland." She declared categorically that "the real goal of the Jews in Palestine is the building up of a Jewish homeland. This goal must never be sacrificed to the pseudo-sovereignty of a Jewish state. . . . The independence of Palestine can be achieved only on a solid basis of Jewish–Arab cooperation. . . . Elimination of all terrorist groups . . . and swift punishment of all terrorist deeds . . . will be the only valid proof that the Jewish people in Palestine has recovered its sense of political reality and that Zionist leadership is again responsible enough to be trusted with the destinies of the Yishuv" (*JP*, 192).

It is Arendt's final proposal that sums up what she took to be the only "realistic" solution for "the political emancipation of Palestine."

> Local self-government and mixed Jewish–Arab municipal and rural councils, on a small scale and as numerous as possible, are the only realistic political measures that can eventually lead to the political emancipation of Palestine. It is still not too late. (*JP*, 192)

This is one of the first sketches of what Arendt took to be a twentieth-century alternative to the outdated nineteenth-century notion of the nation-state and national sovereignty – the council system. This is one of Arendt's most important political themes – her answer to what she saw as the slide from unthinking nationalism to blind chauvinism. In the next chapter I will explore how the council system came alive for Arendt in the unexpected and unprecedented 1956 Hungarian revolution. It was to become central to her analysis of modern revolutions in *On Revolution*. It has rarely even been noted that Arendt's initial thinking about a council system and a federation of local councils first emerged in the concrete political context of what political form a Jewish homeland in Palestine might take. It is her confrontation with the Jewish question, specifically the question of the political structure of a Jewish homeland, that was a primary source for some of her first reflections on the political significance of councils and her vision of a new type of federation. Proposing a federation of local Arab–Jewish councils in May 1948 opened Arendt to the charge of being hopelessly naive and politically irresponsible. Such a plan ignored the ugly realities of suspicion, hostility, and conflict between Jews and Arabs. *Contra* her claim that such local councils "are the only realistic political measures that can eventually lead to the political emancipation of Palestine," her proposal struck many Zionists and non-Zionists as being completely unrealistic. Before examining in greater detail what Arendt meant by the council system, and why it plays such a prominent role in her political thinking, I want to consider her relation with Magnes and her support of Ihud. This is one of the very few times in Arendt's life when she was not a spectator, seeking to understand, but an active participant, supporting a (defeated) political cause.[10]

When Arendt opposed the majority of Zionists and non-Zionists who enthusiastically endorsed the "accomplished fact" of a sovereign state of Israel, she was viciously attacked. Ben Halpern, a committed American Zionist, accused her of having an "enfant-terrible complex" and of indulging in "outrageous sensation-mongering." She was seen as having a "subconscious" intention to discredit prominent Zionists – Herzl, Weizmann, and Ben-Gurion (*YB*, 230). Halpern called her a "collaborationist", a term loaded with ugly overtones ever since the Second World War. This was not the last time that such extreme charges and epithets were hurled at Arendt. It happened again, with even greater vehemence, when she published *Eichmann in Jerusalem*. But Arendt was rarely perturbed by hostile criticism, and it did not stop her close "collaboration" with Magnes, who sought out Arendt's support for the proposals of Ihud.

Count Bernadotte had been asked by the United Nations to try to resolve the crisis in Palestine after the partition plan had failed, and open fighting had broken out between Jews and Arabs. Arendt was asked by Magnes to prepare (along with David Riesman) a proposal to be submitted to the United Nations for consideration. Magnes hoped that Ihud might be appointed as a negotiating group in the event that the United Nations decided to establish a trusteeship in Palestine. He asked Arendt to chair an American political committee representing Ihud, but she turned him down. Arendt, who was well aware of her lack of moderation, wrote to Magnes; "I lack quite a number of qualities a good chairman must have" (*YB*, 230). Elliot Cohen, the imaginative, progressive editor of *Commentary*, requested Magnes to write a response to what seemed to be an encouraging suggestion by Aubrey (Abba) Eban, Israel's representative to the United Nations: that Jewish–Arab cooperation might be possible if the Arabs were willing to recognize the State of Israel. Magnes asked Arendt to help write such a reply. The prospect for a positive initiative by the UN to accept Ihud's proposals was shattered when Count Bernadotte was assassinated by Irgun–Stern terrorists. (These were the terrorists that Arendt insisted must be eliminated and not tolerated in her May 1948 article "To Save the Jewish Homeland.") Count Bernadotte's intervention and proposals had seemed to be one of the last hopes for Magnes and Ihud. Bernadotte's initial recommendations were very close to what Arendt and Ihud were advocating. A few weeks after his assassination, Arendt wrote an article entitled "The Mission of Bernadotte," in which she once again outlined and reiterated the need for a confederation between Jews and Arabs. Bernadotte's chief concern was with peace. He attempted to reason with, and persuade, both Jews and Arabs. Nevertheless, he was "denounced as a British agent by the Jews and as a Zionist agent by the Arabs." "He was of course not the agent of anybody, not even the UN in any narrow sense, since he did not consider himself bound by the textual provisions of the UN decision of November 29, 1947 [the partition plan]." But Jews and Arabs no longer had the will to reason, compromise, and negotiate. Arendt succinctly expressed her admiration for Bernadotte and her disillusionment with the "fanaticism" of both Jews and Arabs:

> Deafened by the incessant noise of their own propaganda, they [Jews and Arabs] could no longer distinguish the voice of integrity; and overheated by their own fanaticism, they had become insensitive to real warmth of heart. Bernadotte, the agent of nobody, died the death of a hero of peace when he was murdered by the agents of war.[11]

Magnes was at once enthusiastic about Arendt's article and depressed by the darkening situation. On October 7, 1948, he wrote to Arendt that her article "might have serious consequences if it were studied and taken to heart by anyone in whose hands decisions lay." The story she told was a "tragic" one. What Magnes wrote about Bernadotte might have been said about Magnes himself: "Here was a great and good man who started out full of hope and ended almost in despair." He plaintively asked, "Is there really no way out?" (*YB*, 232).

Three weeks after writing this letter, Magnes died, on October 27, "without," as Young-Bruehl writes, "having answered his own question about the way out" (*YB*, 232). For a short time, his ideas were kept alive with the establishment of the Judah Magnes Foundation, but Arendt would not accept leadership of it when asked. After speaking in support of Magnes' ideas to a hostile audience and being shouted down, she wrote to Elliot Cohen: "I am not qualified for any direct political work" (*YB*, 233). But she did, as a last public gesture to Magnes, publish an article "Peace or Armistice in the Near East?" with the following note:

> This paper was written in 1948 upon the suggestion of Judah L. Magnes, the late President of the Hebrew University in Jerusalem, who from the close of World War I to the day of his death in October, 1948, had been the outstanding Jewish spokesman for Arab–Jewish understanding in Palestine. It is dedicated to his memory. (*JP*, 193)

"Peace or Armistice in the Near East?" is much more moderate in tone than Arendt's previous writings on Palestine. Nevertheless, she reiterates many of her substantive claims about the necessity of Arab–Jewish negotiations, compromise, and cooperation if there is to be a genuine peace. In the final section of her paper, "Federation or Balkanization?", she elaborates her vision of the true objectives of a nonnationalist policy. "The only alternative to Balkanization is a regional federation" (*JP*, 217). She supported Eban's suggestion of a "Near Eastern League, compromising all the diverse nationalities of the area, each free within its own area of independence and cooperating with others for the welfare of the region as a whole" (*JP*, 218). The best hope for bringing such a federation nearer to realization was to begin with a "Confederation of Palestine," where "two independent political entities" would work together. Such a confederation was in accord with the 1947 minority report of the United Nations' Special Committee on Palestine. She reminded her readers that those who claimed that such a confederation was utopian should remember that there was a model for such a confederation – the Constitution of the United States.

Peace, rather than a precarious armistice, confederation rather than Balkanization: this is what Arendt (and Ihud) called for. She knew already that her cause was a lost one, but, as she pointed out in her reply to Ben Halpern's attack on her, "we deal in politics only with warnings and not with prophecies" (*JP*, 238). She concluded "Peace or Armistice in the Near East?", the last major article that she ever wrote about Palestine (or Israel), with the following warning:

> National sovereignty which so long had been the very symbol of free national development has become the greatest danger to national survival for small nations. In view of the international situation and the geographical location of Palestine, it is not likely that the Jewish and Arab peoples will be exempt from this rule. (*JP*, 222)

Arendt had admired Magnes for his convictions. Shortly before his death, she wrote to him, in a letter that is very revealing about Arendt's own ambivalence toward politics:

> Will you permit me to tell you how grateful I am that the past year brought me the privilege of knowing you. . . . Politics in our century is almost a business of despair and I have always been tempted to run away from it. I wanted you to know that your example prevented me from despairing and will prevent me for many years to come. (*YB*, 233)

Four days after Magnes' death, she described him in a letter to Jaspers (Oct. 31, 1948), in what is Arendt's eulogy of Magnes.

> Magnes, the president of the Hebrew University in Jerusalem, had enlisted me . . . to act as a political adviser for his little American group. Through our correspondence this summer I developed a very close working relationship with Magnes himself, who was a magnificent sort. He died this week. I knew that he was very ill, and he did, too. That was one of my reasons for accepting his offer. What will happen now, I don't know. The man simply cannot be replaced. He was an unusual mix of typically American common sense and integrity along with a genuine, half-religious Jewish passion for justice. He exercised a personal influence on people and had a certain authority among Jews and Arabs, not a real political influence but much more than none at all. His Palestinian group is always in danger of being sucked into the nationalistic wake, and he . . . kept them from that. I'm much afraid that they will now become more "realistic" and will consequently lose all their influence, representing nothing but pallid moderation, with one compromise after another, before they finally dissolve. (*C*, 117)

Arendt, unfortunately, was all too perceptive about what was likely to – and did – occur. She herself withdrew from being a political actor. She had never thought of herself as primarily a political actor – or even as laying out theoretical blueprints for those who were actors. To think that this is (or ought to be) the role of the political thinker, she saw as misguided, arrogant, and dangerous. Her passion was to understand. "There are other people who are primarily interested in doing something. I am not. I can very well live without doing anything. But I cannot live without trying at least to understand whatever happens" (*RPW*, 303).

6

"The Innermost Story of the Modern Age": Revolutions and the Council System

The history of revolutions – from the summer of 1776 in Philadelphia and the summer of 1789 in Paris to the autumn of 1956 in Budapest – which politically spells the innermost story of the modern age, could be told in a parable form as the tale of an age-old treasure which, under the most varied circumstances, appears abruptly, unexpectedly, and disappears again, under different mysterious conditions, as though it were a fata morgana.

BPF

The expresssion that best characterizes Arendt's mode of thinking is one she used over and over again – "thought-trains." All thinking is (or ought to be) grounded in "personal experiences" and events. Thinking is, literally, reflection (*nachdenken*) on such events. They energize our thinking, giving it specificity and concreteness. If we read Arendt carefully, if we make the effort to situate her thinking within the events that make up her life story and follow her trains of thought, we can grasp what she is saying (and why she is saying it) with freshness and critical sharpness. These trains of thought, which frequently have independent sources, crisscross and interweave. They reveal complex patterns in the fabric of her thinking. (Sometimes they also clash and conflict with one another, resulting in dissonances that cannot easily be reconciled. Later, when I explore Arendt's reflections on judgment as it pertains to the problem of evil, I will consider a case of such dissonance.) But here I want to explore Arendt's reflections on councils as an instance of her thought-trains interweaving and furthering her own quest for understanding of politics in the twentieth century.

Let us step back and review some of Arendt's key claims about the nation-state. Originally, Arendt approached the meaning and hidden conflicts of the nation-state from the perspective of the Jewish question and anti-Semitism. The nineteenth-century nation-state flourished after the French Revolution, even though it never adequately resolved the unstable tension between the universal demand for human rights and the more particular demand for national sovereignty. The Jews were caught in this conflict, because as human beings they were presumably entitled to universal human rights, but as a distinct people with their own religion, rituals, and customs, a cloud hung over them. They did not really "belong" to the European nations – or so it was claimed, especially by anti-Semites. The nation-state declined with the rapid growth of imperialism in the last decades of the nineteenth century, and imperialism not only went hand in hand with racist thinking, it also gave rise to a new, much more vicious form of political anti-Semitism. With the triumph of imperialism, both overseas and on the Continent, the stage was set for the subterranean forces of European history to erupt and crystallize into totalitarianism. The event that really signaled the collapse of the nation-state was the First World War. Nevertheless, the peace treaties of 1919 were made as if the nation-state were still a viable political institution. There was a disastrous assumption that one could create new, artificial nation-states by drawing boundaries on a map – even if the territories marked off by these boundaries encompassed the most diverse national, religious, and ethnic groups. There was a catastrophic failure to realize how potentially explosive this might become, a failure to acknowledge that the logic of national sovereignty, especially in its more chauvinistic varieties, meant either coerced assimilation of minority groups into the larger national population or total exclusion. This affected not only the scattered Jewish population, but virtually all minority groups in Europe.

From Arendt's perspective, it was the revisionist Zionist ideology which relied on the outdated nineteenth-century concept of a nation-state as a model for the Jewish state that was so potentially dangerous. It fostered an ugly "racist chauvinism" that tolerated the use of terrorism in order to create panic and "encourage" the Arabs to flee from Palestine, thereby swelling the numbers of Arab refugees. In "Peace or Armistice in the Near East?" Arendt endorsed the claim already made by Magnes:

> If the Palestine Arabs left their homesteads "voluntarily" under the impact of Arab propaganda and in a veritable panic, one may not forget that the most potent argument in this propaganda was the fear of the repetition of the Irgun–Stern atrocities at Deir Yassim, where the Jewish authorities were unable or unwilling to prevent the act or

punish the guilty. It is unfortunate that the very men who could point to the tragedy of Jewish DPs as the chief argument for mass immigration into Palestine should now be ready, as far as the world knows, to help create an additional category of DPs in the Holy Land. (*JP*, 216)

Arendt favored the development of a Jewish homeland in Palestine as strongly as she opposed a sovereign Jewish (or Israeli) state. She actively supported Magnes in advocating a confederation of Arabs and Jews in Palestine, which she hoped would be the basis for a more inclusive Near East federation. What did she mean by confederation? What would be the political structure of a confederation of Jews and Arabs in Palestine? Once again, let me cite the proposal she made at the conclusion of "To Save the Jewish Homeland": "Local self-government and mixed Jewish–Arab municipal and rural councils, on a small scale and as numerous as possible, are the only realistic political measures that can eventually lead to the political emancipation of Palestine" (*JP*, 192). What precisely does Arendt mean by "councils"? In the heat of controversy and given the rapidity with which events were taking place in Palestine, she did not really spell out these "realistic political measures." One might think that such a proposal for Jew–Arab councils was quixotic, utopian, and – despite her claims to the contrary – "unrealistic."

Throughout the 1940s Arendt was beginning to think about a viable political alternative to the failures of the nineteenth-century nation-state (and national sovereignty) and to the all too real successes of twentieth-century totalitarianism. Another independent thought-train was taking shape in her reflections, which crystallized around one event that was quite remote from the politics of the Near East. The 1956 Hungarian revolution provided the occasion to adumbrate what she meant by a council system. Despite its tragic ending, when it was crushed by the Russian army, it raised a faint hope, exposing the vulnerability of Soviet totalitarianism. Here was a tangible manifestation of the creation of those public spaces in which freedom makes its appearance. Arendt decided to include her "Reflections on the Hungarian Revolution" as an epilogue to the 1958 edition of *The Origins of Totalitarianism*.

The spirit that breathes through these "Reflections" is one of enthusiasm, excitement, and hope. It is events that challenge and call into question our normal, standard, commonsense assumptions. In a passage that echoes her earlier critique of the use of social science techniques for understanding the concentration camps, she tells us:

> Events past and present, – not social forces and historical trends, nor questionnaires and motivation research, nor any other gadgets in the arsenal of the social sciences – are the true, the only reliable teachers of political scientists, as they are the most trustworthy source of information for those engaged in politics. Once such an event as the spontaneous uprising in Hungary has happened, every policy, theory and forecast of future potentialities needs re-examination. In its light we must check and enlarge our understanding of the totalitarian form of government as well as of the nature of the totalitarian version of imperialism. (OT_2, 482)

Arendt's sense of the momentousness of this event and the "tragedy it enacted" is vividly expressed in the way she begins her "Reflections."

> As I write this, more than one year has passed since the flames of the Hungarian revolution illuminated the immense landscape of post-war totalitarianism for twelve long days. This was a true event whose stature will not depend upon victory or defeat; its greatness is secure in the tragedy it enacted. For who can forget the silent procession of black-clad women in the streets of Russian-occupied Budapest, mourning their dead in public, the last political gesture of the revolution? And who can doubt the solidity of this remembrance when one year after the revolution the defeated and terrorized people have still enough strength of action left to commemorate once more in public the death of their freedom by shunning spontaneously and unanimously all places of public entertainment, theaters, movies, coffee houses and restaurants? . . . What happened in Hungary happened nowhere else, and the twelve days of the revolution contained more history than the twelve years since the Red Army had "liberated" the country from Nazi domination. (OT_2, 480)

Arendt reviews what happened in the 12-year period that preceded this event, and analyzes what happened in Russia after Stalin's death, in order to establish the historical context for this eruption of "spontaneous revolution." What started out as a harmless student demonstration became an armed uprising in less than 24 hours; the revolution encompassed large segments of the Hungarian people, including workers and the army. "From this moment onward, no programs, points or manifestos played any role; what carried the revolution was the sheer momentum of acting-together of the whole people whose demands were so obvious that they hardly needed elaborate formulation: Russian troops should leave the territory and free elections should determine a new government. The question was no longer how much freedom to permit to action, speech and thought, but how to institutionalize a freedom which was already an accomplished fact" (OT_2, 496).

She describes the rapid disintegration of the whole elaborate, seemingly impenetrable power structure, including party, army, and government bureaucracy. She emphasizes the spontaneous springing up of revolutionary and workers' councils. They were the political institutions that arose when individuals created those public spaces where they could debate and act together with their peers. It was in the councils that public freedom made its appearance. The councils were the "same organization which for more than a hundred years now has emerged whenever the people have been permitted for a few days, or a few weeks or months, to follow their own political devices without a government (or a party program) imposed from above" (OT_2, 497).

> For these councils made their first appearance in the revolution which swept Europe in 1848; they reappeared in the revolt of the Paris Commune in 1871, existed for a few weeks during the first Russian revolution of 1905, to reappear in full force in the October revolution in Russia and the November revolutions in Germany and Austria after the first World War. Until now, they have always been defeated, but by no means only by the "counter-revolution." (OT_2, 497)

Arendt is alluding to what has been a tragic pattern, repeated over and over again, whenever these councils have briefly come into existence. The enemies of these people's councils have been those "professional" revolutionaries who have crushed them.

Arendt's reflections on the emergence of such councils provides a perspective for reassessing her earliest reflections on the failures of a Jewish politics in the modern age. Arendt's hope had been that the Jewish people themselves might create such revolutionary councils, that they might – as Lazare proposed – join with other oppressed groups to fight for and secure their freedom; and that they might do this "without leadership and without [a] previously formulated program" (OT_2, 497). This would have been the fulfillment of the populist strain in her thinking. And this idea of a council system (where Jews and Arabs would work together) is the political alternative to an independent sovereign Jewish or Arab state. Her thought-train concerning a Jewish homeland and her thought-train concerning the council system interweave and reinforce each other.

In describing the council system, she tells us that "the councils were born exclusively out of the actions and spontaneous demands of the people, and they were not deduced from an ideology nor foreseen, let alone preconceived, by any theory about the best form of government" (OT_2, 499). The councils are a paradigm of a democratic institution, "but in a sense never seen before and never thought about" (OT_2, 499).

> Under modern conditions, the councils are the only democratic alternative we know to the party system, and the principles on which they are based stand in sharp opposition to the principles of the party system in many respects. Thus, the men elected for the councils are chosen at the bottom, and not selected by the party machinery and proposed to the electorate either as individuals with alternate choices or as a slate of candidates. . . . The elected, therefore, is not bound by anything except trust in his personal qualities, and his pride is "to have been elected by the workers, and not by the government" or a party, that is, by his peers and from neither above nor below. (OT_2, 499)[1]

The council system helps us to understand two interrelated concepts that are central to Arendt's political thinking: "no-rule" and political equality (isonomy). At first (or even second) glance, Arendt's repeated insistence that politics is not a question of *who* rules *whom* but involves "no-rule" seems strange – if not perverse. But now we can understand what she means. In the councils, members meet as political equals. Even leadership is not a matter of ruling, but of acting and speaking together with one's peers. The councils – indeed, those councils which have spontaneously come into existence in modern times – are the very institutions in which equality or isonomy is created, a political equality which is not to be confused or reduced to the false and dangerous idea of social equality. "No-rule" must not be confused with the bureaucratic rule of "Nobody" – which Arendt took to be such a pervasive trait of modern societies.

If we read Arendt's remarks about the Greek city-states from the perspective of the concrete emergence of revolutionary councils – councils which came into existence once again with the 1956 Hungarian revolution – then we can discern with greater finesse what she intends when she invokes "the Greeks." In *On Revolution*, she tells us that the emergence of public freedom was coeval with the rise of the Greek city-states. It involved a political organization "in which the citizens lived together under conditions of no-rule, without a division between rulers and ruled. This notion of no-rule was expressed by the word isonomy, whose outstanding characteristic among the forms of government, as the ancients enumerated them, was that the notion of rule . . . was entirely absent from it" (*OR*, 30). And this isonomy, this equality, existed only in the artificial institution of the polis. It is this isonomy that Arendt saw as an essential characteristic of the councils.

Arendt envisioned a pyramid structure, whereby local councils arising directly from the people would elect members of higher councils. She argues that there is a great deal of flexibility in the council system:

> In Hungary, we have seen the simultaneous setting-up of all kinds of councils, each of them corresponding to a previously existing group in which people habitually lived together or met regularly and knew each other. Thus neighborhood councils emerged from sheer living together and grew into county and other territorial councils; revolutionary councils grew out of fighting together; councils of writers and artists, one is tempted to think, were born in the *cafés*, students' and youth councils at the university, military councils in the army, councils of civil servants in the ministries, workers' councils in the factories, and so on. The formation of a council in each disparate group turned a merely haphazard togetherness into a political institution. (*OT*₂, 500)

Still, one might protest. What could be more disparate than the 1956 Hungarian revolution and the circumstances that confronted Jews and Arabs in Palestine in 1948? Arendt would certainly not deny this. She always insisted on the need to be concrete and specific about the historical situations in which the councils were spontaneously organized – where "islands of freedom" were created. But one reason why she focused her attention on the council system is precisely because it kept reemerging in the modern age in the most diverse historical situations and the most disparate political contexts.

In ways in which she could never have anticipated, there is an enduring truth in what she wrote to Magnes a few weeks before his death: "Politics in our century is almost a business of despair. . . . I wanted you to know that your example prevented me from despairing and will prevent me for many years to come" (*YB*, 233). What she did not know in 1948 was that the type of politics that she and Magnes were advocating for Palestine at that time would make a brief appearance in a different part of the world in an entirely different political context – with the reemergence of the incipient council system in Hungary.

As a political alternative to the nation-state and totalitarianism, the council system continued to preoccupy Arendt. She probed its meaning and problems in *On Revolution*, especially in her last chapter, "The Revolutionary Tradition and Its Lost Treasure." For all her praise of the American Revolution and her criticism of the French Revolution, she claimed that "the failure of post-revolutionary thought to remember the revolutionary spirit and to understand it conceptually was preceded by the failure of the revolution to provide it with a lasting institution" (*OR*, 232). The central problem of all modern revolutions was how to create a stable institution within which the revolutionary spirit could be preserved. Speaking of the American Revolution, Arendt tells us that "in this republic . . . there was no space reserved, no room left for the exercise of precisely those qualities which had been instrumental in building it" (*OR*, 232). The hard political problem was how to create appropriate political institutions where this treasure (which is always in danger of being lost again) could be housed and preserved – where the revolutionary spirit could be kept alive and continually revitalized. Arendt considers this to be the "paradox of founding." The aim of revolutions is to found a new constitution. The tangible freedom that appears in newly created public spaces is what manifests itself in the very activity of founding a constitution. Yet the danger that faces every revolution is that its success may result in institutions where the treasure of the revolutionary spirit is lost. Thus Arendt tells us that the failure of the founders of the United States Constitution was their failure "to incorporate the township and the town hall meeting into the Constitution, or rather their failure to find ways and means to transform them under radically changed circumstances" (*OR*, 236). The real paradox seemed to be that public freedom existed only for the revolutionary founders. According to Arendt, Jefferson was the American political thinker who "perceived this seemingly inevitable flaw in the structure of the republic with greater clarity and more passionate preoccupation" than anyone else. It was Jefferson who called for dividing the republic into wards (elementary republics or councils) in order to renew the revolutionary spirit of the founding generation.

Had Jefferson's plan of elementary republics been carried out, it would have exceeded by far the feeble germs of a new form of government which we are able to detect in the sections of the Parisian Commune and the popular societies during the French Revolution. However, if Jefferson's political imagination surpassed them in insight and in scope, his thoughts were still traveling in the same direction. Both Jefferson's plan and the French *sociétés révolutionnaires* anticipated with an almost weird precision those councils, *soviets* and *Räte*, which were to make their appearance in every genuine revolution throughout the nineteenth and twentieth centuries. Each time they appeared, they sprang up as the spontaneous organs of the people, not only outside of all revolutionary parties but entirely unexpected by them and their leaders. Like Jefferson's proposals [and like the proposals of Arendt and Magnes for local Jewish–Arab councils in 1948] they were utterly neglected by statesmen, historians, political theorists, and, most importantly, by the revolutionary tradition itself. . . [Historians] failed to understand to what an extent the council system confronted them with an entirely new form of government, with a new public space for freedom which was constituted and organized during the course of the revolution itself. (*OR*, 249)

Arendt distinguished "the people" from "the mob" and "the masses." The creation of atomized masses in the twentieth century was one of the fertile conditions for the emergence of totalitarianism. One must be careful not to confuse Arendt's critique of the mob and the masses with her positive evaluation and faith in the people. Nothing "contradicts more sharply the old adage of the anarchistic and lawless natural inclinations of a people left without the constraint of its government than the emergence of the councils that, wherever they appeared, and most pronouncedly during the Hungarian Revolution, were concerned with the reorganization of the political and economic life of the country and the establishment of a new order" (*OR*, 271).

The Hungarian revolution of 1956 was an exemplar for Arendt of the reemergence of the council system. She was also exhilarated by the early stages of the civil rights movement in the United States. In an interview entitled "Thoughts on Politics and Revolution" that she gave in 1970, she returned once again to the council system, and how she understood it as a political alternative to "national sovereignty" and the modern political party system. She repeated many of the observations she had made in "Reflections on the Hungarian Revolution", and in *On Revolution*. "The council system seems to correspond and to spring from the very experience of political action." The council system "begins from below, continues upward, and finally leads to a parliament" (*CR*, 232).

> The councils say: We want to participate, we want to debate, we want to make our voices heard in public, and we want to have a possibility to determine the political course of our country. Since the country is too big for all of us to come together and determine our fate, we need a number of public spaces within it. The booth in which we deposit our ballots is unquestionably too small, for this booth has room for only one. The parties are completely unsuitable; there we are, most of us, nothing but the manipulated electorate. But if only ten of us are sitting around a table, each expressing his opinion, each hearing the opinion of others, then a rational formation of opinion can take place through the exchange of opinions. There, too, it will become clear which one of us is best suited to present our view before the next higher council, where in turn our view will be clarified through the influence of other views, revised, or proved wrong. (*CR*, 233)

Arendt points out that not everyone wants or needs to be a member of such a council, but "each person must be given the opportunity."

She concludes her comments with a statement that is reminiscent of what she wrote in 1948 about Jewish–Arab councils and the possibility of a confederation in Palestine.

> In this direction I see the possibility of forming a new concept of the state. A council-state of this sort, to which the principle of sovereignty would be wholly alien, would be admirably suited to federations of the most various kinds, especially because in it power would be constituted horizontally and not vertically. But if you ask me now what prospect it has of being realized, then I must tell you: Very slight if at all. And yet perhaps, after all – in the wake of the next revolution. (*CR*, 233)

In 1958, when Arendt revised *The Origins of Totalitarianism* for a new edition for Meridian Books, she added (as I have indicated) her "Reflections on the Hungarian Revolution" as an epilogue. In the house journal of Meridian Books, she wrote a short article about the "new enlarged and revised edition." She sets forth her reasons for adding the epilogue, and acknowledges that there is something awkward about this. "There is in this [epilogue] a certain hopefulness – surrounded, to be sure, with many qualifications – which is hard to reconcile with the assumption of the third part that the only clear expression of the present age's problems up to date has been the horror of totalitarianism."[2] Although she was aware of the importance of the council system when she wrote *Origins*, she "had no hope for its re-emergence and therefore left it out of account." It is what Arendt goes on to say that I find so characteristic of her as a political thinker.

> The Hungarian Revolution taught me a lesson. If we take into account the amazing re-emergence of the council-system during the Hungarian Revolution, then it looks as though we are confronted with two new forms of government in our own time, both of which can be understood only against the bankrupt body politic of the nation-state. The government of total domination certainly corresponds better to the inherent tendencies of a mass society than anything we previously knew. But the council-system clearly has been for a long time the result of the wishes of the people, and not of the masses, and it is just barely possible that it contains the very remedies against mass society and the formation of mass-men for which we look everywhere else in vain.
>
> Thus the last chapter of the present edition is an Epilogue or an afterthought. I am not at all sure that I am right in my hopefulness, but I am convinced that it is as important to present all the inherent hopes of the present as to confront us ruthlessly with all its intrinsic despairs. In any event, to a political writer this must be more important than to present the reader with a well-rounded book.[3]

This passage epitomizes what is distinctive about Hannah Arendt as a political thinker. Many commentators on Arendt (whether sympathetic or hostile) have noted that there are deep tensions, conflicting tendencies – even what appear to be manifest contradictions – in almost every area of her thinking.[4] Furthermore, as the interchange between Hans Morgenthau and Arendt cited in the Introduction indicates, it is virtually impossible to classify and categorize her thinking. Arendt has a way of introducing distinctions that cut through standard ways of classifying positions. She emphatically declares: "I don't think that the real questions of this century will get any kind of illumination by this kind of thing" (*RPW*, 334). Many of the tensions in her thinking revolve around her understanding of twentieth-century politics. Is she a thinker who despairs, a prophet of our darkening times? If one reads her selectively, one can easily come to this conclusion. She ends *Origins* (before she added her epilogue) with the claim "that the crisis of our time and its central experience have brought forth an entirely new form of government which as a potentiality and *an ever-present danger is only too likely to stay with us from now on"* (*OT*$_3$, 478; emphasis added). Her prognosis for a Jewish state demanding national sovereignty was bleak. Even if we turn to *The Human Condition*, it is difficult to resist reading this as a despairing book. It unfolds a narrative whereby, with the triumph of "the social," the traditional hierarchy of activity – action, work, and labor – has been reversed. From this perspective, action, the highest form of human activity, in which we appear to each other in speech and deed, no longer seems to be a real possibility. What is worse, we are no longer even a society of laborers, but a society of "jobholders." One can hardly miss the parallels between Arendt's narrative of this movement from action to fabrication, to labor, to "holding a job" and Heidegger's bleak portrait of *Gestell*, in his "Question Concerning Technology," where even human beings become mere human resources.[5]

There is another, equally distorting reading of Arendt. This is the upbeat reading, the one that focuses on her categories of natality, spontaneity, new beginnings, and freedom. It is tempting to read her enthusiastic descriptions of the revolutionary spirit, elementary republics, and local councils as a blueprint for radical political action.

Although one can find (with selective emphasis) plenty of evidence to support these opposed readings of Arendt, they miss what is most characteristic about her as a political thinker. She is neither despairing nor a thinker of hope. She insists that we must hold on to the unstable, unpredictable tension between these extremes. Her most profound insight is that the human condition is such that the same human beings are capable of both radical evil and creating "islands of freedom." It is human beings (not monsters) who "created" the total domination and terror of totalitarianism. But human beings are also capable of creating elementary republics in which public freedom makes its appearance. It is the very *same* capacities that can create these diametrically opposite extremes. In political terms, this means that we must realize that the modern age is the age out of which *both* totalitarianism and the council system emerged. Both are responses to "the bankrupt body politic of the nation-state." Totalitarianism has been defeated, but there is no guarantee that we will not be tempted to use totalitarian methods to solve the intractable problems of mass society that are still with us. The council system has been defeated over and over again, but this is no reason to believe that it cannot someday be housed in stable political institutions. "It is just barely possible that the [council system] contains the very remedies against mass-society and the formation of mass-men for which we look everywhere else in vain."[6]

Arendt refuses to be pushed to either extreme. She insists on what might be called the ontological openness that is quintessential to our being-in-the-world. This is why I have suggested that the above passage can be read as an encapsulation of Arendt. As a political thinker, one has an obligation to confront honestly the "intrinsic despairs" of the present, as well as its "inherent hopes," and to do this in a way in which one does not lose one's judgmental balance. I believe that this is why Arendt felt that the epigraph she took from Jaspers for *The Origins of Totalitarianism* was so appropriate: "Weder dem Vergangenen an heimfallen noch dem Zukünftigen. Es kommt darauf an, ganz gegenwärtig zu sein" (To succumb neither to the past nor the future. What matters is to be entirely present) (OT_1, vii).[7] As she tells us, *Origins* "has been written against a background of both reckless optimism and reckless despair. It holds that Progress and Doom are two sides of the same medal; that both are articles of superstition, not of faith" (OT_3, vii).

We seem to have come a long way from Arendt's preoccupation with the question of a Jewish homeland or a Jewish state. Her first suggestions regarding a council system arose in her proposals for an alternative to a Jewish nation-state and how Arabs and Jews might work together in local councils. Her insights into elementary republics and the council system had other, independent sources, especially when she seeks to understand the lost treasure of the revolutionary spirit that has reemerged over and over again since the eighteenth century. Arendt's early struggles with the Jewish question, specifically the political structure of a Jewish homeland, eventually led her to more general insights into the meaning of politics and the "inherent hopes of the present."

Elisabeth Young-Bruehl makes a perceptive judgment about Arendt's hopes for "the homeland of the Jews":

In the homeland of the Jews, Hannah Arendt wished to see all of the elements which formed the foundations of her political theory: new social forms, local political councils, a federation, and international cooperation. It had been exhilarating for her to think that her own people, the victims of a totalitarian regime, could offer the world models for institutions that might prevent totalitarianism from making another appearance. As always, the defeat of her greatest expectations and of her deepest wish for her people to be heroic was registered by Hannah Arendt in a rush of anger and irony. (*YB*, 229)

I would add one, not insignificant emendation to this claim. Most of the "elements which formed the foundations of [Arendt's] political theory," including her reflections on the council system were themselves forged originally in her confrontation with the Jewish question. This is why her sense of exhilaration and her extreme disappointment were so intense when her "cause" was defeated. *Victrix causa diis placuit, sed victa Catoni.*

7

From Radical Evil to the Banality of Evil: From Superfluousness to Thoughtlessness

In 1945, Arendt declared: "The problem of evil will be the fundamental question of postwar intellectual life in Europe" (*EU*, 134). She was wrong. Most postwar intellectuals avoided any direct confrontation with the problem of evil. But it did become fundamental for Arendt. She returned to it over and over again, and she was still struggling with it at the time of her death.

It is well known that Arendt used the phrase "the banality of evil," and presumably abandoned her earlier understanding of "radical evil"; but there has been enormous confusion over what she may have meant by these expressions. The narrative of her struggle to probe the problem of evil in the twentieth century is far more complex and subtle than it might seem. Following its twists and turns is like reading a detective story in which there are all sorts of misleading clues, and some of the misleading clues come from Arendt herself. It is not one of those detective stories where all the loose ends are tied up neatly, however. Like all independent thinking – thinking without banisters – there is no finality. In this chapter I want to focus primarily on what she meant by absolute, or radical, evil. In the next chapter, I will explore her thinking about the banality of evil. The question we need to confront is twofold: what does Arendt mean by radical evil? And did she change her mind about the meaning of evil?

Let me plunge in by citing what appears to be conclusive evidence that Arendt changed her mind about the meaning of evil – her own testimony. Shortly after the publication of *Eichmann in Jerusalem*, a now famous exchange of letters between Gershom Scholem and Hannah Arendt was published. Scholem concludes his letter with a damning critique of Arendt's "thesis" concerning the banality of evil. I want to cite Scholem's critique and Arendt's response at length, because these texts are vital for everything that follows. Scholem, barely restraining his disgust and disdain, sarcastically remarks:

> After reading your book I remain unconvinced by your thesis concerning the "banality of evil" – a thesis which, if your sub-title is to be believed, underlies your entire argument. This new thesis strikes me as a catchword: it does not impress me, certainly, as the product of profound analysis – an analysis such as you give us so convincingly, in the service of a quite different, indeed contradictory thesis, in your book on totalitarianism. At that time you had not yet made your discovery, apparently, that evil is banal. Of that "radical evil," to which your then analysis bore such eloquent and erudite witness, nothing remains but this slogan – to be more than that it would have to be investigated, at a serious level, as a relevant concept in moral philosophy or political ethics. I am sorry – and I say this, I think, in candor and in no spirit of enmity – that I am unable to take the thesis of your book more seriously. I had expected, with your earlier book in mind, something different. (*JP*, 245)

Scholem here sums up what many of Arendt's critics at the time were saying in a much more hysterical fashion. For the very phrase "the banality of evil" was offensive. It seemed to trivialize not only what Eichmann had done, but the full horror of the Holocaust. Speaking directly to the issues raised above, Arendt replies:

> In conclusion, let me come to the only matter where you have not misunderstood me, and where indeed I am glad that you have raised the point. You are quite right: I changed my mind and do no longer speak of "radical evil." It is a long time since we last met, or we would perhaps have spoken about that subject before. (Incidentally, I don't see why you call my term "banality of evil" a catchword or slogan. As far as I know no one has used the term before me; but that is unimportant.) It is indeed my opinion now that evil is never "radical," that it is only extreme, and that it possesses neither depth nor any demonic dimension. It can overgrow and lay waste the whole world precisely because it spreads like a fungus on the surface. It is "thought-defying," as I said, because thought tries to reach some depth, to go to the roots, and the moment it concerns itself with evil, it is frustrated

because there is nothing. That is its "banality." Only the good has depth and can be radical. But this is not the place to go into these matters seriously: I intend to elaborate them further in a different context. Eichmann may very well remain the concrete model of what I have to say. (*JP*, 250–1)

What could be clearer and more explicit? Arendt affirms that she has changed her mind. She now (1964) believes that "evil is never 'radical'." Even Elisabeth Young-Bruehl reaffirms what Arendt says here. She comments: "Arendt rejected the concept she had used in *The Origins of Totalitarianism* to point at the incomprehensible nature of the Nazis – 'radical evil.' As she did this, she freed herself of a long nightmare; she no longer had to live with the idea that monsters and demons had engineered the murder of millions" (*YB*, 367). So it would seem! But if we step back and reflect on the exchange between Scholem and Arendt, it is striking how *little* is said about the meaning of "radical evil." Only the barest hint is given. If we are to answer the question, Did Hannah Arendt change her mind?, we must first find out what precisely *she* meant by "radical evil." Our detective work must begin here if the relevant evidence is to be gathered.

In Chapter 4, "The Descent into Hell," I discussed Arendt's important essay entitled "The Concentration Camps," which was originally published in *Partisan Review* in 1948. This article was revised for inclusion in *The Origins of Totalitarianism*, and revised again for the second (1958) edition. A careful examination of these various texts shows the stages of her thinking about absolute or radical evil. Arendt does not use the phrase "radical evil" in her original 1948 article, but she does speak of "absolute evil." She writes:

Murder in the camps is as impersonal as the squashing of a gnat, a mere technique of management, as when a camp is overcrowded and is liquidated – or an accidental by-product, as when a prisoner succumbs to torture. Systematic torture and systematic starvation create an atmosphere of permanent dying, in which death as well as life is effectively obstructed.

The fear of the *absolute Evil* which permits of no escape knows that this is the end of dialectical evolutions and developments. It knows that modern politics revolves around a question which, strictly speaking, should never enter into politics, the question of all or nothing: of all, that is, a human society rich with infinite possibilities; or exactly nothing, that is, the end of mankind. (*CC*, 748; emphasis added)

The first edition of *Origins* ends with some perfunctory "Concluding Remarks." She deleted this section from subsequent editions, although she incorporated some of her remarks in the main body of her text. But in the original "Concluding Remarks" this is what she writes about radical evil:

> Until now the totalitarian belief that everything is possible seems to have proved only that everything can be destroyed. Yet, in their effort to prove that everything is possible, totalitarian regimes have discovered without knowing it that there are crimes which man can neither punish nor forgive. When the impossible was made possible it became the unpunishable, unforgivable absolute evil which could no longer be understood and explained by the evil motives of self-interest, greed, covetousness, resentment, lust for power, and cowardice; and which therefore anger could not revenge, love could not endure, friendship could not forgive. Just as the victims in the death factories or the holes of oblivion are no longer "human" in the eyes of their executioners, so this newest species of criminals is beyond the pale even of the solidarity in human sinfulness.
>
> *Difficult as it is to conceive of an absolute evil even in the face of its factual existence, it seems to be closely connected with the invention of a system in which all men are equally superfluous.* The manipulators of this system believe in their own superfluousness as much as in that of all others, and the totalitarian murderers are all the more dangerous because they do not care if they themselves are alive or dead, if they ever lived or never were born. The danger of the corpse factories and holes of oblivion is that today, with populations and homelessness everywhere on the increase, masses of people are continuously rendered superfluous if we continue to think of our world in utilitarian terms. (*OT*₁, 433; emphasis added)

When Arendt dropped her "Concluding Remarks" from the revised, second (1958) and subsequent editions of *Origins*, she incorporated most of the above passage in her discussion of "Total Domination." But she also made a very significant addition. Immediately after the first paragraph cited above, she added the following sentences:

> It is inherent in our entire philosophical tradition that we cannot conceive of a "radical evil," and this is true both for Christian theology, which conceded even to the Devil himself a celestial origin, as well as for Kant, the only philosopher who, in the word he coined for it, at least must have suspected the existence of this evil even though he immediately rationalized it in the concept of a "perverted ill will" that

could be explained by comprehensible motives. Therefore, we actually have nothing to fall back on in order to understand a phenomenon that nevertheless confronts us with its overpowering reality and breaks down all standards we know. There is only one thing that seems to be discernible: we may say *that radical evil has emerged in connection with a system in which all men have become equally superfluous.* (*OT*₂, 459; emphasis added)

Before attempting to make sense of these several texts, I want to cite one further piece of evidence in order to clarify what Arendt meant by "absolute evil" or "radical evil."[1]

In early 1951, before *The Origins of Totalitarianism* appeared in bookstores, Arendt sent a copy to Karl Jaspers, so that he would receive it for his birthday. Delighted that his former gifted student had used a quotation from his writings as the epigraph to the book, he immediately acknowledged receiving it. After a first reading of the preface and concluding remarks of the book, he added a note with the following cryptic question: "Hasn't Jahwe faded too far out of sight?" (*C*, 145). In her next letter to him, Arendt wrote that his question "has been on my mind for weeks now without my being able to come up with an answer to it." But the question did provoke the following reflections on radical evil:

> Evil has proved to be more radical than expected. In objective terms, modern crimes are not provided for in the Ten Commandments. Or: the Western Tradition is suffering from the preconception that the most evil things human beings can do arise from the vice of selfishness. Yet we know that the greatest evils or radical evil has nothing to do anymore with such humanly understandable, sinful motives. *What radical evil really is I don't know, but it seems to me it somehow has to do with the following phenomenon: making human beings as human beings superfluous (not using them as means to an end, which leaves their essence as humans untouched and impinges only on their human dignity; rather, making them superfluous as human beings). This happens as soon as all unpredictability – which, in human beings, is the equivalent of spontaneity – is eliminated.* And all this in turn arises from – or, better, goes along with – the delusion of the omnipotence (not simply with the lust for power) of an individual man. If an individual man qua man were omnipotent, then there is in fact no reason why men in the plural should exist at all – just as in monotheism it is only God's omnipotence that makes him ONE. So, in this same way, the omnipotence of an individual man would make men superfluous. (*C*, 166; emphasis added)

What are we to make of these claims about absolute or radical evil? Initially, what is most striking is what Arendt does not say. There is no suggestion in any of these passages that radical evil is to be understood as the "idea that monsters and demons had engineered the murder of millions." I want to be even more emphatic. There is no evidence that Arendt ever held anything like this belief. On the contrary, she categorically rejected such a claim – and long before she witnessed the Eichmann trial. Already in her 1948 article, "The Concentration Camps," she distinguishes sharply between what happened when the camps were run by the SA and what happened when they were taken over by the SS. The SA (the infamous Nazi "brown-shirts") represented a "criminal and abnormal" mentality. They might well be thought of as sadistic monsters.

> Behind the blind bestiality of the SA, there often lay a deep hatred and resentment against all those who were socially, intellectually, or physically better off than themselves, and who now, as if in fulfillment of their wildest dreams, were in their power. This resentment, which never died out entirely in the camps, strikes us as a last remnant of humanly understandable feeling. (*CC*, 758)

But although such behavior was perverse and sadistic, it was still *humanly* understandable. This was not yet the real horror – the transformation that took place when the "desk murderers" took control. In a passage that sounds very much like, and seems to anticipate, Foucault, Arendt writes:

> The real horror began, however, when the SS took over the administration of the camps. The old spontaneous bestiality gave way to an absolutely cold and systematic destruction of human bodies, calculated to destroy human dignity; death was avoided or postponed indefinitely. The camps were no longer amusement parks for beasts in human form, that is, for men who really belonged in mental institutions and prisons; the reverse became true: they were turned into "drill grounds" . . . on which perfectly normal men were trained to be full-fledged members of the SS. (*CC*, 758)

Arendt not only rejects categorically the all too popular image of the Nazis as "insane" monsters, she makes a much stronger and more provocative claim – that "radical evil" cannot be accounted for by "evil motives." This is compatible with one of her main points in the later *Eichmann in Jerusalem*, where she emphatically states that "one cannot extract any diabolical or demonic profundity from Eichmann" (*EJ*, 288).

Now it might be thought that Arendt's reference to Kant would be helpful in grasping what she means by "radical evil." After all, she tells us that it was Kant who coined the expression "radical evil." It is, of course, true that Kant speaks of radical evil in his *Religion within the Limits of Reason Alone*, and there are commentators who have argued that this is an essential concept for understanding Kant's moral philosophy, particularly his analysis of human freedom. So it would seem sensible in trying to grasp what Arendt means by radical evil to first probe what Kant meant by it, and then focus attention on what Arendt appropriated from Kant.[2] This, however, is one of those misleading clues that could divert our attention from the business in hand. Arendt indicates that her understanding of radical evil is quite different from Kant's. Consider once again what she says in her all too brief reference to Kant. "Kant, the only philosopher who, in the word he coined for it, at least must have suspected the existence of this evil *even though he immediately rationalized it in the concept of a 'perverted ill will' that could be explained by comprehensible motives*" (*OT₃*, 459; emphasis added). Whether Arendt is being fair to Kant is debatable. But it is clear that Arendt does not think that Kant grasped what *she* intends by "radical evil." Kant's analysis is based on the presupposition that there are comprehensible motives that can explain radical evil. But this is precisely what Arendt is calling into question. This is why she goes on to say that "we actually have nothing to fall back on in order to understand a phenomenon that nevertheless confronts us with its overpowering reality" (*OT₃*, 459).

The question that must be asked is: What does *Arendt* mean by radical evil? She provides an essential clue in her letter to Jaspers: "It seems to me it somehow has to do with the following phenomenon: making human beings as human beings superfluous (not using them as means to an end, which leaves their essence as humans untouched and impinges only on their human dignity; rather, making them superfluous as human beings)." This is also the point she makes when she introduces the expression "radical evil" in *The Origins of Totalitarianism*. So the question now becomes: What does Arendt mean when she says that "radical evil has emerged in connection with a system in which all men have become equally superfluous" (*OT₃*, 459)?

Superfluousness is one of the most pervasive themes in *The Origins of*

Totalitarianism. This theme is crucial for her analysis of the decline of the nation-state and the end of the Rights of Man, as too for her analysis of statelessness and what happens when human beings are stripped of the right to have rights. In her analysis of total domination, Arendt is most explicit about the new phenomenon of superfluousness that characterizes totalitarian regimes. To make human beings superfluous is to eradicate the very conditions that make humanity possible. Arendt sums this up in the paragraph that immediately precedes her brief discussion of absolute or radical evil:

> What totalitarian ideologies therefore aim at is not the transformation of the outside world or the transmutation of society, but the transformation of human nature itself. The concentration camps are the laboratories where changes in human nature are tested, and their shamefulness therefore is not just the business of their inmates and those who run them according to strictly "scientific" standards; it is the concern of all men. Suffering, of which there has been always too much on earth, is not the issue, nor is the number of victims. Human nature as such is at stake, and even though it seems that these experiments succeed not in changing man but only in destroying him, by creating a society in which the nihilistic banality of *homo homini lupus* is consistently realized, one should bear in mind the necessary limitations to an experiment which requires global control in order to show conclusive results. (*OT*₃, 458–9)

Earlier I suggested that the kernel of Arendt's understanding of the human condition, especially her emphasis on plurality as the condition for human action, is contained in this culminating chapter of *The Origins of Totalitarianism.*[3] It is as if by "dwelling on the horrors" she came to the shocking realization that the not so hidden aim of totalitarianism was the deliberate attempt to make human beings *qua human* superfluous, to transform human nature so that what is essential to live a *human* life – plurality, spontaneity, natality, and individuality – is destroyed. This is what Arendt meant by "radical evil" – a new, unprecedented phenomenon that "confronts us with its overpowering reality and breaks down all standards we know." Mass murder, genocide, unbearable large-scale suffering by innocent people, systematic torture and terror had happened before in history. But the aim of totalitarianism was not oppression, not even "total domination" if this is still understood as the total domination of *human beings.* Totalitarianism, as Arendt understands it, strives to obliterate people's humanity. This is one of the main reasons why she insisted that Nazi crimes (if we can speak of them as "crimes") are "crimes against *humanity*." She tells us in *Eichmann in Jerusalem* that "there was not the slightest doubt that Jews had been killed *qua* Jews, irrespective of their nationalities at the time," and that this unprecedented crime "was a crime against humanity, perpetrated upon the body of the Jewish people" (*EJ*, 269). Radical evil differs from the main traditional Western understandings of evil because it has nothing to do with humanly understandable "evil motives" – indeed, it has nothing to do with *human* motives at all. And this is precisely what Arendt says about Eichmann when she speaks of the "banality of evil." "Except for an extraordinary diligence in looking out for his personal advancement, he had no motives at all. . . . He *merely*, to put the matter colloquially, *never realized what he was doing*" (*EJ*, 287). Radical evil, as Arendt so devastatingly phrases it, is making human beings "superfluous as human beings." As Margaret Canovan tells us, Arendt "never *had* thought in terms of 'monsters and demons,' and 'banality' was really a more accurate way of describing the self-abandonment to inhuman forces and the diminution of human beings to an animal species . . . ."[4]

Nevertheless, it looks as if there is a crucial gap at this stage of Arendt's thinking. Even if one accepts the claim that totalitarianism aims at "the transformation of human nature itself" and that "the concentration camps are the laboratories where changes in human nature are tested," we may still ask why she calls this radical or absolute evil. Arendt, it would seem, is presupposing a normative concept of human nature which is itself in need of justification. But this way of putting the issue is misleading, for it misses the poignancy of her shocking insight. It is, of course, true that in *The Origins of Totalitarianism*, she does not hesitate to speak about "human nature" and the "transformation of human nature." But in *The Human Condition* she is much more cautious.

> To avoid misunderstanding: the human condition is not the same as human nature, and the sum total of human activities and capabilities which correspond to the human condition does not constitute anything like human nature. . . .
>
> The problem of human nature, the Augustinian *quaestio mihi factus sum* ("a question have I become for myself"), seems unanswerable in both its individual psychological sense and its general philosophical sense. It is highly unlikely that we, who can know, determine, and

define the natural essences of all things surrounding us, which we are not, should ever be able to do the same for ourselves – this would be like jumping over our own shadows. Moreover, nothing entitles us to assume that man has a nature or essence in the same sense as other things. In other words, if we have a nature or essence, then surely only a god could know and define it, and the first prerequisite would be that he be able to speak about a "who" as though it were a "what." (*HC*, 9–10)

Arendt expresses a philosophical motif that she found in Augustine, one which had been reinforced by her philosophic mentors, Heidegger and Jaspers. But there is another important dimension of doubt about a fixed human nature. Arendt, who insisted that her thinking was rooted in her own experience, claimed that with the advent of totalitarianism, one could no longer believe in the fixity of human nature, or that there is something deep down in human beings that will resist the totalitarian impulse to prove that "everything is possible" – even the most radical transformation of "human beings" into a species which is not quite human. When Eric Voegelin sharply criticized her for claiming that "human nature as such is at stake," she replied:

The success of totalitarianism is identical with a much more radical liquidation of freedom as a political and as a human reality than anything we have ever witnessed before. Under these conditions, it will hardly be consoling to cling to an unchangeable nature of man and conclude that either man himself is being destroyed or that freedom does not belong to man's essential capabilities. Historically we know of man's nature only insofar as it has existence, and no realm of eternal essences will ever console us if man loses his essential capabilities.[5]

In many places Arendt affirms how profoundly she was affected by the realization that what she had been brought up to believe was impossible had turned out not only to be possible but also to be all too real. She began her 1965 New School lecture course, "Some Questions of Moral Philosophy," by citing a passage she admired from Winston Churchill: "Scarcely anything material or established, which I was brought up to believe was permanent and vital, has lasted. Everything I was sure or taught to be sure was impossible, has happened." This was the bitter lesson of totalitarianism. Even more significant for questioning the meaning of evil was the near universal collapse of moral standards in the face of totalitarianism. She declared: "We . . .

have witnessed the total collapse of all established moral standards in public and private life during the thirties and forties." "Without much notice all this collapsed almost overnight and then it was as though morality suddenly stood revealed . . . as a set of *mores*, customs and *manners* which could be exchanged for another set with hardly more trouble than it would take to change the table manners of an individual or a people."[6] Arendt makes a similar point in the introduction to *The Life of the Mind*.

> The fact that we usually treat matters of good and evil in courses in "morals" or "ethics" may indicate how little we know about them, for morals comes from *mores* and ethics from *ēthos*, the Latin and Greek words for customs and habit, the Latin word being associated with rules of behavior, whereas the Greek word is derived from habitat, like our "habits." (*LM*, 5)

Consequently, it is not accurate to say that Arendt is presupposing uncritically a normative conception of human nature as the basis for her conception of radical or absolute evil. Rather, it is more perspicacious to say that Arendt's own thinking was deeply affected by the traumatic experience of witnessing what had seemed to be impossible – that an unprecedented totalitarian movement could arise whose ideology was based on the principle that "everything is possible," including the transformation of the human species into something less than human. And, what is even more frightening, totalitarian regimes sought to prove this "principle" in the laboratories of the concentration camps. The specter that haunted Arendt, the specter of totalitarianism, was one in which human beings would become superfluous, and even the concept of humanity itself would be obliterated.

Against Scholem, who states that radical evil and the banality of evil are *contradictory*, I want to argue for the *compatibility* of these conceptions of evil. I want to pursue a clue which, initially, does not even appear to be a clue. Let us return to Arendt's reply to Scholem. She casually remarks: "(Incidentally, I don't see why you call my term 'banality of evil' a catchword or a slogan. As far as I know no one has used the term before me; but that is unimportant.)" Arendt is wrong again. The "banality" of evil had been used before, in a very significant context which Arendt seems to have forgotten. In 1946, some 15 years prior to *Eichmann in Jerusalem*, Arendt discussed the question of Nazi war crimes in her correspondence with Jaspers.

In 1946, a year after Arendt and Jaspers resumed their correspondence, which had been interrupted by the war, Jaspers sent
Arendt his monograph *Die Schuldfrage* which dealt with the question of
Nazi war crimes and German guilt. Commenting on the book, this is
what she wrote about Nazi "crimes" (Aug. 17, 1946):

> Your definition of Nazi policy as a crime ("criminal guilt") strikes me
> as questionable. The Nazi crimes, it seems to me, explode the limits of
> the law; and that is precisely what constitutes their monstrousness. For
> these crimes, no punishment is severe enough. . . . That is, this guilt, in
> contrast to all the criminal guilt, oversteps and shatters any and all
> legal systems. (*C*, 54)

Responding to this criticism, Jaspers wrote:

> You say that what the Nazis did cannot be comprehended as "crime" –
> I'm not altogether comfortable with your view, because a guilt that
> goes beyond all criminal guilt inevitably takes on a streak of
> "greatness" – of satanic greatness – which is, for me, as inappropriate
> for the Nazis as all the talk about the "demonic" element in Hitler and
> so forth. It seems to me that we have to see those things in their total
> banality, in their prosaic triviality, because that's what truly character-
> izes them. Bacteria can cause epidemics that wipe out nations, but they
> remain merely bacteria. I regard any hint of myth and legend with
> horror. (*C*, 62)

These are the words of Jaspers in 1946, but they could very well be the
words used by Arendt in her reply to Scholem in 1964. There is even
an uncanny echo of Jaspers's comparison with bacteria and Arendt's
comparison of the spread of evil to a fungus: "Evil . . . possesses
neither depth nor any demonic dimension. It can overgrow and lay
waste the whole world precisely because it spreads like a fungus on the
surface" (*JP*, 251).[7]

Returning to the question, Did Arendt change her mind?, we may
ask how Arendt understood the evil of Nazi "criminality" in 1946,
when she discussed the issue with Jaspers, before she wrote publicly
about radical evil and long before she wrote about the banality of evil.
Nor do we have to speculate. In her December 17, 1946, letter to
Jaspers she says:

> I found what you say about my thoughts on "beyond crime and
> innocence" in what the Nazis did half convincing; that is, I realize

completely that in the way I've expressed this up to now I come dangerously close to that "satanic greatness" that I, like you, totally reject. But still, there is a difference between a man who sets out to murder his old aunt and people who without considering the economic usefulness of their actions at all (the deportations were very damaging to the war effort) built factories to produce corpses. One thing is certain: We have to combat all impulses to mythologize the horrible, and to the extent that I can't avoid such formulations, I haven't understood what actually went on. Perhaps what is behind it all is only that individual human beings did not kill other individual human beings for human reasons, but that an *organized attempt was made to eradicate the concept of the human being.* (*C*, 69; emphasis added)

It is difficult to imagine a more forceful rejection of "satanic greatness" as an appropriate concept for describing Nazi crimes. This is what Arendt "totally rejects." Like Jaspers, she strongly affirms the need to combat all impulses to mythologize the horrible. She is even self-critical of her own formulation, insofar as it suggests this misleading type of demonization. The problem is to find a language that can comprehend the incomprehensible, represent the unrepresentable, *without* making it into a "negative" sublime. For the problem one faces in speaking about evil bears a strong family resemblance to the way in which Kant speaks of the sublime. But there is nothing sublime about radical evil. Radical evil is the systematic attempt to make human beings (in their plurality) superfluous; it is the organized attempt to eradicate the concept and *reality* of being a human being. In theological language, it is the audacious attempt to destroy God's creation and to transform human beings into "perverted animals."

Radical evil, strictly speaking, is neither punishable nor forgivable, because punishment and forgiveness presuppose what radical evil eradicates: that is, *human* action. In *The Human Condition*, Arendt writes:

The alternative to forgiveness, but by no means its opposite, is punishment, and both have in common that they attempt to put an end to something that without interference could go on endlessly. It is therefore quite significant, a structural element in the realm of human affairs, that men are unable to forgive what they cannot punish and they are unable to punish what has turned out to be unforgivable. This is the true hallmark of those offenses which, since Kant, we call "radical evil" and about whose nature so little is known, even to us who have been exposed to one of their rare outbursts on the public scene. All we know is that we can neither punish nor forgive such offenses and that they therefore transcend the realm of human affairs and the potentialities of human power, both of which they radically destroy wherever they make their appearance. (*HC*, 241)

Arendt thought that the so-called Nazi crimes and the radical evil of totalitarianism break the bounds of our traditional concepts and standards. But to say this is not to say that "satanic greatness" is the character of these "crimes." For "satanic greatness" is itself a human – all too human – category. The radical evil of totalitarianism must not be either mythologized or aestheticized.

The 1946 exchange between Arendt and Jaspers helps to clear up another, closely related confusion concerning the meaning of radical evil, a confusion which some of Arendt's rhetorical constructions actually help to generate. Jaspers criticizes Arendt for coming close to taking the "path of poetry" in describing Nazi crimes. "The way you do express it, you've almost taken the path of poetry. And a Shakespeare would never be able to give adequate form to this material – his instinctive aesthetic sense would lead to falsification of it – and that's why he couldn't attempt it" (*C*, 62). Jaspers's reference to Shakespeare is illuminating, because it was Shakespeare who created some of the greatest and most compelling characters exemplifying "satanic greatness." Arendt herself frequently refers to Shakespeare when speaking about evil, especially when she attempts to distinguish the banality of evil from traditional conceptions of evil.[8] Because her rhetorical constructions sometimes suggest that the alternative to the banality of evil is evil which is theologically or aesthetically categorized as "satanic greatness," one can easily be misled into thinking that she identifies radical evil with satanic greatness. Thus, in one of her first attempts to explain and clarify what she means by the banality of evil, she wrote:

> Eichmann was not Iago and not Macbeth, and nothing would have been farther from his mind than to determine with Richard III "to prove a villain. . . ." [Eichmann] was not stupid. It was sheer thoughtlessness – something by no means identical with stupidity – that predisposed him to become one of the greatest criminals of that period. . . . That such remoteness from reality and such thoughtlessness can wreak more havoc than all the evil instincts taken together which, perhaps, are inherent in man – that was, in fact, the lesson one could learn in Jerusalem. (*EJ*, 287–8)

We find a similar rhetorical contrast more fully elaborated in the introduction to *The Life of the Mind*.

Factually, my preoccupation with mental activities has two rather different origins. The immediate impulse came from my attending the Eichmann trial in Jerusalem. In my report of it I spoke of "the banality of evil." Behind that phrase, I held no thesis or doctrine, although I was dimly aware of the fact that it went counter to our tradition of thought – literary, theological, or philosophic – about the phenomenon of evil. Evil, we have learned, is something demonic; its incarnation is Satan, a "lightning fall from heaven" (Luke 10:18), or Lucifer, the fallen angel ("The devil is an angel too" – Unamuno) whose sin is pride ("proud as Lucifer"), namely, that *superbia* of which only the best are capable: they don't want to serve God but to be like Him. Evil men, we are told, act out of envy; this may be resentment at not having turned out well through no fault of their own (Richard III) or the envy of Cain, who slew Abel because "The Lord had regard for Abel and his offering, but for Cain and his offering he had no regard." Or they may be prompted by weakness (Macbeth). Or, on the contrary, by the powerful hatred wickedness feels for sheer goodness (Iago's "I hate the Moor: my cause is hearted"; Claggart's hatred for Billy Budd's "barbarian" innocence, a hatred considered by Melville a "depravity according to nature"), or by covetousness, "the root of all evil" (*Radix omnium malorum cupiditas*). However, what I was confronted with was utterly different and still undeniably factual. I was struck by a manifest shallowness in the doer that made it impossible to trace the uncontestable evil of his deeds to any deeper level of roots or motives. The deeds were monstrous, but the doer – at least the very effective one now on trial – was quite ordinary, commonplace, and neither demonic nor monstrous. There was no sign in him of firm ideological convictions or of specific evil motives, and the only notable characteristic one could detect in his past behavior as well as in his behavior during the trial and throughout the pre-trial police examination was something entirely negative: it was not stupidity but *thoughtlessness*. (*LM*, 3–4)

This passage shows how strikingly Arendt departs from the traditional, entrenched conception of evil understood as a manifestation of "evil motives." This departure from the tradition is what is so disturbing in her analysis of the banality of evil. But she had already made the same point about radical evil: it was not a matter of "evil motives," but rather of seeking "to eradicate the concept of the human being," making human beings superfluous *qua* human beings. Arendt also indicates here what she takes to be the essential clue for understanding Eichmann's "monstrous deeds": his thoughtlessness, by which she means his inability to think and to judge.

Let me return to the question, Did Arendt change her mind? Phrased in this unqualified manner, the question is too vague and ambiguous; it invites misleading answers. But we can analyze this vague question into more specific, determinate questions that *can* be answered. Does radical evil as Arendt presents it in *The Origins of Totalitarianism* "contradict" (as Scholem claims) Arendt's notion of the banality of evil? No! I have argued that what Arendt means by radical evil is making human beings superfluous, eradicating the very conditions required for living a human life. This is entirely compatible with what she says about the banality of evil. Eichmann lacked the thoughtfulness to grasp that this was the consequence of his "monstrous deeds." Did Arendt ever believe that Nazi crimes could be adequately explained as the "deeds of monsters and demons"? No! She explicitly and consistently "totally rejects" such an understanding of Nazi criminality. Did Arendt ever think that anything like "satanic greatness" was a relevant concept for understanding the evil of totalitarian domination? No! Already in 1946 she makes it perfectly clear that she rejects such a notion – and even criticizes those formulations she uses that suggest such an understanding of Nazi evil. Arendt resists all tendencies to mythologize or aestheticize the radical evil of totalitarianism.

To answer these questions emphatically in the negative is not to deny that there was a change and a shift of focus when she spoke of "the banality of evil." Indeed, the shift was major. The key concept in her earlier analysis of radical evil was *superfluousness*. After she witnessed the Eichmann trial, she turned her attention to *thoughtlessness*.[9] It is as if Arendt had initially felt the need to understand what was unprecedented in the evil that erupted with the advent of twentieth-century totalitarianism. Her response was that never before had there been such a thorough, systematic attempt to change human nature, to make human beings in their plurality, spontaneity, and individuality superfluous. But after the Eichmann trial she became preoccupied with a new and different question: how to account for the "monstrous deeds" committed by persons who in other circumstances seemed so "normal" and "ordinary."

Following the Eichmann trial, Arendt revised her understanding of the role of Nazi ideological indoctrination. As she says in the passage quoted above, "there was no sign in [Eichmann] of firm ideological convictions." What Arendt took to be the indisputable phenomenon of the banality of evil opened up an entirely new line of questioning for her. She now asked by what right she possessed this concept of the banality of evil. The full story of her struggle with the meaning and consequences of that concept is as complex and nuanced as her struggle with the meaning of radical evil.

The crystallized event of twentieth-century totalitarianism brought a new, unprecedented type of regime into existence, one which strives to achieve total domination by means of total terror. This new regime of totalitarianism opens for us the abyss of radical evil, the evil that seeks to make human beings superfluous and even to eradicate the concept of humanity. What is most frightening is that this monstrous deed, this deliberate attempt to destroy and transform the human condition, does not require monstrous or "evil motives." It can result from the thoughtlessness – the inability to think – of ordinary, normal people. Even after the collapse of Soviet totalitarianism, we remain haunted by the specter of radical evil erupting again in unforeseen circumstances. There is no ontological guarantee, no "fact of the matter" about human nature that is a guarantee against this all too real possibility. On the contrary, the one lesson that totalitarianism should have taught us is that it is an illusion to think that radical evil is impossible. "Everything is possible." All of Arendt's thinking is directed against the ever present, real *danger* of the eruption of radical evil.

8

Evil, Thinking, and Judging

On May 23, 1960, David Ben-Gurion, the Israeli Prime Minister, made a sensational announcement to the Knesset (the Israeli parliament). Adolf Eichmann, the notorious Nazi war criminal, had been captured in Argentina. Eichmann, who had been living in a suburb of Buenos Aires under the assumed name of Ricardo Klement, was tracked down by the Israeli secret service and flown to Israel. At the very moment when Ben-Gurion was making his announcement to the world, Eichmann was already in an Israeli prison.

The infamous name of Adolf Eichmann was well known. Eichmann had played a key role in implementing "the final solution," a policy he carried out with "murderous zeal" and bureaucratic efficiency. Even in the summer and fall of 1944, when it was clear that the Nazis were losing the war, having suffered defeats on two major fronts, Eichmann coolly continued to arrange for the transportation of hundreds of thousands of Jews to death camps. The evidence gathered since the end of the war, documenting in detail what Eichmann and his section, R.S.H.A. IV-B-4 had done, was overwhelming. Just as "Auschwitz" had imprinted itself as the name for all death camps, so "Eichmann" had become a place-holder for all Nazis responsible for the deaths of millions of Jews. Eichmann, who had a flair for the melodramatic, offered to hang himself in public, without a trial. But this was not to be. He would be tried by an Israeli court for "crimes against humanity" and "crimes against the Jews with the intent to destroy the people."

Eichmann's trial promised to be even more sensational and significant than the Nuremberg trials. Attention would be focused on the deeds of a single individual. There would be an opportunity to tell the full story of what the Nazis had done to the Jews and what the Jews had suffered. Before the trial, Ben-Gurion himself made it clear that the trial was intended to serve several purposes. It would document in detail how "the final solution" was carried out; it would serve as a lesson to the world regarding the consequences of anti-Semitism; and it would educate Jews living in Israel, as well as those living in the Diaspora. It would show the world why Israel was so vital for the survival of the Jewish people.

When it became clear that Eichmann would be tried in Jerusalem, Hannah Arendt decided to attend the trial. She said "to attend this trial is somehow, I feel, an obligation I owe my past" (*YB*, 329). And when Karl Jaspers expressed his apprehension about the trial, Arendt wrote to him: "I would never be able to forgive myself if I didn't go and look at this walking disaster face to face in all his bizarre vacuousness, without the mediation of the printed word" (*C*, 409–10). Arendt approached William Shawn, editor of the *New Yorker*, offering to write a "report" of the trial. Shawn quickly accepted. She was free to write whatever she thought appropriate.

In the decade prior to the Eichmann trial, Arendt had not written publicly about Jewish, Zionist, or Israeli affairs. Her last major article on these topics had been "Peace or Armistice in the Near East?" (1950), the article that she had dedicated to Magnes in which she outlined his hope for a Jewish homeland founded on Arab–Jewish cooperation. This was the article that signaled Arendt's withdrawal from active Zionist debate. For she knew that the cause she had fought for with Magnes was already a defeated one. The decade of the 1950s was when Arendt was achieving prominence as a political thinker. Her rise to prominence began with the publication of *Origins*. In 1958, she published *The Human Condition*. And when the announcement of Eichmann's capture was made, she was in the process of writing *On Revolution*.

Although Arendt had not published anything about Jewish affairs for some time, developments in Israel were never far from her thoughts. This is clear from her correspondence, especially her letters to Jaspers and Blumenfeld. She had accepted the factual existence of the State of Israel, and even taken pride in its accomplishments. But she had continued to be critical of Israeli chauvinism, the successes of revisionist ideology, the distortions of Jewish history encouraged by Israeli authorities, the lack of concern for Palestinian Arabs by the Israeli political leaders, and the failures of Israelis to engage in direct Israeli–Arab discussions and negotiations. She strongly objected to the "theocratic rule of the rabbis" and the willingness of secular politicians to compromise on issues of civil liberties in order to gain the political support of the small, but powerful, orthodox religious parties. In her ongoing correspondence with Jaspers, she points out his naiveté about Israel. She felt he was "blind concerning Israel." The following passage from her November 16, 1958, letter to Jaspers is typical of her critical stance toward Israel, and shows the continuity of her thinking with the articles that she wrote during the 1940s.

> A few days ago I came across the sheet of paper on which I'd noted what you wanted to know about Israel. I'm enclosing the circular letter of the rabbinate apropos of the immigration of Jewish refugees from Poland with their non-Jewish wives (to whom most of them owed the fact that they survived the Hitler years!). A friend said to me a few days ago that there are more and more people in Israel now who are finding the theocratic rule of the rabbis intolerable. Another point: The name of the village where an army regiment staged a massacre on the day before the Suez Campaign is Kfar Kassim. The story is this: A state of siege was declared for all the Arab villages in Israel, and all the inhabitants had to be in their houses by 5 PM. Violators, whether men, women, or children, would be shot. This announcement wasn't made in Kfar Kassim until 4:30, however; and the villagers were in the fields and couldn't be notified in time. The village was consequently almost completely wiped out – everybody, women, children, etc. When the soldiers were given this order, they asked what they should do with the people who couldn't be notified in time. The Jewish officer's answer was: May Allah have mercy upon them! – The matter was finally settled in court a few weeks ago, and the soldiers were all sentenced to life imprisonment. A decision has finally been made too, to try the officer who gave the order. People are afraid about this because nobody knows where the order originated; that is, people are afraid because they probably in fact do know. The public does not know. – And finally: The first Arab village to be wiped out at the beginning of the Arab–Jewish war (about 1947) in order to set an example was called Deir Jassim. The mass exodus of Arabs from Palestine was largely prompted by this massacre. It was widely characterized as a second Lidice. (*C*, 358)[1]

Arendt's independent, critical attitude toward the State of Israel was not well known to the wider public when she went to Jerusalem to attend the Eichmann trial. (Most of her articles on Palestine written during the 1940s had appeared in specialized Jewish periodicals.) She never thought of herself as an anti-Zionist, but rather as a member of the "loyal opposition."[2] In the months preceding the trial there was an extensive international debate about the legal, moral, and political issues concerning the propriety of the trial – questions concerning the legality of Eichmann's capture and abduction without any attempt at formal extradition, questions concerning which court (if any) had legal jurisdiction to try him, what laws were relevant in judging him, and whether Eichmann could receive a fair trial in Israel. It was also asked how one could justify Eichmann being tried by an Israeli court when the State of Israel did not even exist when he committed his crimes.

Jaspers and Arendt discussed many of these issues in their correspondence.[3] Jaspers did not think that Eichmann should be tried by an Israeli court. He proposed instead that there should be a public inquiry into "the historical facts," but not a legal trial. He was apprehensive that an Israeli court might make Eichmann a martyr for anti-Semites. Arendt sought to rebut Jaspers's objections point by point. She agreed with Jaspers that Israel did not have the "right to speak for the Jews of the world," but she argued that "Israel has the right to speak for the victims, because the large majority of them (300,000) are living in Israel now as citizens." Sounding like a committed Zionist, she countered the objection that Israel did not exist when Eichmann's crimes were committed by declaring: "One could say that it was for the sake of these victims that Palestine became Israel." Arendt also conceded that, theoretically, it might be better for Eichmann to be tried in "an international court with appropriate powers," but unfortunately no such court existed. And she presented an argument showing that an Israeli court did have "competence" to try Eichmann. (See Arendt's Dec. 23, 1960, letter, *C*, 414–18.) I mention these details because – especially in light of the savage criticism of *Eichmann in Jerusalem* and some of the slanderous claims leveled at Arendt – it is important to set the historical record straight, to know that even before the trial Arendt defended Israel's right to abduct Eichmann and try him in an Israeli court. We shall also see that she endorsed the crucial part of the judgment of the court and the correctness of the death sentence.

Arendt did, however, express her uneasiness about the Israeli propaganda surrounding the trial. After giving her arguments for the appropriateness and legitimacy of Eichmann being tried by an Israeli court, she comments:

> As to the conduct of the trial itself, I share your fears. . . . It's a pretty sure bet that there'll be an effort to show Israeli youth and (worse yet) the whole world certain things. Among others, that Jews who aren't Israelis will wind up in situations where they'll let themselves be slaughtered like sheep. Also: that the Arabs were hand in glove with the Nazis. There are other possibilities for distorting the issue itself. (*C*, 416)

Jaspers and Arendt agreed that "the concept of *hostes humani generis . . .* is more or less indispensable to the trial. The crucial point is that although the crime at issue was committed primarily against the Jews, it is in no way limited to the Jews or the Jewish question" (*C*, 423).

On April 11, 1961, the trial of Adolf Eichmann began in the Beth Ha'am, the House of the People, the largest auditorium in Jerusalem, with Hannah Arendt seated with other "members of the press." The trial lasted until August. (Arendt attended only for short periods.) The court then adjourned for four months, and judgment was pronounced on December 11. Eichmann was condemned to death by hanging. The case was appealed. On May 29, 1962, a second judgment was handed down by the Court of Appeal, Israel's Supreme Court. Eichmann submitted a plea for mercy, which was promptly denied. On Thursday, May 31, 1962, he was hanged.

On February 16, 1963, the first installment of Hannah Arendt's five-part report on the Eichmann trial was published in the *New Yorker*. Following the *New Yorker* policy, the series was entitled "A Reporter at Large: Eichmann in Jerusalem." But even before the installments started appearing, they created a scandal. It was rumored that Arendt exonerated Eichmann and blamed the Jews for their own extermination. She was accused of being anti-Zionist and anti-Semitic. She was "soulless," "malicious," "arrogant," and "flippant." She distorted the facts. She trivialized the entire Holocaust with her catchword "the banality of evil." There were those who accused her of making Eichmann seem much more attractive than the Jews he murdered. Arendt was attacked, threatened, vilified, and excoriated. Some of her closest friends broke with her. The Eichmann controversy raged for

years. Even today, more than 30 years after the appearance of
Eichmann in Jerusalem: A Report on the Banality of Evil, there are those
who cannot forgive her for what she wrote.[4]

I want to clarify my intentions in reexamining Arendt's report and
her understanding of the banality of evil. I have no interest in putting
Arendt on trial or in condemning or exonerating her. My goal is to
understand what she is saying and why. I want to follow some of the
basic thought-trains that arose from her encounter with Eichmann in
Jerusalem. There is a great deal in her book that can legitimately be
criticized – both what she says and how she says it. Throughout, she
employed sarcastic irony. She did not attempt to tone down her strong
opinions. She did not hide her disdain for the chief prosecutor, Gideon
Hauser, or her criticism of Ben-Gurion. In the opening pages of her
report she wrote: "This courtroom is not a bad place for the show trial
David Ben-Gurion, Prime Minister of Israel, had in mind when he
decided to have Eichmann kidnapped in Argentina and brought to
the District Court of Jerusalem to stand trial for his role in the 'final
solution' of the Jewish question." And: "Ben-Gurion . . . remains the
invisible stage manager of the proceedings" (*EJ*, 4–5). This is scarcely
the type of rhetoric to achieve a sympathetic reading of her report.
One of the central themes in Arendt's writing is the inescapability of
personal responsibility. I believe Arendt herself bears some of the
responsibility for how her book was read (and even misread), and why
it caused so much pain and anger.

I also believe that the reason why Arendt's report is so troubling is
because it compels us to face up to painful questions about the
meaning of evil in the contemporary world, the moral collapse of
respectable society, the ease with which mass killing becomes
"normal," acceptable behavior, the feebleness of the so-called voice of
conscience, the subtle forms of complicity and cooperation that "go
along" with murderous deeds. These, unfortunately, are not issues
restricted to Nazi horrors. They are still with us, and demand that we
struggle with them over and over again.

It is important to remember that even though Arendt was critical –
even scornful – of the chief prosecutor, Gideon Hauser, and the case
he presented, she expressed the highest admiration for the three
judges who tried Eichmann. She completely endorsed their judgment
concerning Eichmann's responsibility. She wrote: "What the judgment had to say on this point was more than correct, it was the truth."
She cited the following passage from their judgment:

[I]n such an enormous and complicated crime as the one we are now considering, wherein many people participated, on various levels and in various modes of activity – the planners, the organizers, and those executing the deeds, according to their various ranks – there is not much point in using ordinary concepts of counseling and soliciting to commit a crime. For these crimes were committed en masse, not only in regard to the number of victims, but also in regard to the numbers of those who perpetrated the crime, and the extent to which any one of the many criminals was close to or remote from the actual killer of the victim means nothing, as far as the measure of his responsibility is concerned. On the contrary, in general *the degree of responsibility increases as we draw further away from the man who uses the fatal instrument with his own hands.* (*EJ*, 246–7; Arendt's emphasis)

This is one of the main points that Arendt stressed throughout her report. She did not think that the prosecution had proved "beyond a reasonable doubt" that Eichmann had committed an overt act of murder with "his own hands." She strongly objected to what she took to be the prosecutor's melodramatic attempt to demonize Eichmann, to portray him as a "sadistic monster" who was possessed by an "insane hatred of the Jews." By relying on such conventional categories, the prosecutor (unlike the judges) obscured the character of this "desk criminal" and his crimes. Eichmann was neither "perverted nor sadistic." He was "terrifyingly normal." He was a "new type of criminal, who is in actual fact *hostis generis humani*, [and who] commits his crimes under circumstances that make it well-nigh impossible for him to know or to feel that he is doing wrong" (*EJ*, 276). This is what Arendt thought was so unprecedented, and what needed to be confronted squarely to understand Eichmann's deeds and responsibility.

But if it is true, as I want to argue, that Arendt's judgment of Eichmann was far more damning than that of "monster" which the prosecutor leveled, why was Arendt so severely and bitterly attacked? Many of her critics claimed that her report was filled with factual errors – errors so egregious that they undermined her claims and judgments.[5] But this was not the main reason for the scandal. Gershom Scholem in his open letter to Arendt spoke for many when he touched on several major concerns. There was the question of the tone of her book. Scholem accused her of being "malicious" and "flippant." She was lacking in love for her people and in *Herzenstadt* in dealing with the sufferings of the Jewish people. He also questioned her account of the role of the *Judenräte*, the Jewish councils appointed by the Nazis to organize the Jewish communities and carry out the Nazi directives. This was the part of her report that caused the greatest uproar, especially in the Jewish community. Scholem claimed that Arendt was guilty of "a kind of demagogic will-to-overstatement." He questioned whether "our generation is in a position to pass any kind of historical judgment" on what the Jews under the Nazis had suffered and done. Finally, Scholem expressed his disdain for Arendt's "thesis concerning the 'banality of evil'," a phrase which he said was a slogan and a catchword (*JP*, 240–5).

Scholem's key objections can be used to probe the basic issues with which Arendt was struggling. Consider the basis for what became the most vehement attacks on Arendt: her discussion of the *Judenräte* (Jewish councils). Although this took up only a few brief pages, it is here that she *seemed* to be soulless and heartless, apparently blaming the victims for their own destruction. Members of these councils were typically selected from local Jewish leaders who were given the responsibility of policing and regulating their own communities. There is extensive documentary evidence detailing the Nazi directives for establishing these councils, who was selected, and what they did and did not do. Despite objections, protests, and even suicides by some council members, the Nazis were remarkably successful in organizing these councils and seeing that they functioned properly. At the beginning of her discussion of the Jewish councils, Arendt writes: "To a Jew this role of the Jewish leaders in the destruction of their own people is undoubtedly the darkest chapter of the whole dark story" (*EJ*, 117). But the statement that many of her critics found the most offensive and outrageous is the following:

> Wherever Jews lived, there were recognized Jewish leaders, and this leadership, almost without exception, cooperated in one way or another, for one reason or another, with the Nazis. The whole truth was that if the Jewish people had really been unorganized and leaderless, there would have been chaos and plenty of misery but the total number of victims would hardly have been between four and a half and six million people. (*EJ*, 125)

Because this claim is so provocative and disturbing, it is important to scrutinize carefully what Arendt is saying and what she is not saying. For she is *not* passing moral judgment on the reasons or motives of the members of the Jewish councils. She is not even denying that millions of Jews would have been murdered even if there had been no Jewish councils. She herself reported the "effectiveness" of the SS *Einsatzgruppen* (mobile killing units) in murdering Jews even where there were no councils.

One of the ironies of the accusations brought against Arendt is that, quite early in her report, she castigated the prosecutor for "asking witness after witness – 'Why did you not protest?' " She said that this question was "cruel and silly" (*EJ*, 11–12). It ignored the dire consequences of any protest or resistance, the totality of *Nazi* terror. To emphasize her point, she said one needed only to permit one's

> imagination to dwell for a few minutes on the fate of those Dutch Jews who in 1941 . . . dared to attack a German security police detachment. Four hundred and thirty Jews were arrested in reprisal and they were literally tortured to death. . . . For months on end they died a thousand deaths. . . . There exist many things considerably worse than death, and the S.S. saw to it that none of them was ever very far from their victims' minds and imaginations. (*EJ*, 12)

But Arendt did think that many Jewish leaders in the councils had crossed an "abyss" when they cooperated in the selection of Jews to be sent for "resettlement" – that is, deportation to forced labor camps and death camps.[6] Her brief discussion does not do justice to the ways in which some leaders sought to subvert Nazi directives. In this context she does not mention what she shows later in her report: that when Jews found themselves in situations in which they had the support of the surrounding population, their leaders acted quite differently. In Denmark, Jewish leaders were able, with the co-operation of Danes, to save most of the relatively small Danish Jewish population who escaped to Sweden.[7] In claiming that "if the Jewish people had been unorganized and leaderless" there would have been far fewer victims of Nazi murder, Arendt is making one of those striking counterfactual historical judgments which it is almost impossible to confirm or falsify by an appeal to hard evidence. Nevertheless, one should not deny the kernel of truth in what she is affirming. Although Arendt was one of the first to reach a wide public in discussing the role of the Jewish councils, much of what she says was already well known to scholars of the Holocaust. Moreover, there is considerable scholarly support for her judgment. The evidence amassed by Isaiah Trunk in his detailed study dedicated exclusively to the *Judenräte* in Eastern Europe, written, in part, to refute Arendt, actually supports the core of Arendt's claim. He tells us:

> The situation became morally unbearable when, during the mass "resettlement actions," the Germans forced the Councils and the Jewish police to carry out the preparatory work and to participate in the initial stages of the actual deportation. The latter task was forced mainly upon the Jewish police. The Councils then faced a tragic dilemma never before experienced by a community representative organ. Cooperation then reached the morally dangerous borderline of collaboration. The Councils were called upon to make fateful decisions on the life and death of certain segments of their coreligionists.[8]

Even Walter Z. Laqueur, who was among Arendt's sharpest critics, concludes his article "Hannah Arendt in Jerusalem: The Controversy Revisited" with a statement that might have been written by Arendt herself:

> But if in many cases mitigating circumstances can be found, if some leaders in fact behaved heroically, the *Judenrat* phenomenon, as a whole, has acquired a negative connotation, and rightly so. From the moment at the very latest that the Jewish Councils were used by the Nazis to help in the "final solution" their action became indefensible.[9]

But why does Arendt raise the question of the Jewish councils in her report? What did this "darkest chapter of the whole dark story" (at least for the Jewish people) have to do with Eichmann? Paradoxically, the question – the rationale for discussing the Jewish councils – has rarely even been considered in the Eichmann controversy. Yet Arendt is quite explicit. She writes:

> I have dwelt on this chapter of the story, which the Jerusalem trial failed to put before the eyes of the world in its true dimensions, because it offers the most striking insight into the totality of the moral collapse the Nazis caused in respectable European society – not only in Germany but in almost all countries, not only among the persecutors but also among the victims. (*EJ*, 125–6)

This is the crucial point that Arendt wants to emphasize: "the totality of the moral collapse" in "respectable society." Arendt was damning in her judgment of the moral collapse of respectable German society. She was scornful of what she called the "post-war fairy-tale" repeated by many Nazis, as well as by other Germans, that they were always "inwardly opposed" to Hitler and were only trying to "mitigate" worse horrors. It was the *totality* of moral collapse "among the persecutors but also among the victims" that she wants us to confront.

This moral collapse is something that Arendt experienced personally when she fled from Germany in 1933. Reflecting on this period in her life, she said: "[T]he problem, the personal problem, was not what our enemies did but what our friends did. In the wave of *Gleichschaltung* (co-ordination) which was relatively voluntary – in any case, not yet under the pressure of terror – it was as if an empty space formed around one" (*EU*, 10–11).[10]

Consider the context in her report in which Arendt discusses the Jewish councils. She is examining Eichmann's claim that "Nobody . . . came to me and reproached me for anything in the performance of my duties" (*EJ*, 131). The question of the "voice of conscience" and Eichmann's conscience became an important issue in the trial. Arendt did not think that Eichmann, as the court's judgment phrased it, had "closed his ears to the voice of conscience." On the contrary, his "conscience" was like an empty cipher that spoke with the voice of "respectable society." And what he heard is that there is nothing intrinsically wrong with murdering millions of innocent victims. "His conscience was indeed set at rest when he saw the zeal and eagerness with which 'good society' everywhere reacted as he did" (*EJ*, 126).

The issues for moral reflection raised by this "total moral collapse" continued to haunt Arendt for the rest of her life. In her 1965 course of lectures delivered at the New School, "Some Questions of Moral Philosophy," she began by discussing the "basic experiences" that lay behind her concern with moral questions. She said that the dominant belief of her generation had been that "moral conduct is a matter of course." But "no one in his right mind can any longer [believe] this."[11] For Arendt, the most intractable moral questions arose not from the Nazis' behavior, but from the behavior of ordinary respectable people. Margaret Canovan succinctly summarizes what so troubled Arendt.

Although these [ordinary respectable] people would never have dreamed of committing crimes as long as they lived in a society where such activities were not usual, they adapted effortlessly to a system in which blatant crimes against whole categories of people were standard behaviour. In the place of "thou shalt not kill" which had seemed the most indisputable rule of civilian existence, such people had no difficulty in accepting the Nazis' rule according to which killing was a moral duty for the sake of the race.[12]

Totalitarian domination called into question the very presuppositions of traditional moral philosophies. Despite her indebtedness to Aristotle, Arendt felt that we could no longer accept the classical understanding of virtue and character whereby, with a proper education and training, a virtuous disposition becomes constitutive of what we are. "Only habits and customs can be taught, and we know only too well the alarming speed with which they are unlearned and forgotten when new circumstances demand a change in manners and patterns of behavior" (*LM*, 5). Aristotle himself realized that virtuous activity presupposes a polis or community in which the virtues can flourish. But the advent of totalitarianism showed how terror and violence could so rapidly obliterate the very conditions required for such an *ethos*.

Furthermore, for all Arendt's admiration of Kant and the inspiration she drew from him, she was skeptical about Kant's "official" moral philosophy. She did not think that telling right from wrong, or distinguishing good from evil, was based solely on the faculty of practical reason. The type of reflective judgment, judgment of particulars, analyzed in the *Critique of Judgment* was required to distinguish not only the beautiful from the ugly, but also right from wrong. Mores, customs, habits, rules, traditional standards, could all change "effortlessly." They provided no barrier to committing evil deeds. This was the frightening "lesson" of twentieth-century totalitarianism. She stresses how little questions concerning good and evil have to do with what have traditionally been called morals and ethics.

Arendt's study of totalitarianism, and especially the concentration camps, led her to question what she called "the optimistic view of human nature" which "presupposes an independent human faculty, unsupported by law and public opinion, that judges anew in full spontaneity every deed and intent whenever the occasion arises."[13] In Arendt's view there are reasons for *wanting* to believe that there is such an independent faculty. Such a belief underlies most traditional understandings of morality and legality. But even if we have reasons for believing that such a human faculty exists, twentieth-century totalitarianism, with its ideological conviction that "everything is possible", has taught us that we can no longer believe that it is impossible to destroy and eliminate such a capacity.

Increasingly, Arendt came to believe that the very capacity to distinguish right from wrong, good from evil, presupposes the exercise of the mental activities of thinking and judging. These are the very activities that Eichmann was incapable of. This is how Arendt accounts for the phenomenon that she calls "the banality of evil." But what precisely does Arendt mean by this provocative phrase which so deeply offended so many of her readers – the phrase which Scholem calls a "slogan" and a "catchword"?

If we turn to the main text of *Eichmann in Jerusalem*, there is scarcely any explicit discussion of what she means by either evil or the banality of evil. As I have already indicated, the subtitle, *A Report on the Banality of Evil*, did not even appear in the *New Yorker* articles. There are only two passages in her report that explicitly mention evil. The first is directly relevant to the discussion of the so-called voice of conscience.

> And just as the law in civilized countries assumes that the voice of conscience tells everybody "Thou shalt not kill," even though man's natural desires and inclinations may at times be murderous, so the law of Hitler's land demanded that the voice of conscience tell everybody: "Thou shalt kill," although the organizers of the massacres knew full well that murder is against the normal desires and inclinations of most people. Evil in the Third Reich had lost the quality by which most people recognize it – the quality of temptation. (*EJ*, 150)

The expression "the banality of evil" appears only once, in the final sentence of her report (just before her epilogue). Arendt comments on "the grotesque silliness" of Eichmann's final words before being hanged. Eichmann is reported to have said: "After a short while, gentlemen, *we shall all meet again*. Such is the fate of all men. Long live Germany, long live Argentina, long live Austria. *I shall not forget them*." This is Arendt's comment:

> In the face of death, he had found the cliché used in funeral oratory. Under the gallows, his memory played him the last trick; he was "elated" and he forgot that this was his own funeral.
>
> It was as though in those last minutes he was summing up the lesson that this long course in human wickedness had taught us – the lesson of the fearsome, word-and-thought-defying *banality of evil*. (*EJ*, 252)

That's it! There is no further commentary or explanation of what

Arendt means by "the banality of evil." When her critics attacked her, she made several attempts to clarify her meaning. But these clarifications introduce further problems. In her postscript to the 1965 edition of the book, she wrote:

> [W]hen I speak of the banality of evil, I do so only on the strictly factual level, pointing to a phenomenon which stared one in the face at the trial. Eichmann was not Iago and not Macbeth, and nothing would have been farther from his mind than to determine with Richard III "to prove a villain." Except for an extraordinary diligence in looking out for his personal advancement, he had no motives at all. . . . He *merely*, to put the matter colloquially, *never realized what he was doing.* (*EJ*, 287)

It simply is not at all clear in what sense Arendt is speaking "on the strictly factual level." This is precisely what is being contested. For to speak of the banality of evil is not simply to report a fact, but – in Arendt's term – to make a *judgment* about the character of Eichmann's motives (or lack thereof). Furthermore, at the very least, it is misleading to say that "Eichmann never realized what he was doing." For Eichmann certainly knew, as Arendt acknowledges, that his actions had led to the murder of millions of innocent victims. In what sense is it accurate to claim that he merely "never realized what he was doing"?

Arendt's reply to Scholem, which we have already discussed in Chapter 7, gives a hint about the meaning of "the banality of evil" but is still not completely satisfactory. She writes:

> It is indeed my opinion now that evil is never "radical," that it is only extreme, and that it possesses neither depth nor any demonic dimension. It can overgrow and lay waste the whole world precisely because it spreads like a fungus on the surface. It is "thought-defying," as I said, because thought tries to reach some depth, to go to the roots, and the moment it concerns itself with evil, it is frustrated because there is nothing. (*JP*, 250)[14]

The clearest, most judicious statement about the meaning of "the banality of evil" occurs in her 1971 essay "Thinking and Moral Considerations."

> Some years ago, reporting the trial of Eichmann in Jerusalem, I spoke of "the banality of evil" and meant with this no theory or doctrine but

something quite factual, the phenomenon of evil deeds, committed on a gigantic scale, which could not be traced to any particularity of wickedness, pathology, or ideological conviction in the doer, whose only personal distinction was a perhaps extraordinary shallowness. However monstrous the deeds were, the doer was neither monstrous nor demonic, and the only specific characteristic one could detect in his past as well as in his behavior during the trial and the preceding police examination was something entirely negative: it was not stupidity but a curious, quite authentic inability to think. (*TM*, 417)[15]

This claim is repeated in the introduction to *The Life of the Mind*, where Arendt tells us that it was one of the sources of her preoccupation with mental activities. Arendt's portrait of Eichmann is damning, but not because he was a "sadistic monster" or exhibited demonic or "satanic greatness." It was his "ordinariness" and "normality" that she found so troubling. His primary motivations seemed to be petty ambition, a desire to please his superiors, to show how dedicated he was in carrying out orders and fulfilling his "duty."

What was so thought-defying for Arendt was Eichmann's inability to think and to judge. The phenomenon that needed to be confronted was how "an average 'normal' person, neither feeble-minded nor indoctrinated, nor cynical, could be perfectly incapable of telling right from wrong." Eichmann was incapable of uttering anything but clichés and stock phrases. Without the slightest difficulty he could switch from one set of rules to an entirely different set. When he was brought to trial, "he knew that what he had once considered his duty was now called a crime, and he accepted this new code of judgment as though it were nothing but another language rule" (*TM*, 417). Arendt agreed with the judges when they declared that what Eichmann said was "empty talk," but she did not think that this emptiness was feigned in order to cover up hideous thoughts. There was no depth to be plumbed here, there was only thought-defying shallowness and superficiality.

> The longer one listened to him, the more obvious it became that his inability to speak was closely connected with an inability to *think*, namely, to think from the standpoint of somebody else. No communication was possible with him, not because he lied but because he was surrounded by the most reliable of all safeguards against the words and the presence of others, and hence against reality as such. (*EJ*, 49)

To understand the phenomenon that Arendt seeks to describe when she speaks of the banality of evil, I want to step back and reflect on something that Heidegger wrote. One of the many shocking revelations in the recent controversy about Heidegger and the Nazis has been the discovery of a sentence from the unpublished version of one of Heidegger's most famous and influential essays, "The Question Concerning Technology." Published in 1953, it is in this essay that Heidegger characterizes *Gestell* (Enframing), the essence of modern technology, as a mode of revealing which he calls "challenging-forth." He contrasts "challenging-forth" with the mode of revealing which he calls "bringing-forth." To illustrate what he means by *Gestell*, Heidegger's published text reads:

> But meanwhile even the cultivation of the field has come under the grip of another kind of setting-in-order, which *sets upon* nature. It sets upon it in the sense of challenging it. Agriculture is now [motorized] food industry.[16]

In the original manuscript of what began as a lecture, there is a clause that was deleted from the published version. The original sentence reads:

> Agriculture is now motorized food industry – in essence the same as the manufacturing of corpses in gas chambers and extermination camps, the same as blockading and starving of nations, the same as the manufacture of hydrogen bombs.[17]

When Thomas Sheehan brought this passage to the attention of the American public, he declared that it is characterized by a rhetoric, a cadence, a point of view, that is damning beyond commentary.[18] But Sheehan is overlooking something that is extremely important here, which is relevant for understanding what Arendt means by the banality of evil.

In the passage quoted, Heidegger is graphically portraying what he takes to be the essence (*Wesen*) of modern technology, in which there is "setting-in-order" and everything becomes "standing-reserve" (*Bestand*) to be manipulated, ordered, and transformed. Even human beings are treated as "human resources." So when Heidegger writes the above disturbing sentence, he is *describing* what is happening in the mode of revealing he names *Gestell* – "the supreme danger." But what does this have to do with the "banality of evil?" The crucial phrase here is "in essence the same" (*im Wesen das Selbe*).[19] Heidegger is describing a type of *mentalité* in which motorized agriculture, arranging for the shipment of human material to death camps, and manufacturing corpses in gas chambers are "in essence the same." This is what is characteristic of the way in which Eichmann (and others like him) conceived of what he was doing. From the perspective of common sense and traditional conceptions of morality and conscience, this is scandalous. We may find it almost impossible to imagine how someone could "think" (or rather, not think) in this manner, whereby manufacturing food, bombs, or corpses are "in essence the same" and this can become "normal," "ordinary" behavior.[20] This is the mentality that Arendt believed she was facing in Eichmann, and which she claims we must confront if we are to understand the new type of criminal that he represents.[21] There is no suggestion of exonerating Eichmann from his crimes and responsibility, only of trying to comprehend what appears so incomprehensible. Arendt completely rejects all versions of what she calls "the cog theory" as an evasion of personal responsibility. In response to the claim that one was merely a cog or a wheel in a system, it is always appropriate to ask (in matters of law and morality): "And why did you become a cog or continue to be a wheel in such circumstances?"[22]

Concerning the banality of evil, it is helpful to distinguish two issues which have frequently been confused. The first might be called the conceptual issue: that is, showing that individuals can commit evil deeds on a gigantic scale without these deeds being traceable to evil or monstrous motives. This is the primary issue for Arendt. But there is a second, specific issue: that is, whether Eichmann fits this description. I think that Arendt tends to overstate her case about Eichmann. Ironically, she was always deeply skeptical about the ability to penetrate the "darkness of one's heart," to say with confidence what one's own or another's "real" motives are. So on *her* own grounds, it is a bit extreme to say that "except for an extraordinary diligence in looking out for his personal advancement, he had no motives at all." Furthermore, some of the evidence suggests that Eichmann was far more fanatical in carrying out his duties than Arendt indicates.[23] But even if we have doubts about the adequacy of Arendt's depiction of Eichmann's motives or lack thereof, we must still face the conceptual issue that she raises so forcefully.

Arendt claims that what was most striking about Eichmann was something negative, "his total absence of thinking." He was trapped in his own clichés, stock phrases, conventional language rules. He seemed to be incapable of that "enlarged mentality" that would have allowed him to think from "the standpoint of somebody else." This is what led Arendt to ask a series of questions concerning the relationship of evil, thinking, and judging.

> Is evil-doing, not just the sins of omission but the sins of commission, possible in the absence of not merely "base motives" (as the law calls it) but of any motives at all, any particular promoting of interest or volition? Is wickedness, however we may define it, this being "determined to prove a villain," *not* a necessary condition for evil-doing? Is our ability to judge, to tell right from wrong, beautiful from ugly, dependent upon our faculty of thought? Do the inability to think and a disastrous failure of what we commonly call conscience coincide? The question that imposed itself was: Could the activity of thinking as such, the habit of examining and reflecting upon whatever happens to come to pass, regardless of specific content and quite independent of results, could this activity be of such a nature that it "conditions" men against evil-doing? (*TM*, 418)

Arendt was inclined to answer all these questions, especially the last one, which sums up the others, in the affirmative. These questions are among her primary reasons for writing *The Life of the Mind*. I cannot fully explore here Arendt's rich, suggestive, although inconclusive, reflections on thinking and judging. She never wrote what was to have been the last part of *The Life of the Mind*, on judging, although, in my view, her lectures on Kant's *Critique of Judgment* and her occasional remarks about judgment provide essential clues as to what she might have written. I want to focus on a single strand in her own questioning: the relation between thinking, judging, and evil. The more tenaciously we follow the pathways of *her* thinking, the deeper the perplexities we encounter. To anticipate, I do not think that Arendt ever gave a fully satisfactory answer to the questions she raised about the relation of thinking and evil.

The problem Arendt sought to address is whether there is an "inner connection between the ability or inability to think and the problem of evil" (*TM*, 425). Thinking must not be confused with knowing. The radical distinction between thinking and knowing was anticipated in Kant's distinction of *Vernunft* and *Verstand*. The type of thinking that Arendt is speaking about is not something that is the prerogative of philosophers or "professional thinkers," but one that can be practised by everyone. Thinking involves an internal dialogue – what Arendt calls a "two-in-one" – in which there is a dialogue between me and myself. "The business of thinking is like the veil of Penelope: it undoes every morning what it had finished the night before" (*TM*, 425).[24] In "Thinking and Moral Considerations" Arendt uses Socrates as an example of someone who engages in this type of thinking. The thinking he exhibited has "a destructive, undermining effect on all established criteria, values, measurements for good and evil, in short on those customs and rules of conduct we treat of in morals and ethics" (*TM*, 434). Thinking is itself dangerous. But if this is so, then our perplexity about "the inner connection between the ability or inability to think and the problem of evil" only increases. To understand what Arendt means by this inner connection, we need to introduce the crucial third term – judging. It was the ability to judge, to tell right from wrong in particular concrete circumstances, that was lacking in Eichmann – as too in those members of respectable society who switched from one set of mores and customs to another with such ease. Arendt emphasizes that "those few who were still able to tell right from wrong went really only by their own judgments, and they did so freely; there were no rules to be abided by, under which the particular cases with which they were confronted could be subsumed. They had to decide each instance as it arose because no rules existed for the unprecedented" (*EJ*, 295).

The above characterization of judging provides the clue to why Arendt was drawn to Kant's *Critique of Judgment*. Kant's analysis of the *sensus communis* and reflective judgment whereby we have the ability to judge a particular without subsuming it under a general or universal rule provides Arendt with a model for what she wants to claim about judgment. She acknowledges that Kant was concerned primarily with aesthetic judgments – "This is beautiful, this is ugly" – but claims that his analysis is applicable to such reflective judgments as this is right, this is wrong.

Still we may ask what is the precise relation between thinking and judging. At times Arendt seems to think of judging as itself a form of thinking. Thus she writes:

> The presupposition for this kind of judging is not a highly developed intelligence or sophistication in moral matters, but merely the habit of living together explicitly with oneself, that is, of being engaged in that silent dialogue between me and myself which since Socrates and Plato we usually call thinking. This kind of thought, though at the root

of all philosophical thinking, is not technical and does not concern theoretical problems. The dividing line between those who judge and those who do not strikes across all social and cultural or educational differences.[25]

But when Arendt was writing *The Life of the Mind*, she emphasized that thinking and judging are independent mental activities. The closest we come to an explicit answer about the relation of thinking and judging is in the final paragraph of her lecture "Thinking and Moral Considerations" (repeated with slight variations in *The Life of the Mind*).

> The faculty of judging particulars (as Kant discovered it), the ability to say, "this is wrong," "this is beautiful," etc. is not the same as the faculty of thinking. Thinking deals with invisibles, with representations of things that are absent; judging always concerns particulars and things close at hand. But the two are interrelated in a way similar to the way consciousness and conscience are interconnected. If thinking, the two-in-one of the soundless dialogue, actualizes the difference within our identity as given in consciousness and thereby results in conscience as its by-product, then judging, the by-product of the liberating effect of thinking, realizes thinking, makes it manifest in the world of appearances, where I am never alone and always much too busy to be able to think. The manifestation of the wind of thought is not knowledge; it is the ability to tell right from wrong, beautiful from ugly. And this indeed may prevent catastrophes, at least for myself, in the rare moments when the chips are down. (*TM*, 446)

What Arendt says here is at once extremely suggestive, yet unsatisfactory. The very intelligibility of her claims depends on the assertion that thinking does have this liberating effect on the faculty of judging. But Arendt does not really provide any arguments to justify this assertion. At times it seems as if she is at war with herself – as if she never quite reconciles the tensions in her own internal dialogue. On the one hand, she insists that thinking by itself does not yield moral knowledge and "produce usable practical wisdom," on the other, that it does have an all-important indirect, practical by-product – insofar as it liberates the faculty of judging.[26] But why should we expect such a liberating relation between thinking and judging in moments of crisis? Even if we stay with her example of Socrates, Arendt herself notes that the perplexities he aroused in Alcibiades and Critias did not liberate *their* faculties of judgment: "What they had been aroused to was license and cynicism" (*TM*, 434).[27] Much more damaging to Arendt's thesis is her own blindness concerning Heidegger's "error" in supporting Hitler and the Nazis. Ironically, in the very same year that she published "Thinking and Moral Considerations," she also published her tribute to Heidegger on his eightieth birthday. Recalling her experience in the 1920s, she tells us that "the rumor about Heidegger put it quite simply: thinking has come to life again. . . . There exists a teacher; one can perhaps learn to think."[28] So Arendt actually proposes *two* models or exemplars of thinking: Socrates and Heidegger. The thinking performed by Socrates, who is at once a "gadfly," an "electric ray," and a "midwife," is a thinking that has "political and moral significance which comes out only in those rare moments in history when 'Things fall apart; the centre cannot hold; / Mere anarchy is loosed upon the world'." Arendt tells us that

> [A]t these moments, thinking ceases to be a marginal affair in political matters. When everybody is swept away unthinkingly by what everybody else does and believes in, those who think are drawn out of hiding because their refusal to join is conspicuous and thereby becomes a kind of action. The purging element in thinking, Socrates' midwifery, that brings out the implications of unexamined opinions and thereby destroys them – values, doctrines, theories, and even convictions – is political by implication. For this destruction has a liberating effect on another faculty, the faculty of judgment, which one may call, with some justification, the most political of man's mental abilities. (*TM*, 445–6)

These remarks take on a bitter irony when we juxtapose them with the actions of Heidegger, whom Arendt considers to be the thinker *par excellence* of the twentieth century. Regardless of how one tries to explain what Arendt euphemistically calls Heidegger's "error" concerning his judgment about Hitler and the Nazis, I do not see how anyone can claim that his thinking "liberated" his faculty of judging. The very least one could say about Heidegger in 1933–4 is that he completely failed to *judge* accurately what was happening. One might try to get around the disparity between Arendt's portraits of Socrates and Heidegger by claiming that the type of thinking she ascribes to Heidegger is categorially different from that she ascribes to Socrates. But Arendt never makes any such sharp distinction. On the contrary, the way in which she characterizes any thinking, including that of Socrates, is heavily indebted to Heidegger's characterization of thinking.[29] She appeals to both of them as exemplifying the type of thinking which must be distinguished from "professional thinking." Arendt desperately wants to show that thinking has moral consequences – at least indirectly, by liberating the faculty of judging whereby we *judge* this is right and this is wrong. But although she asserts this categorically, she never gives us sufficient grounds for making this connection.

There are further problems. We can see that the faculty that is most important for preventing catastrophes to the self is the faculty of judging – "the ability to tell right from wrong, beautiful from ugly." One must be cautious about reconstructing or second-guessing what Arendt might have said had she completed the final part of *The Life of the Mind*. But there are perplexities in what she does in fact say. The reason why Arendt was so drawn to Kant's analysis of reflective judgment in the *Critique of Judgment* is because Kant analyzes a type of judgment of particulars which is made without subsuming the particulars under a universal principle or general rule. But whereas Kant was concerned primarily with aesthetic judgment, Arendt is concerned more with moral judgment and wishes to extend his analysis to such particular judgments as this is right, this is wrong. In her Eichmann report, Arendt professes herself struck by those few who resisted evil, by those who in discriminating between right and wrong "went really only by their own judgments" because there were "no rules to be abided by, under which the particular cases with which they were confronted could be subsumed. They had to decide each instance as it arose, because no rules existed for the unprecedented" (*EJ*, 295). If we grant Arendt's point that this is beautiful, this is ugly, this is right, this is wrong, are all examples of reflective judgments, we still want to understand the differences among them. What precisely are we asserting when we say that this is right, this is wrong? Arendt never really answers this question. On the contrary, she seems to gloss over and obscure two separate issues. The first is how we are to characterize the *type* of judgment we are making when we judge something to be right or wrong. She tells us that this type of judgment is a reflective judgment. But if we agree with her that this is a reflective judgment wherein we judge particulars directly, without subsuming them under some universal or general rule, we can still ask – and this is the second issue – what we mean by "right" and "wrong," and how these predicates are to be distinguished from "beautiful" and "ugly."

But perhaps the most troublesome perplexity in Arendt's attempt to account for the banality of evil, the phenomenon she claimed to have witnessed in Eichmann, concerns what she has left *unsaid*. On the one hand, she tells us that thinking and judging are faculties that can be ascribed to everyone, in that everyone *potentially* has the capacity to think and to judge. This is a crucial presupposition in her attempt to show that there is an "inner connection between the ability or inability to think and the problem of evil." On the other hand, she claims that Eichmann's specific characteristic was "a curious, quite authentic inability to think." Presumably this is also true of all the members of "respectable society" who could switch so effortlessly from one set of mores to another – from the conviction that one ought not to kill to the conviction that killing was permissible or even required for racial reasons. Suppose we accept Arendt's claim about Eichmann's inability to think. The primary question that confronts us is how we are to *account* for this lack. More generally, if indeed every human being has the potential for thinking and judging, how are we to account for Eichmann (and all the others) who do not think and judge? The question can be generalized. Despite Arendt's constant references to "total moral collapse," she believed that there were those few (all too few) who did not lose their ability to judge and to act accordingly.[30]

In one of the most moving chapters of *Eichmann in Jerusalem*, almost as a counterpoint to her unrelenting portrayal of Eichmann, Arendt tells the story of Anton Schmidt, a sergeant in the German army who helped Jewish partisans by supplying them with forged papers and military trucks until he was arrested and executed by the Germans. She relates how when the story of Anton Schmidt was told in the Jerusalem court, it was as though those present observed a two-minute silence in honor of this man who helped save Jewish lives. Arendt comments:

> And in those two minutes, which were like a sudden burst of light in the midst of impenetrable, unfathomable darkness, a single thought stood out clearly, irrefutably, beyond question – how utterly different everything would be today in this courtroom, in Israel, in Germany, in all of Europe, and perhaps in all countries of the world, if only more such stories could have been told. (*EJ*, 231)[31]

In the end, despite what Arendt tells us about thinking, judging, and evil, the question she does not answer – which, indeed, may be unanswerable – is how we can account for the differences between Adolf Eichmann and Anton Schmidt. Why is it that there are so few stories to be told about people like Anton Schmidt who, under conditions of totalitarian terror, did not lose their ability to judge what is right and wrong, and to act in accord with their judging?

I have been arguing that Arendt never satisfactorily answers the questions she raises concerning the "inner connection of thinking and the problem of evil." She asserts that our ability to judge, to tell right from wrong, is "dependent upon the faculty of thought" – "the habit of examining and reflecting upon whatever happens to come to pass" – but she never *justifies* the crucial claim that thinking has this liberating effect on the faculty of judging. When she turns to judgment and shows the relevance of Kant's analysis of reflective aesthetic judgments and the *sensus communis*, she does not really explain what we are *asserting* when we judge a particular deed to be right and distinguish it from what is wrong. Ultimately, she leaves us with a profound, unsettling perplexity. Even if we accept the role she assigns to thinking and judging in preventing evil in moments of crisis, we are left with no account of why – even in instances of extreme totalitarian terror – some persons (a few) maintain their ability to judge, while most lose or show no signs of the ability to think.

The unprecedented event of twentieth-century totalitarianism has taught us a terrifying lesson. For totalitarian domination based on the "principle" that everything is possible revealed that there is nothing about human nature or the human condition that cannot be altered or obliterated. Totalitarian terror aims at "the transformation of human nature itself." Even our ability to think and judge can be obliterated. Indeed, Arendt thought that one of the major dangers of modern society was that it threatened to eliminate the capacity for independent thinking and judging. We can no longer believe that traditional mores, customs, or habits are sufficient to prevent evil. For these "*mores*, customs and manners . . . could be exchanged for another set with hardly more trouble than it would take to change the table manners of an individual or people." Under extreme conditions, there is nothing that can prevent "total moral collapse." We may desperately want to believe that there is something about human beings that cannot be transformed, something deep about the human self, the voice of conscience or a sense of responsibility that cannot be obliterated. But after totalitarianism, we can no longer hold on to these beliefs. This is the specter that now haunts us – the all too real possibility of this *danger*. Arendt was herself critical of what she once called the "optimistic view of human nature," which "presupposes an independent human faculty, unsupported by law and public opinion, that judges anew in full spontaneity every deed and intent whenever the occasion arises."[32] Yet, ironically, it is Arendt herself who (in one part of the dialogue with herself) *wants to believe* that there is such a human faculty. This is what she calls the faculty of judging. I emphasize "wants to believe," because here is where she is at war with herself. For she claims that Eichmann did not possess this ability to judge.

Yet we do know that even under conditions of the most extreme terror, some individuals are capable of resisting, judging what is right and wrong, and acting according to their consciences. The question that eludes Arendt – and may always elude us – is how we are to explain (in a noncircular way) the differences between those who remain capable of judging what is evil and acting according to conscience and those who have lost or never had this ability.

When Arendt tells the story of Anton Schmidt, the German sergeant who was executed for helping Jewish victims, and contrasts his behavior with "the hollowness of respectability" of those Germans who argued that it was "practically useless" to oppose the Nazis, she writes:

> For the lesson of such stories is simple and within everybody's grasp. Politically speaking, it is that under conditions of terror most people will comply but *some people will not*, just as the lesson of the countries to which the Final Solution was proposed is that "it could happen" in most places but *it did not happen everywhere*. Humanly speaking, no more is required, and no more can reasonably be asked, for this planet to remain a place fit for human habitation. (*EJ*, 233)

9

Concluding Remarks:
Blindness and Insight

The Good Lord did not create religion; he created the world.
Franz Rosenzweig, cited in Lévinas, *Difficile Liberté*

The world as God created it seems to me a good one.
Arendt, letter to Kurt Blumenfeld

Hannah Arendt began her 1944 article "The Jew as Pariah: A Hidden Tradition" by describing Jewish pariahs as those who are "great enough to transcend the bounds of nationality and to weave the strands of their Jewish genius into the general texture of European life." These are "the bold spirits who tried to make the emancipation of the Jews that which it really should have been – an admission of Jews *as Jews* to the ranks of humanity" (*JP*, 67–8). It is difficult to imagine a more apt description of Arendt herself. Quite early in her career, she identified with this hidden tradition, and she became one of its outstanding exemplars in the twentieth century. There was nothing parochial or constricting about Arendt's concern with the Jewish question and her Jewish identity. On the contrary, her self-affirmation as a Jew situated her concretely and historically; it opened her up to the wider horizon of the horrendous events of the twentieth century. When she felt bashed over the head by history, when she felt attacked as a Jew, she resisted and rebelled as a Jew. As a Jew, she was thrust into the very storm center of world politics. She became a conscious pariah, a rebel, and an independent thinker – even among her own people.

Arendt's education in politics and history began when she fled Germany in 1933, and she was tutored by Kurt Blumenfeld and her husband, Heinrich Blücher. When writing her study of Rahel Varnhagen, she discovered the significance of the distinction between society and politics. She became acutely aware of the self-deception, hypocrisy, and failure of the project of social assimilation – a project that arose as a result of the Enlightenment and came to a shattering end for German Jews in 1933. Like her "friend" Rahel, Hannah rebelled against a false emancipation which, when unmasked, was nothing but "Jewish suicide." But, unlike Rahel, she was never tempted to "belong" to society; she never wanted to be the "exceptional Jew"; she never exhibited any parvenu tendencies. She wrote to Jaspers: "I'm more than ever of the opinion that a decent human existence is possible today only on the fringes of society" (*C*, 29). Like her hero, Bernard Lazare, she argued fiercely that the only proper response to anti-Semitism, the only way in which Jews could assume their political responsibility, was to fight for their rights *as Jews*.

One must understand the ways in which Jewish history, especially modern Jewish history, has been entwined with modern European history. Confronting the Jewish question required a broader analysis of the subterranean streams of modern European history. It was from this perspective that Arendt first began to explore the conflicting tendencies of the modern age. This is what compelled her to focus on the vicissitudes of the nation-state – its birth, hidden conflicts, and disintegration when it was partially displaced by nineteenth-century imperialism. European Jewry was completely unprepared for the new phenomenon of political anti-Semitism that arose in the nineteenth century. There was a "secret conflict" built into the very core of the nation-state, a conflict between the demand for the universal Rights of Man and the growing conviction that rights are national, that they can be guaranteed and protected only for those who truly belong to a nation. The Jews were caught in this conflict because it was claimed by political anti-Semites that the Jews did not "really" belong to any European nation. Furthermore, with the increasing conflict between society and the state, the Jews were identified as the financial power behind existing states.

A much more vicious and lethal form of political anti-Semitism arose with the growth of racist imperialism. The supranational ideological anti-Semitism of the pan-Germanic and pan-Slavic movements sought not only to exclude the Jews from European nations, but to eliminate the Jewish people altogether. What started as a marginal, almost crackpot movement became one of the subterranean elements that was to crystallize into Nazi ideology and policy. The Nazis knew what a powerful weapon anti-Semitism had become in galvanizing the masses.

Arendt's deepest convictions about history and politics were also shaped by her concern with the Jewish question. She opposed all (sophisticated or vulgar) appeals to historical necessity or inevitability. The belief that there is a logic at work in historical development is a false and dangerous doctrine. It obscures and suppresses the very possibility of political initiative and action. Action always presupposes a new beginning that ruptures historical continuities. Arendt was a relentless critic of the fatalistic doctrine of eternal anti-Semitism, and rejected all scapegoat theories of anti-Semitism. Her concern was to open the space for the possibility of a Jewish politics. She knew that the doctrines of historical necessity and inevitability which had become so fashionable in the nineteenth century were the deadly enemy of political initiative.

I have sought to identify the most persistent strand in Arendt's understanding of politics – the populist strand. It manifested itself in her summons for the Jewish people to organize themselves collectively "from below," to assume political responsibility, and to fight against political anti-Semitism. She learned this lesson from Bernard Lazare, and she favored the type of revolutionary Zionism that he advocated (in opposition to that favored by Herzl). At the beginning of the Second World War she became a strong advocate of an independent Jewish army to fight the Nazis, thinking that this might be the "beginning of a Jewish politics." She was enthusiastic about the Sabbatian movement because Scholem had shown that the Jews were not exclusively "history-sufferers," but could also be "history-makers." She interpreted the Sabbatian movement as a popular political Jewish movement that ended in the catastrophe of the Jews withdrawing from politics. Her populist strand was manifested in her support for a Jewish homeland where there would be a new political structure of confederation based upon local Arab–Jewish councils. Arendt's advocacy of the "council system" was inspired by the sudden appearance of "islands of freedom" – the appearance (and disappearance) of the lost treasure of the revolutionary spirit. She claimed that the creation of councils in the most diverse historical circumstances by the spontaneous action of the people was the "innermost story of the modern age."

Beginning in 1933, Arendt engaged in a quest for the meaning of politics, a quest that lasted for the rest of her life. Her reflections on statelessness – on her own personal experiences, those of other European Jews, as well as many others of the millions of stateless – led her to the conviction that the most fundamental right of human beings is the "right to have rights" – the right to belong to a polity. She was a devastating critic of abstract humanism and abstract conceptions of right which maintain that human beings possess inalienable rights simply by virtue of being human. Totalitarianism exposed the emptiness of this abstract talk of human rights, and it taught us how dangerous it is· to be a "naked human being" unprotected by a political community. To be suddenly stripped of legal and political rights is to be stripped of a necessary condition for leading a human life. Arendt knew that the twentieth century was becoming the century of mass statelessness. Like a series of catastrophic earthquakes, every significant political event of the century had led to creating new masses of stateless persons.

Dwelling on the horrors of totalitarian terror – looking into the abyss of the concentration and death camps – led Arendt to her most profound insights about the very conditions required to lead a human life. The real horror of totalitarianism was not only the suffering, torture, and murder of millions, but the systematic attempt to eliminate all plurality, natality, spontaneity, and individuality. It was the attempt to prove that everything is possible, including the transformation of human nature – to demonstrate that human beings as (plural) human beings are superfluous.

Arendt's attraction to – and break with Zionism – was motivated by her concern with, and understanding of, politics. She identified herself with the Zionists in the 1930s and early 1940s because they were the only group among the Jews who shared her conviction that the Jewish people must take political initiative. But even when she most identified with them, she saw herself as a dissenting critic, a member of the "loyal opposition." She had an almost visceral reaction against any and all forms of ideology, including Zionist ideology. She was most critical of what she detected as the creeping dominance of revisionist Zionist ideology. She castigated her fellow Zionists for their failure to face up honestly to the need for direct Arab–Jewish negotiations and cooperation. She warned against growing Jewish nationalism and chauvinism. She opposed the idea of a Jewish nation-state as based upon an outdated and dangerous concept of national sovereignty. She accused her fellow Zionists of abandoning and betraying the *revolutionary promise* of the Zionist movement. It was

Arendt's confrontation with "really existing Zionism" that provoked her to think about the political alternative of federation and confederation based upon the council system. This was the political structure that might provide a real alternative to the nation-state and totalitarian regimes. She was never afraid to champion the defeated cause – and she knew the consequences of doing so.

Arendt's thinking about the Jewish question, political anti-Semitism, and totalitarian terror reached its culmination in her struggle to confront the problem of evil. In 1952, in a review of a book by Léon Poliakov, she wrote:

> Only if the reader continues, after everything about the exterminations has been made tangible and plausible, to feel his first reaction of outraged disbelief, only then will he be in the position to begin to understand that totalitarianism, unlike all other known modes of tyranny and oppression, has brought into the world a *radical* evil characterized by its divorce from all humanly comprehensible motives of wickedness.[1]

But what does Arendt mean by "radical evil"? She confesses (to Jaspers) that she is not certain what radical evil really is, "but it seems to me it somehow has to do with the following phenomenon: making human beings as human beings superfluous" (*C*, 166). I have sought to follow the twists and turns of her thinking about radical evil and to clarify what she means by making human beings as human beings superfluous. The heart of the matter is the deliberate attempt to eradicate human plurality – and to substitute the delusion of an omnipotent *Führer*.

Finally, I turn to a reexamination of the central themes in *Eichmann in Jerusalem: A Report on the Banality of Evil*. The controversy provoked by this book (which still goes on) blinds many to Arendt's real Jewish concerns. I have argued that Arendt's harsh judgment of the Jewish councils in the camps must be understood in the context of her wider and deeper concern with the "total moral collapse" that resulted from Nazi totalitarian terror. Arendt, who never shied away from confronting what she called "realities," argued that if we really want to understand Nazi totalitarianism and how successful the Nazis were, then we must face up to the extent of the moral collapse of all involved: persecutors, victims, and bystanders. In considering what Arendt means by "the banality of evil," I have tried to show that although there is a significant change of focus in her questions concerning evil, the concept of the banality of evil is compatible with her earlier thoughts about radical evil. What she had done is to shift her emphasis from superfluousness to thoughtlessness. Once she had described the phenomenon of the banality of evil, she wanted to understand the conditions for its possibility. Focusing her attention on Eichmann in this context, she became convinced that his capacity to commit such monstrous deeds without monstrous motives could be accounted for by his inability to think and to judge.

The question that Arendt sought to answer was: "Could the activity of thinking as such, the habit of examining whatever happens to come to pass or to attract attention, regardless of results and specific content, could this activity be among the conditions that made men abstain from evil-doing or even actually 'condition' them against it?" (*LM*, 5). Arendt's own hesitance and tentativeness are indicated in the highly qualified way in which she raises the question. It is the question with which she was still struggling at the time of her sudden death. Thinking with (and against Arendt), entering into the dialogue she was still having with herself, I have indicated some of her unresolved questions concerning evil, thinking, and judging.

In our so-called postmodern age, we are becoming much more aware of the subtle interplay of blindness and insight. We discover in the texts of the most imaginative thinkers that their insight is based upon a certain blindness, that at the core of their insight are blind spots, and, indeed, that insight is achieved at the cost of blindness. This is especially true of Arendt's thinking about Judaism and Jewishness. We first encountered this phenomenon in the very dubious way in which Arendt draws the distinction between Judaism as a "religious" set of beliefs, rituals, and practices and Jewishness as primarily a "factual" matter of being born a Jew. The crucial question – and Arendt's blind spot – is the relation between Judaism and Jewishness. What does it mean to be a Jew if one insists on a sharp distinction between Judaism and Jewishness? For all Arendt's insistence on affirming herself as a Jew, and her conviction that one can truly resist and rebel as a Jew, the question that must be asked is: What precisely is being affirmed in asserting one's identity as Jewish? As we have observed, the pariah as a human type is not limited to the Jewish people. Arendt always seems to focus on the existential status of the pariah, as a person who lives on the margins of society who is at once an outsider and yet never completely an outsider. So the question can be focused more narrowly: What is distinctive about the *Jewishness* of the Jewish pariah? How does the Jewish conscious pariah differ from other kinds of conscious pariahs? This is a question that must (or rather should) be asked by anyone who identifies herself as a secular Jew. Here, the consistent advocate of assimilation has an advantage. For she can say, "My being born a Jew is simply an accident of birth (on a par with other accidents such as color of hair or eyes). It has no meaning or significance for me. Therefore this accident should not stand as an obstacle preventing me from belonging to society." This is *not* Arendt's position. She affirms (and even takes pride in) being a secular Jew. So it is proper to ask: What, then, is the substance of the claim that one is a Jew? In these final remarks I want to reflect on some of the perplexities, lacunae, and blind spots in Arendt's reflections on Judaism and Jewishness.

Let us recall that Arendt's earliest intellectual passion was for theology, Christian theology. As an adolescent, she developed an enthusiasm for Kierkegaard. She wrote her dissertation on a Christian saint, St Augustine. At crucial points in her career she returned to Christian theological themes – or, more precisely, the philosophical and political implications of these themes. St Augustine is important for her not only because of her early interest in his concept of neighborly love, but also for her own understanding of beginnings, natality, freedom, and will. He is central not only in her first book (her dissertation), but also in her last (posthumous) book, *The Life of the Mind*.

At times Arendt was scathing in her criticism of Christianity, especially of the aspects of Christian religious thought that were "other worldly," turning one away from a concern with the affairs of the world. Like Machiavelli, she warned against the dangers of mixing and confusing Christian religion with politics. She tells us that "with the rise of Christianity, the emphasis shifted entirely from care for the world and the duties connected with it to the care for the soul and its salvation."[2] At the same time, she wrote with great insight and feeling about Jesus of Nazareth, especially with regard to his understanding of forgiveness. "The discoverer of the role of forgiveness in the realm of human affairs was Jesus of Nazareth" (*HC*, 238).

I mention this early, ongoing concern with Christian theological and religious themes because it stands in striking contrast with the paucity of any serious discussion of Judaism or the Jewish religious tradition in her writings. Arendt never really studied her own tradition; nor did she ever seem to feel any need to do so. Even her interest in Scholem's work on Jewish mysticism was directed primarily to the political significance and consequences of the Sabbatian movement.

It is almost as if the religious question of Judaism was never even a serious intellectual or personal issue for Arendt. She identified with those secular Jews (like Lazare and Herzl) who "stood outside the religious tradition of Judaism" and did not wish "to return to it" (*JP*, 126). I noted earlier that Arendt was "shocked" when Golda Meir said to her, "You will understand that as a Socialist, I, of course, do not believe in God; I believe in the Jewish people"; but Arendt never satisfactorily answers the question of what it means to be a (secular) Jew such that one can demand a right to be recognized as a Jew. She fails to confront the normative (and not only the "factual" issue) of being a Jew. When Arendt was pressed on this issue, as she repeatedly was by Jaspers in their correspondence, her answers were always evasive and lame. At one point she wrote to Jaspers: "About the Jews: Historically, you are correct in everything you say. But the fact remains that many Jews such as myself are religiously completely independent of Juda*ism* yet are still Jews nonetheless" (*C*, 98). Such a response does not at all address the question of in what *sense* one is still a Jew. What is the content of being a Jew if Jewishness is severed from Judaism? It is precisely here that Arendt's blindness is so striking. It is as if her reasoning went something like the following: for me, the religious issue of Judaism is not (to use William James's phrase) a "live option." I am not a religious Jew, and I have no interest in returning to Judaism. Yet I am a Jew. I affirm myself as a member of the Jewish people. But what, then, is the Jewish question for such a secular Jew living in the modern age? It takes either a social or a political form. But to think of the Jewish question as an exclusively social question is disastrous. It involves the self-deception and hypocrisy characteristic of the Jewish parvenu. Social assimilation is not Jewish emancipation; it is Jewish suicide. The only live option for a secular Jew is political. And this requires an understanding of both the failures and the possibilities of a Jewish politics. Jewish emancipation requires bringing "about political circumstances that do not make [the continuing existence of the Jewish people] impossible" (*C*, 98). This seems to be the underlying, skeletal structure of Arendt's belief that in the modern age the Jewish question is primarily a political question.

When Arendt was asked to explain in what sense she saw herself as a Jew, she would typically reply that being Jewish was simply one of the indisputable factual data of her life (*JP*, 246). But even this response is disingenuous. For the issue is not one of fact, but of the significance or *meaning* of this fact. Indeed, Arendt herself – in a very different context – provides the most biting criticism of this type of answer. In her discussion of Disraeli, she tells us:

> Judaism, and belonging to the Jewish people, degenerated into a simple fact of birth only among assimilated Jewry. Originally it had meant a specific religion, a specific nationality, the sharing of specific memories and specific hopes. . . . Secularization and assimilation of the Jewish intelligentsia had changed self-consciousness and self-interpretation in such a way that nothing was left of the old memories and hopes but the awareness of belonging to a chosen people. (*OT₃*, 73)

Arendt, of course, disparaged assimilation, and expressed disdain for the secularized concept of a chosen people. But it is difficult to see why the brunt of her criticism should not apply also to her. After all, is *she* not asserting that her Jewishness is "a simple fact of birth"?

The portrait I have just presented of Arendt does not quite ring true, however. It is too flat, too undifferentiated; it does not do justice to the tensions in her thinking, her own subtlety and inner complexity. We gain a more robust, three-dimensional understanding of Hannah Arendt as a Jew, who wove the strands of her Jewish genius into the general texture of European life, if we return, for one last time, to the famous interchange with Scholem.

At one point in his letter Scholem writes: "I regard you wholly as a daughter of our people, and in no other way." In her response, Arendt quotes this sentence and then comments:

> The truth is I have never pretended to be anything else or to be in any way other than I am, and I have never even felt tempted in that direction. It would have been like saying that I was a man and not a woman – that is to say, kind of insane. I know, of course, that there is a "Jewish problem" even on this level, but it has never been my problem – not even in childhood. I have always regarded my Jewishness as one of the indisputable factual data of my life, and I have never had the wish to change or disclaim facts of this kind. There is such a thing as a basic gratitude for everything that is as it is; for what has been *given* and was not, could not be, *made*. (*JP*, 246)

There is something about Arendt's phrasing that recalls the words that Rahel Varnhagen is alleged to have said on her death bed: "Having been born a Jewess – this I should on no account have missed." The sentence which epitomizes Arendt's blindness/insight, which has deep resonances within the tradition of Judaism, is: "*There is such a thing as a basic gratitude for everything that is as it is.*" This is not the first time that Arendt spoke of such gratitude. In a letter to Jaspers (Aug. 6, 1955), anticipating one of her cherished visits to him and telling him about the book she was then writing (*The Human Condition*), she suddenly bursts forth:

> Yes, I would like to bring the wide world to you this time. I've begun so late, really only in recent years, to truly love the world that I shall be able to do that now. Out of gratitude, I want to call my book on political theories "Amor Mundi" (*C*, 264).[3]

The fact that Arendt uses the Latin phrase "Amor Mundi" is almost symbolic of how thoroughly Arendt was a product of, and appropriated, European life and culture. But the spirit that breathes through this passage reverberates with one of the most glorious strands in the tradition of Judaism. It is a strand that is central and dominant in Franz Rosenzweig and Emmanuel Lévinas when they remind us that "The Good Lord did not create religion; he created the world." Arendt's a-theological secular faith is one that is world-centered, not God-centered. She rebelled against the modern obsession with the self and with the salvation of the self, tracing this back to the influence of Christianity. For all her indebtedness to Heidegger's concept of the world, her own concept is a world that is given to us, a world which is a source of joy and tragedy, a world that we share with our fellow human beings which itself comes into tangible reality through care, responsibility and action, is a world to be cherished. Arendt's faith, like that of so many Jews before her, is directed more to creation than to the creator. Even her notion of radical evil takes on a richer meaning when viewed from this perspective. For the unprecedented phenomena of the twentieth century which compel us to speak of radical evil are not only mass destruction, murder, and torture on a scale never before experienced, but the delusion of omnipotence whereby an attempt was made to transform and debase the world as created. The horror we face when we confront the banality of evil is how this monstrous debasement can result from sheer thoughtlessness.

Scholem was right in ways which even he did not recognize. In her love of the world, in her gratitude for all that is as it is, in her "half-religious Jewish passion for justice"[4] and tangible public freedom, in the pride she takes in the accomplishments of her people, as well as in her passionate critiques of their failures, in her hope (and disappointment) that the Jews might set an example and bring some illumination to other peoples in these "dark times," in keeping alive the tradition of independent thinking and the conscious Jewish pariah, Hannah Arendt was truly "a daughter of our people."

Notes

Preface

1 See Introduction for a discussion of the literature dealing with Arendt's historical context and her grappling with Jewish issues.
2 Ann Lane, "The Feminism of Hannah Arendt," *Democracy*, 3 (Summer 1983): 109.
3 Hanna Pitkin, "Conformism, Housekeeping, and the Attack of the Blob: Hannah Arendt's Concept of the Social" (paper presented at the 1990 annual meeting of the American Political Science Association), 19. This paper has been revised and included in *Feminist Interpretations of Hannah Arendt*, ed. Bonnie Honig (University Park, Pa.: Pennsylvania University Press, 1995), 51–81. The sentences quoted are from the original typescript.
4 For an analysis of the history of the expression "the Jewish Question," see Jacob Toury, " 'The Jewish Question': A Semantic Approach," *Leo Baeck Institute Year Book*, 11 (1966): 85–107.

Introduction

1 Hannah Arendt discussed the question of fame and notoriety many times. One of her most eloquent statements appears in her Introduction to the writings of Walter Benjamin, *Illuminations*. She begins her essay by declaring: "*Fama*, that much-coveted goddess, has many faces, and fame comes in many sorts and sizes – from the one-week notoriety of the cover

story to the splendor of an everlasting name. Posthumous fame is one of *Fama's* rarer and least desired articles, although it is less arbitrary and often more solid than the other sorts, since it is only seldom bestowed upon mere merchandise." She goes on to tell us, in a remark that is applicable not only to Benjamin but to Arendt herself: "Posthumous fame seems, then, to be the lot of the unclassifiable ones, that is, those whose work neither fits the existing order nor introduces a new genre that lends itself to future classification" (*MD*, 153, 155).

2 Both Margaret Canovan and Jeffrey C. Isaac provide excellent discussions of why such a "cold war" reading of the book is seriously mistaken. See ch. 2, "The Origins of Totalitarianism," in Canovan's *Hannah Arendt: A Reinterpretation of Her Political Thought* (Cambridge: Cambridge University Press, 1992); and ch. 2, "Totalitarianism and the Intoxication of Power," in Isaac's *Arendt, Camus, and Modern Rebellion* (New Haven: Yale University Press, 1992).

3 "Hannah Arendt on Hannah Arendt," *RPW*, 333.

4 For the meaning and significance of "world alienation," see *HC*, 248–56.

5 For recent feminist interpretations of Arendt, see Bonnie Honig (ed.), *Feminist Interpretations of Hannah Arendt* (University Park, Pa.: Pennsylvania State University Press, 1995). Arendt followed the standard practice of using masculine nouns and pronouns when referring to human beings. To avoid stylistic awkwardness, I have followed her practice when discussing passages from her writings.

6 During the past few years, there has been an intensive exploration of the intellectual and personal relationship between Heidegger and Arendt. There are now several excellent studies examining the ways in which Arendt appropriated, transformed and responded to Heideggerian themes from the time when she was his student (and his lover) through her mature critique of Heidegger in the posthumously published *The Life of the Mind*. I share the views of those interpreters who emphasize that the centrality of the concepts of plurality, action, narrative, politics and *praxis* in Arendt represent a strong response and serious challenge to basic themes in Heidegger's thinking. See Jacques Taminiaux, *La Fille de Thrace et le penseur professionnel: Arendt et Heidegger* (Paris: Éditions Payot, 1992); and Seyla Benhabib, *The Reluctant Modernism of Hannah Arendt* (Newbury Park, Calif.: Sage Publications, 1996). For a different "postmodern" reading of the Heidegger–Arendt relationship, see Dana R. Villa, *Arendt and Heidegger: The Fate of the Political* (Princeton: Princeton University Press, 1995).

My own critique of Heidegger is developed basically from an Arendtian perspective. I do not think that Heidegger had a deep sense of what Arendt meant by plurality – the most basic concept of her political thought. Furthermore, I argue there is an "oblivion of *praxis*" and an excessive valorization of *poiesis* in Heidegger's obsession with the destiny of metaphysics, humanism and technology. This critique is developed in "Heidegger on Humanism," in *Philosophical Profiles: Essays in a Pragmatic Mode* (Cambridge: Polity Press, 1986), 197–220, and "Heidegger's Silence?: *Êthos* and Technology," in *The New Constellation: The Ethical-Political Horizons of Modernity/Postmodernity* (Cambridge: Polity Press, 1991), 79–141.

Until recently, scholars have not been permitted to examine the Arendt–Heidegger correspondence. Elzbieta Ettinger (*Hannah Arendt and Martin Heidegger* (New Haven: Yale University Press, 1995)) is the first person to have been allowed to publish excerpts from this correspondence. I agree with Seyla Benhabib when she writes: "Unfortunately, Ms. Ettinger's interpretation of this material is psychologistic, partial, and from the standpoint of philosophical scholarship, naive" (*The Reluctant Modernism of Hannah Arendt*, "Introduction – Why Hannah Arendt," n. 5). In Ettinger's voyeuristic "exposé," which appears to have been written for the purpose of creating a scandal and dismissing Heidegger and Arendt as serious thinkers, Ettinger amply demonstrates that she has little interest in, and no understanding of, the intellectual contributions of either Heidegger or Arendt. Perhaps the most desirable consequence of the furor created by Ms Ettinger's book is that the literary executors of the Arendt and the Heidegger estates have promised the publication of the entire Arendt–Heidegger correspondence. This will allow serious scholars the opportunity for a more careful, open, and nuanced examination of the human and intellectual relationship between Heidegger and Arendt.

7 Unfortunately, Feldman's collection, *The Jew as Pariah* (New York: Grove Press, 1978), has long been out of print. Jerome Kohn is now preparing a new collection of Arendt's Jewish writings.

8 Ann Lane, "The Feminism of Hannah Arendt," *Democracy*, 3 (Summer 1983): 109.

9 Isaac, *Arendt, Camus, and Modern Rebellion*, 2.

10 Canovan, *Hannah Arendt*, 3, 7.

11 Many commentators and critics of Arendt have located unresolved tensions, conflicts, and even contradictions in her writings. Some of these are only apparent, and some do not lend themselves to easy resolution. I agree with Margaret Canovan that the most illuminating way to understand Arendt's thinking is to follow her "thought-trains." Canovan writes: "Her thinking about politics took the form of a set of complex and interrelated trains of thought, in the course of which she did indeed establish a great many settled positions, firm conceptual distinctions and interconnected commitments, but which remained open-ended and incomplete" (*Hannah Arendt*, 6).

12 "Nightmare and Flight," *Partisan Review*, 12/2 (Spring 1945): 259; repr. in *EU*.
13 See her discussion of Socrates as a "midwife," "gadfly," and "electric ray" (*LM*, 166–79).

Chapter 1 The Conscious Pariah as Rebel and Independent Thinker

1 From "What Remains? The Language Remains: An Interview with Günter Gaus" (translation of "Was Bleibt? Es bleibt die Muttersprache," in Günter Gaus, *Zur Person: Porträts in Frage und Antwort* (Munich: Feder Verlag, 1964), 13–32. In *EU*, 6–7. For details concerning Arendt's youth see Young-Bruehl's biography. See also Dagmar Barnouw, *Visible Spaces: Hannah Arendt and the German-Jewish Experience* (Baltimore: Johns Hopkins University Press, 1990).
2 Hannah Arendt and Gershom Scholem, " 'Eichmann in Jerusalem': Exchange of Letters between Gershom Scholem and Hannah Arendt," *Encounter*, 22/1 (1964); repr. in *JP*, 246.
3 This remark occurs in one of Arendt's early letters to Karl Jaspers. Jaspers had sent her a copy of his book on Max Weber. Arendt objected to Jaspers's claim to have found the "German essence" in Weber and to have identified this essence with "rationality and humanity originating in passion." This led to a lively exchange about the "German character" and the relations between Germans and Jews, a topic to which they returned many times in the course of their long correspondence. See especially the letters dated Jan. 1, 3, and 6, 1933, 15–19.
4 Unfortunately, the superbly edited edition of the letters exchanged by Hannah Arendt and Kurt Blumenfeld, '. . . *in keinem Besitz verwurzelt,' Die Korrespondenz*, ed. Ingeborg Nordmann and Iris Pilling (Hamburg: Rotbuch Verlag, 1995), was published when my book was already in production. This correspondence has a very different character from that of either Arendt and Jaspers or Arendt and McCarthy. The letters are more playful, and they are ruthlessly frank concerning Jewish, Zionist, and Israeli issues. Most of the letters were written during the period from the 1950s until Blumenfeld's death in 1963 when Arendt published scarcely anything dealing directly with the Jewish question. But the correspondence with Blumenfeld shows how deeply concerned she was with this question throughout this period. (See also the discussion of the relation between Arendt and Blumenfeld in Barnouw, *Visible Spaces*.)
5 See Arendt, "Martin Heidegger at 80," *New York Review of Books*, 17/6 (Oct. 21, 1971): 50–4; repr. in *Heidegger and Modern Philosophy*, ed. M. Murray (New Haven: Yale University Press, 1978), 293–303.

6 Arendt edited and wrote an introduction to an English translation of Lazare's writings, *Job's Dungheap* (New York: Schocken Press, 1949).

7 For a detailed and perceptive analysis of the meaning of "society," especially as it is used in Arendt's biography of Rahel Varnhagen, see Pitkin, "Conformism, Housekeeping, and the Attack of the Blob." See also Seyla Benhabib's discussion of society in "The Pariah and Her Shadow," *Political Theory*, 23 (Feb. 1995): 5–24.

8 See "The Social Question" in *OR*, 59–114. See also Richard J. Bernstein, "Rethinking the Social and the Political," in *Philosophical Profiles: Essays in a Pragmatic Mode* (Cambridge: Polity Press, 1986), 238–59.

9 Arendt, "We Refugees," *Menorah Journal*, 31 (Jan. 1943); repr. in *JP*, 66.

10 See Arendt's discussion of the editing of Rahel's letters in her preface to *RH*. See also her objections to Karl Jaspers's portrait of Rahel in *C*, 198.

11 Several commentators have emphasized Arendt's identification with Rahel Varnhagen. There is no doubt that Arendt found Rahel both fascinating and "insufferable." She even referred to Rahel as "my closest friend, though she has been dead for some one hundred years" (*YB*, 56). But unlike Rahel, Arendt was never tempted to play the role of the parvenu. She never experienced her Jewishness as a source of shame.

12 Writing to Jaspers in 1952, Arendt gives a more accurate statement of her approach: "What I meant to do was argue further with her, the way she argued with herself, and always within the categories that were available to her and that she somehow accepted as valid" (*C*, 200). There are several excellent discussions of *RH*. See *YB*, ch. 3, "The Life of a Jewess"; Barnouw, *Visible Spaces*, ch. 2, "Society, Parvenu and Pariah: The Life of a German Jewess"; Pitkin, "Conformism, Housekeeping, and the Attack of the Blob"; Benhabib, "The Pariah and Her Shadow." See also Sybille Bedford, "Emancipation and Destiny," review of *RH*, *Reconstructionist*, 24 (Dec. 1958): 22–6.

13 For the details concerning Arendt's arrest, interrogation, and escape from Germany, see *YB*, 102–10.

14 Arendt did not publish the book at this time, although she finally agreed to publish an English translation in 1958. The German edition was published in 1959. The American edition appeared in 1974.

15 After the Second World War, when they renewed their correspondence, Arendt wrote to Jaspers explaining what she took to be the "fundamental contradiction" in the United States. In her letter dated Jan. 29, 1946, she writes:

> The fundamental contradiction in this country is the coexistence of political freedom and social oppression. The latter is ... not total; but it is dangerous because society organizes and orients itself along "racial lines." And that holds true without exception at all social levels, from the bourgeoisie on down to the working class. This racial issue has to do with a

person's country of origin, but it is greatly aggravated by the Negro question; that is, America has a real "race" problem and not just a racial ideology. You doubtless know that social anti-Semitism is taken completely for granted here and that antipathy towards Jews is, so to speak, a consensus omnium.

This is the same letter in which Arendt explains to Jaspers why she continues to use her own name and not her (Gentile) husband's name: "I continue to use my old name. That's quite common here in America when a woman works, and I have gladly adopted this custom out of conservatism (and also because I wanted my name to identify me as a Jew)" (*C*, 29–31).

16 Arendt is reporting a conversation she had with Golda Meir. When she agreed to the publication of what was originally a personal letter to Scholem, she (at Scholem's request) agreed to delete the reference to Golda Meir and use a masculine pronoun. See *YB*, 332; and Barnouw, *Visible Spaces*, 302–3, n. 62.

17 This quotation from Lazare is cited in *DA*, 239.

18 "The Jew as Pariah: A Hidden Tradition," *Jewish Social Studies*, 6/2 (Apr. 1944): 99–122; repr. in *JP*, 67–90.

19 The first chapter of *Rahel Varnhagen* is entitled "Jewess and Schlemihl."

20 Arendt writes: "Chaplin has recently declared that he is of Irish and Gypsy descent, but he has been selected for discussion because, even if not himself a Jew, he has epitomized in an artistic form a character born of the Jewish pariah mentality" (*JP*, 69, n.1).

21 Compare this statement written in 1944 with a statement from her 1965 (unpublished) New School lectures, "Some Questions of Moral Philosophy," Arendt Archives, Library of Congress:

The greatest evil perpetuated is the evil committed by Nobodies, committed, to be sure, by human beings, but by human beings who refused to be persons. Within the conceptual framework of these considerations we could say: Wrong doers who refused to think by themselves what they were doing and who also refuse in retrospect to think about it, that is, to go back, return to and remember what they did, which is *teshuvah* or repentance, have actually failed to constitute themselves into somebodies, and by stubbornly remaining nobodies prove to be unfit for intercourse with others, who, good, bad or indifferent, are at the very least persons.

22 See her discussion of "tribal nationalism" in *OT₃*, 227–43.

Chapter 2 Anti-Semitism as a Political Ideology

1 *DA* was written in German and translated into English.

2 Although Arendt is critical of Sartre, she does not do justice to the

subtleties of his analysis in *Anti-Semite and Jew* (New York: Schocken Books, 1948). She fails to note how Sartre's analysis reinforces and complements her own distinction between the parvenu and the pariah. Sartre does say that "the Jew is one whom other men consider a Jew" and "thus it is no exaggeration to say that it is the Christians who have *created* the Jew in putting an abrupt stop to his assimilation and in providing him, in spite of himself, with a function in which he has prospered" (p. 68). Such statements, when ripped from their context, seem to support Arendt's interpretation. But even here, Sartre's main point is that it is the anti-Semite who ascribes the pariah status to the Jews. "The [anti-Semite] wishes to destroy him as a man and leave nothing in him but the Jew, the pariah, the untouchable" (p. 57).

Sartre's distinction between the "inauthentic" and the "authentic" Jew closely parallels Arendt's distinction between the parvenu and the conscious pariah. He highlights a crucial feature that is implicit in Arendt's distinction. This is the way in which Sartre characterizes authenticity:

> If it is agreed that man may be defined as a being having freedom within the limits of a situation, then it is easy to see that the exercise of this freedom may be considered as *authentic* or *inauthentic* according to the choices made in the situation. Authenticity . . . consists in having a true and lucid consciousness of the situation, in assuming the responsibilities and risks that it involves, in accepting it in pride or humiliation, sometimes in horror and hate. (p. 90)

The following description of the "inauthentic Jew" describes what Arendt calls the parvenu.

> Thus, no matter what he may do, the inauthentic Jew is possessed by the consciousness of being a Jew. At that very moment when he is forcing himself by his whole conduct to deny the traits ascribed to him, he feels that he can see these traits in others, and thus they return to him indirectly. He seeks and flees his coreligionists; he affirms that he is only one man among others, and like others, yet he feels himself compromised by the demeanor of the first passer-by, if that passer-by is a Jew. He makes himself an anti-Semite in order to break all his ties with the Jewish community; yet he finds that community again in the depths of his heart, for he experiences in his very flesh the humiliations that the anti-Semites impose upon other Jews. (pp. 106–7)

Sartre's contrasting portrait of the "authentic" Jew not only closely corresponds to the "conscious pariah," but brings into sharp relief Arendt's own emphasis on the choice to assume responsibility to fight anti-Semitism.

Jewish authenticity consists in choosing oneself *as Jew* – that is, in realizing one's Jewish condition. The authentic Jew abandons the myth of the universal man; he knows himself and wills himself into history as a historic and damned creature; he ceases to run away from himself and to be ashamed of his own kind. . . . He knows that he is one who stands apart, untouchable, scorned, proscribed – and it is *as such* that he asserts his being. (pp. 136–7)

Sartre, like Arendt, is critical of the "myth of the universal man." "Democrat" is the label that Sartre assigns to the person who fails to see the particular case and thinks of all individuals as an "ensemble of universal traits." The "democrat" who thinks he is protecting the Jew actually "wishes to destroy him as a Jew and leave nothing in him but the man, the abstract and universal subject of the rights of man and the rights of the citizen" (p. 57). "It follows that his defense of the Jew saves the latter as a man and annihilates him as a Jew" (p. 56). "This means that he wants to separate the Jew from his religion, from his family, from his ethnic community, in order to plunge him into the democratic crucible whence he will emerge naked and alone, an individual and solitary particle like all the other particles" (p. 57).

3 See Seyla Benhabib's perceptive remarks on the methodological puzzles of Arendt's analysis of totalitarianism in "Hannah Arendt and the Redemptive Power of Narrative," *Social Research*, 57/1 (Spring 1990): 168–96. She writes that "Arendt's work defies categorization while violating a lot of rules. It is too systematically ambitious and overinterpreted to be strictly a historical account; it is too anecdotal, narrative, and ideographic to be considered social science; and although it has the vivacity and the stylistic flair of a work of political journalism, it is too philosophical to be accessible to a broad public" (p. 173).

4 Not only are there layers of *The Origins of Totalitarianism* that date back to the study of anti-Semitism which Arendt began during her Paris years, but it is clear that she changed her mind several times in the course of writing the book. For a discussion of how the book was written and finally composed, see *YB*, 199–211; and Margaret Canovan, *Hannah Arendt*, 17–23. In my discussion I focus primarily on Nazi totalitarianism. Arendt herself came to realize the tensions and disparities in her treatment of Nazi totalitarianism and Stalinist totalitarianism. As late as Feb. 13, 1948, she was planning to divide her "Imperialism" book into three parts: on anti-Semitism, imperialism, and Nazism. There is no indication that she intended to discuss totalitarianism in the Soviet Union. In her (unpublished) letter to Paul Brooks, editor of Houghton Mifflin, she wrote:

You may remember from our talks and correspondence that I intend to give an historical analysis of those elements which finally crystallized into

Nazism. The three parts of the book, accordingly, have not only a logical but also a chronological order. The first part deals with roughly the nineteenth century, the second with the four decades following 1884 ("scramble for Africa") and the third part will analyze Nazism as the racist type of totalitarian regime. (Arendt to Brooks, New York, Feb. 13, 1948, in Arendt Archives, Library of Congress)

The book was published ultimately by Harcourt, Brace, and Co. Between 1948 and her submission of the completed manuscript in 1950, Arendt changed her emphasis to focus on both Nazi and Stalinist versions of totalitarianism, but she did not significantly change the first two parts of her book: "Antisemitism" and "Imperialism."

5 Eric Voegelin's review and Arendt's reply were published in *Review of Politics*, 15/6 (Jan. 1953): 68–85; citation from pp. 77–8.

6 "Understanding and Politics," originally entitled "The Difficulties of Understanding," *Partisan Review*, 20/4 (1954); repr. in *EU*, 319.

7 See Margaret Canovan's illuminating analysis of what Arendt means by "totalitarianism" in *Hannah Arendt*, 23–8.

8 It is the various "elements" of totalitarianism that provide what Arendt called the "hidden structure" of her book. These include "antisemitism, decay of the national state, racism, expansion for expansion's sake, alliance between capital and mob." Margaret Canovan gives a subtle analysis of these elements in *Hannah Arendt*, 28–44. Canovan, who is one of the first to make extensive use of Arendt's unpublished writings in her reinterpretation, argues that "virtually the entire agenda of Arendt's political thought was set by her reflections on the political catastrophes of the mid-century." I agree with Canovan's thesis, but I strongly disagree with her claim that "although it played a key part . . . antisemitism was not actually an essential factor" in totalitarianism. This contradicts Arendt's emphatic claim that "Nazi ideology centered around anti-semitism and that Nazi policy, consistently and uncompromisingly, aimed at the persecution and finally the extermination of the Jews."

9 In her reflections on totalitarianism, Arendt warns us about the *déformation professionnelle* of historians "to see in history a story with many ends and no beginning; and this inclination becomes really dangerous only when . . . people begin to make a philosophy out of history as it presents itself to the professional eyes of the historian. Nearly all modern explications of the so-called historicity of man have been distorted by categories which, at best, are working hypotheses for arranging the material of the past." Arendt herself does not succumb to this "dangerous inclination," she sharply contrasts what is central for all political thought and genuine politics. "The great consequence which the concept of beginning and origin has for all strictly political questions comes from the simple fact that political action, like all action, is essentially always the

beginning of something new; as such, it is, in terms of political science, the very essence of human freedom. The central position which the concept of beginning and origin must have in all political thought has been lost only since the historical sciences have been permitted to supply the field of politics their methods and categories" (*EU*, 320–1). This thesis concerning the autonomy of politics and the modern danger of confusing politics with the philosophy of history is one that Arendt reiterates throughout her writings. Much of her thinking about politics can be seen as a defense of the autonomy and dignity of politics, based upon the concept of spontaneously beginning something new which she sees as "the very essence of human freedom." This theme was first developed in Arendt's lament for the failure of Jewish politics and her summons to the Jewish people to initiate political action.

10 *Aufbau*, 7/47 (Nov. 14, 1941): 1–2. See Elisabeth Young-Bruehl's discussion of Arendt's call for organizing a Jewish Army in *YB*, 173–81.

11 "Totalitarianism," *Meridian*, 2/2 (Fall 1958): 1. Compare this statement with what she says in her reply to Eric Voegelin's criticism:

> The problem originally confronting me was simple and baffling at the same time: all historiography is necessarily salvation and frequently justification; it is due to man's fear that he may forget and to his striving for something which is even more than remembrance. . . . Thus my first problem was how to write historically about something – totalitarianism – which I did not want to conserve but on the contrary felt engaged to destroy. ("Reply to Eric Voegelin," 77)

Arendt's attempt to break the continuity of historical narrative bears a strong resemblance to Walter Benjamin's understanding of history and counter-history. See Seyla Benhabib's discussion of Arendt and Benjamin in "Hannah Arendt and the Redemptive Power of Narrative."

12 Arendt was frequently accused of exaggeration. To my knowledge, the first to make such a charge was Karl Jaspers. Arendt had claimed that the anti-Semitic forgery "The Protocols of the Elders of Zion" was a source for Nazi policy to establish a fascist international. Writing to Arendt (June 27, 1946), Jaspers says: "You exaggerate – and even as I use this word I find it wrong, because you *don't* exaggerate in your overall picture but, for instance, in regard to the [Protocols of the Elders of Zion] as a source for Nazi policy, or so it seems to me" (*C*, 44). In their correspondence, Arendt and Jaspers frequently return to this issue of exaggeration. Arendt gives one of the most forceful defenses of her tendency to exaggerate in her Jan. 25, 1952, letter. She writes:

> "Exaggeration" – of course. "Relationships between ideas," as you say, can hardly be presented any other way. And then they are not really exaggerations either. They're products of dissection. It's the nature of

thought to exaggerate. When Montesquieu says that republican government is based on the principle of virtue, he is "exaggerating" too. Besides,
reality has taken things to such great extremes in our century that we can
say without exaggeration that reality is "exaggerated." Our thinking,
which after all likes nothing better than rolling along its accustomed paths,
is hardly capable of keeping up with it. My "exaggerated" kind of thinking,
which is at least making an effort to say something adequate in a tone that
is, if possible, itself adequate, will of course sound wildly radical if you
measure it not against reality but against what other historians, going on
the assumption that everything is in the best of order, have said on the
same subject. (*C*, 175–6)

13 Canovan, *Hannah Arendt*, 276.
14 "The Jewish State, Fifty Years After: Where Have Herzl's Politics Led?,"
    Commentary, 1 (May, 1946): 1–8. Repr. in *JP*, 166.
15 "Jewish History, Revised," *Jewish Frontier*, 15 (Mar. 1948), repr. in *JP*, 96.
16 In her letter to Jaspers, Arendt continues by declaring:

As far as the two-thousand-year-old history of hatred for the Jews is
concerned, it rests primarily on the claim of the Jewish people to be the
chosen people. This history – like all Jewish history – has unfortunately
been so falsified, with a few major exceptions, being presented by the
Jewish side as the history of an eternally persecuted people and by the anti-
Semitic side as the history of the devil, that we somehow have to revise
everything in it. (*C*, 55)

Arendt is alluding to the doctrine of eternal anti-Semitism, but she
connects this with "the claim of the Jewish people to be the chosen
people." Arendt was always troubled by this claim. She viewed the
secularization of the idea of chosenness as double-edged. In her
discussion of Disraeli's race doctrines, she claims that, as a result of the
secularization of assimilated Jewry, "two basic elements of Jewish piety –
the Messianic hope and the faith in Israel's chosenness" were being
transformed.

Without the Messianic hope, the idea of chosenness meant eternal
segregation; without faith in chosenness, which charged one specific people
with the redemption of the world, Messianic hope evaporated into the dim
cloud of general philanthropy and universalism which became so
characteristic of specifically Jewish political enthusiasm.
    The most fateful element in Jewish secularization was that the concept of
chosenness was being separated from Messianic hope, whereas in Jewish
religion these two elements were two aspects of God's redemptory plan for
mankind. Out of Messianic hope grew that inclination toward final
solutions of political problems which aimed at nothing less than
establishing a paradise on earth. Out of the belief in chosenness by God
grew that fantastic delusion, shared by unbelieving Jews and non-Jews

alike, that Jews are by nature more intelligent, better, healthier, more fit for survival – the motor of history and the salt of the earth. (*OT*₃, 74)

17 See her analysis of the decline of the nation-state and the birth of anti-Semitism in *OT*₃, "The Jews, the Nation-State and the Birth of Antisemitism."

18 Arendt distinguishes continental imperialism from overseas imperialism. She tells us:

> The chief importance of continental, as distinguished from overseas, imperialism lies in the fact that its concept of cohesive expansion does not allow for any geographic distance between the methods and institutions of colony and of nation, so that it did not require boomerang effects in order to make itself and all its consequences felt in Europe. Continental imperialism truly begins at home. If it shared with overseas imperialism the contempt for the narrowness of the nation-state, it opposed to it not so much economic arguments, which after all quite frequently expressed authentic national needs, as an "enlarged tribal consciousness" which was supposed to unite all people of similar folk origin, independent of history and no matter where they happened to live. Continental imperialism, therefore, started with a much closer affinity to race concepts, enthusiastically absorbed the tradition of race-thinking, and relied very little on specific experiences. (*OT*₃, 224-5)

19 Benhabib, "Hannah Arendt and the Redemptive Power of Narrative," 181–2.

20 Lisa J. Disch, "More Truth than Fact," *Political Theory*, 21 (Nov. 1993): 683.

Chapter 3 Statelessness and the Right to Have Rights

1 For a fuller account of Arendt's life as a stateless person, see ch. 4, "Stateless Persons," in *YB*; see also "What Remains? The Language Remains" (*EU*, 1–23).

2 Walter Benjamin, "Theses on the Philosophy of History," in *Illuminations*, ed. and introduced by Hannah Arendt (New York: Schocken Press, 1969), 257–8. See Arendt's discussion of this thesis in "Franz Kafka: A Reevaluation," *Partisan Review*, 11/4 (1944); repr. in *EU*, 74–5.

3 In a review of J. T. Delos's book, *La Nation*, Arendt states bluntly:

> Nationalism signifies essentially the conquest of the state through the nation. This is the sense of the national state. The result of the XIX century identification of nation and state is twofold: while the state as a

legal institution has declared and must protect the rights of men, its identification with the nation implied the identification of the national and the citizen and thereby resulted in the confusion of the Rights of Men with the rights of nationals or national rights. . . .

The conquest of the state through the nation started with the declaration of the sovereignty of the nation. This was the first step transforming the state into an instrument of the nation which finally has ended in those totalitarian forms of nationalism in which all laws and the legal institutions of the state as such are interpreted as means for the welfare of the nation. It is therefore quite erroneous to see the evil of our times in a deification of the state. It is the nation which has usurped the traditional place of God and religion. ("The Nation," *Review of Politics*, 8/1 (Jan. 1946): 139)

4 See Arendt's discussion of opinion in *OR*, 227–8, 268.

5 In *On Revolution*, Arendt shows the web of connection between "freedom," "no-rule," "isonomy," and political equality. See *OR*, 21–8.

Chapter 4 The Descent into Hell

1 It was during the 1940s that Arendt most explicitly thought of herself as a *Jewish* intellectual. She worked for various Jewish organizations, and published frequently in Jewish journals. In one of her first letters to Jaspers when they renewed their correspondence after the war (Nov. 18, 1945) she wrote: "Since I've been in America – that is, since 1941 – I've become a kind of free-lance writer, something between a historian and a political journalist. In the latter capacity I've focused primarily on questions of Jewish politics" (*C*, 23–4).

2 Unless otherwise noted, I refer to the 3rd edn, rev., of *The Origins of Totalitarianism* (*OT*₃). Occasionally, when there are variations, I cite the 1st edn published in 1951 (*OT*₁) or the 2nd edn of 1958 (*OT*₂). Arendt dropped her "Concluding Remarks" in the "second enlarged edition," and added an epilogue entitled "Reflections on the Hungarian Revolution." She decided to eliminate this epilogue in the 3rd edn, rev., of 1968.

3 I discuss what Arendt means by absolute or radical evil in Ch. 7.

4 In making this claim, Arendt does not mean that concentration camps originated with totalitarian regimes. What she stresses is the distinctive nonutilitarian function of these camps in totalitarian regimes.

Not even concentration camps are an invention of totalitarian movements. They emerge for the first time during the Boer War, at the beginning of the century, and continued to be used in South Africa as well as India for "undesirable elements"; here, too, we first find the term "protective custody" which was later adopted by the Third Reich. These camps correspond in many respects to the concentration camps at the beginning of totalitarian rule; they were used for "suspects" whose offenses could not be proved and who could not be sentenced by ordinary process of law. All this clearly points to totalitarian methods of domination; all these are elements they utilize, develop and crystallize on the basis of the nihilistic principle that "everything is permitted," which they inherited and already took for granted. But wherever these new forms of domination assume their authentically totalitarian structure they transcend this principle, which is still tied to the utilitarian motives and self-interest of the rulers, and try their hand in a realm that up to now has been completely unknown to us: the realm where "everything is possible." (*OT*₃, 440)

5 "Social Science Techniques and the Study of Concentration Camps," *Jewish Social Studies*, 12 (1950); repr. in *EU*, 234. This article was written as a companion piece to "The Concentration Camps." It reiterates and expands some of the key points made in the first article.

6 This is the argument that Arendt develops in "Social Science Techniques and the Study of Concentration Camps." She writes:

It is the contention of this paper that the institution of concentration and extermination camps, that is, the social conditions within them as well as their function in the larger terror apparatus of totalitarian regimes, may very likely become that unexpected phenomenon, that stumbling-block on the road toward the proper understanding of contemporary politics and society which must cause social scientists and historical scholars to reconsider their hitherto unquestioned fundamental preconceptions regarding the course of the world and human behavior. (*EU*, 232)

7 For the details of what happened in Hungary and Eichmann's role in organizing the "resettlement" of Hungarian Jews, see Raul Hilberg, *The Destruction of the European Jews* (Chicago: Quadrangle Books, 1961), 509–54.

8 This is not the first time that Arendt compared the death camps to Hell. In 1946, Arendt wrote a review of *The Black Book: The Nazi Crime Against the Jewish People*, entitled "The Image of Hell." She wrote:

The facts are: that six million Jews, six million human beings, were helplessly, and in most cases unsuspectingly, dragged to their deaths. The method employed was that of accumulated terror. First came calculated neglect, deprivation, and shame, when the weak in body died together with those strong and defiant enough to take their own lives. Second came outright starvation, combined with forced labor, when people died by the thousands but at different intervals of time, according to their stamina. Last came the death factories – and they all died together, the young and the old, the weak and the strong, the sick and the healthy; not as people, not as men and women, children and adults, boys and girls, not as good and bad, beautiful and ugly – but brought down to the lowest common denominator of organic life itself, plunged into the darkest and deepest abyss of primal equality, like cattle, like matter, like things that had neither body nor soul, nor even a physiognomy upon which death could stamp its seal.

It is in this monstrous equality without fraternity or humanity – an equality in which cats and dogs could have shared – that we see, as though mirrored, the image of hell. (*EU*, 198)

9 In characterizing the concentration camps, Arendt frequently describes them as "holes of oblivion." However, by the time she wrote *Eichmann in Jerusalem*, she had changed her mind. "The holes of oblivion do not exist. Nothing human is that perfect, and there are simply too many people in the world to make oblivion possible. One man will always be left alive to tell the story" (*EJ*, 232–3). In her letter to Mary McCarthy (Sept. 20, 1963), Arendt acknowledges this shift. She also comments on her original evaluation of the impact of totalitarian ideology.

> If one reads [*Eichmann in Jerusalem*] carefully, one sees that Eichmann was much less influenced by ideology than I assumed in the book on totalitarianism. The impact of ideology upon the individual may have been overrated by me. Even in the totalitarian book, in the chapter on ideology and terror, I mention the curious loss of ideological content that occurs among the elite of the movement. The movement itself becomes all important; the content of anti-semitism for instance gets lost in the extermination policy, for extermination would not have come to an end when no Jew was left to be killed. In other words, extermination per se is more important than anti-semitism or racism. (*BF*, 147–8)

10 Arendt is quoting a passage from David Rousset, *Les Jours de notre mort* (Paris: Éditions du Pavois, 1947). Throughout her analysis of concentration camps, she relies heavily on this report by a survivor.

11 For the distinction between truth and meaning see *LM*, 57–65.

12 In *OT₃* Arendt characterizes the aim of totalitarian ideologies as "the transformation of human nature itself. The concentration camps are the laboratories where changes in human nature are tested" (*OT₃*, 458). Arendt dropped her references to "human nature" after *OT₃*. In *HC* she explains why she no longer speaks of "human nature" (*HC*, 9–11). But this change does not substantially alter the significance of her claims about what totalitarianism seeks to accomplish.

13 Claude Lefort, "Hannah Arendt and the Question of the Political," in *Democracy and Political Theory* (Minneapolis: University of Minnesota Press, 1988), 50. My one caveat about Lefort's statement concerns his reference to a "theory of politics." *Theory* tends to suggest something far more definitive than the "meaning of politics." Even more important, a close reading of Arendt reveals just how complex her understanding of

action and politics is. Margaret Canovan is especially helpful in tracking the many strands that are woven into Arendt's web of understanding of politics and action. See especially her discussion "The Complexities of Arendt's Account of Action," in *Hannah Arendt*, 136–43.

Chapter 5 Zionism: Jewish Homeland or Jewish State?

1 See Elisabeth Young-Bruehl's account of Arendt's first trip to Palestine, *YB*, 138–9.
2 This is how Arendt describes the kibbutz movement in "Zionism Reconsidered":

> Out of these social ideals grew the *chalutz* and *kibbutz* movement. Its members, a small minority in their native lands, are a hardly larger minority in Palestine Jewry today. But they did succeed in creating a new type of Jew, even a new kind of aristocracy with newly established values: their genuine contempt for material wealth, exploitation, and bourgeois life; their unique combination of culture and labor; their rigorous realization of social justice within their small circle; and their loving pride in the fertile soil, the work of their hands, together with an utter and surprising lack of any wish for personal possession. (*JP*, 138)

Many years later, when Mary McCarthy wrote to Arendt about Nathalie Sarraute's enthusiastic response to Israel, Arendt wrote back as follows (letter of Oct. 17, 1969):

> Nathalie's reaction to Israel: quite understandable. I still remember my first reaction to the kibbutzim very well. I thought: a new aristocracy. I knew even then, of course, as she probably does too, that one could not live there. "Rule by your neighbors," that is of course what it finally amounts to. Still, if one honestly believes in equality, Israel is very impressive. (*BF*, 248–9)

It is in this same letter that Arendt also comments: "But even I know that any real catastrophe in Israel would affect me more deeply than almost anything else."
3 Although Arendt consistently objected to Herzl's claim that anti-Semitism was the " 'propelling force' responsible for all Jewish suffering since the destruction of the Temple and it would continue to make the Jews suffer until they learned how to use it for their own advantage," she did think that "Herzl's lasting greatness lay in his very desire to do something about the Jewish question, his desire to act and to solve the problem in political terms" (*JP*, 166).

4 It is an extremely bitter irony that the term "revisionists," used to identify the extreme wing of the Zionist movement whose original goal had been a Jewish state that would include the whole of Palestine and Transjordan, is the very term that has recently been used to identify the fringe, but vociferous, group who deny that the Holocaust ever occurred.

5 "Zionism Reconsidered," which was submitted to *Commentary* in 1944, was published in a journal barely known outside Jewish circles, the *Menorah Journal*, 33 (Aug. 1945): 162–96 (repr. in *JP*, 131–63). Many of the rhetorical devices that Arendt employed in it were used again in *Eichmann in Jerusalem*. In the latter, she does not hide her disdain for Ben-Gurion's attempt to use the trial to further Zionist goals. She was vehemently attacked for her *alleged* "anti-Zionism," "antisemitism," and "Jewish self-hatred."

6 Arendt attributed this statement to Cato, but it is actually from Lucan, *Pharsalia* (Bellum civile I, line 128). She cited it in her first book, *Rahel Varnhagen*, and it appears on a sheet that was found in her typewriter when she died, bearing the title "The Life of the Mind. Part III. Judging." In a letter to Jaspers she cites it in the description of her Zionist friend Kurt Blumenfeld:

> To give you an idea of the man: a number of articles appeared on the occasion of his seventieth birthday, and an anecdote in one of them has stuck with me because it was so typical of him. When he was a young man he tried to make a Zionist out of someone who objected: "But you have to admit that this cause has no prospect of success." Whereupon Blumenfeld said: "Whoever said I was interested in success?" . . . You must know that quote from Cato that Gentz always cited: *Victrix causa diis placuit sed victa Catoni*. That is the spirit of republicanism." (*C*, 244)

For further comments on the use and meaning of this quotation in Arendt, see the editors' note 2 in *C*, 735–6; and Jerome Kohn's introduction to *EU*, xxiii.

7 The meaning and centrality of opinion for politics is explored in *PP*. Here Arendt relates *doxa* to opinion and fame. "The word *doxa* means not only opinion but also splendor and fame. As such, it is related to the political realm, which is the public sphere in which everybody can appear and show who he himself is" (*PP*, 80).

8 For the distinction between truth (especially the truth sought by philosophers) and opinion, see *PP*. In this lecture Arendt speaks of the "tyranny of truth" in Plato, which she claims results from Plato's reflections on the implications of the trial and condemnation of Socrates. She carefully distinguishes Socrates from Plato. "To Socrates, maieutic was a political activity, a give and take, fundamentally on a basis of strict equality, the fruits of which could not be measured by the result of

arriving at this or that general truth." Socrates "wanted to help others give birth to what they themselves thought anyhow, to find the truth in their *doxa*" (*PP*, 81).

9 The nation-state in this European sense presupposed a homogeneous national population. Arendt claimed that "the political structure of the United States . . . is not a national state in the European sense of the word." Consequently, "the American body politic can afford a far greater tolerance for community life of the numerous nationalities which all together form and determine the life of the American nation" (*JP*, 158–9).

10 For a fuller account of Arendt's relations with Magnes and her activities in support of Ihud, see *YB*, 225–33.

11 "The Mission of Bernadotte," *New Leader*, 31 (Oct. 1948): 819.

Chapter 6 "The Innermost Story of the Modern Age": Revolutions and the Council System

1 Arendt is quoting here from a report on the Hungarian revolution: *The Revolt of Hungary: A Documentary Chronology of Events* (New York: Free Europe Committee, n.d.).

2 "Totalitarianism," 1.

3 Ibid.

4 See my discussion of some of these contradictions in "Judging – the Actor and the Spectator," in *Philosophical Profiles: Essays in a Pragmatic Mode*, (Cambridge: Polity Press, 1986), 221–37.

5 For an exploration of these similarities, as well as some of the significant differences between Heidegger and Arendt, see my "Heidegger's Silence."

6 "Totalitarianism," 1.

7 See also her commentary on Kafka's parable in her preface to *BPF*.

Chapter 7 From Radical Evil to the Banality of Evil: From Superfluousness to Thoughtlessness

1 Arendt uses "absolute evil" and "radical evil" as synonyms, although she favors the latter.

2 For interpretations of the meaning of radical evil in Kant, see John Silber, "The Ethical Significance of Kant's *Religion*," introductory essay to *Kant's Religion within the Limits of Reason Alone* (New York: Harper & Row, 1960), lxxix–cxxxiv; Henry E. Allison, *Kant's Theory of Freedom* (Cambridge: Cambridge University Press, 1990); idem, "Reflections on the Banality of (Radical) Evil: A Kantian Analysis," *Graduate Faculty Philosophy Journal*, 18/2 (Winter 1995): 141–58; and Sharon Anderson-

Gold, "Kant's Rejection of Devilishness: The Limits of Human Volition," *Idealistic Studies*, 14 (1989): 35–48. Anderson-Gold even claims "there is a certain parallel between Kant's concept of radical evil and Arendt's concept of 'banal' evil in *Eichmann in Jerusalem*" (p. 48, n. 30).

3 In "Ideology and Terror: A Novel Form of Government," which Arendt added to the third (1968) edition of *Origins* in place of her original "Concluding Remarks," she stresses how total terror seeks to destroy all plurality and spontaneity.

> [Total terror] substitutes for the boundaries and channels of communication between individual men a band of iron which holds them so tightly together that it is as though their plurality had disappeared into One Man of gigantic dimensions. . . . In the iron band of terror, which destroys the plurality of men and makes out of many the One who unfailingly will act as though he himself were part of the course of history or nature, a device has been found not only to liberate the historical and natural forces, but to accelerate them to a speed they never would reach if left to themselves. (OT_3, 465–6).

4 Canovan, *Hannah Arendt*, 24, n. 30. Canovan also brings out another aspect of Arendt's conception of superfluousness. Totalitarian murderers are dangerous because they believe in their *own* superfluousness. They abandon themselves to "superhuman laws of Nature and History."

5 Arendt, "Reply to Eric Voegelin," 83–4.

6 "Some Questions of Moral Philosophy," in Arendt Archives, Library of Congress.

7 These "biological" metaphors of bacteria and fungi are double-edged, in that they are virtually identical with the biological characterization of the Jews by the Nazis.

8 Although Arendt totally rejected any comparison between Nazi crimes and poetic representations of "satanic greatness," she could have appealed to Shakespeare for his understanding of superfluousness. Recall Lear's response to Goneril and Regan:

> "O reason not the need! Our basest beggars
> Are in the poorest thing superfluous."
> *King Lear, II.* iv. 263–4

9 To be "thoughtless," as Mary McCarthy (who frequently corrected Arendt's English) informed her, most commonly means to be inconsiderate or heedless. Nevertheless, Arendt insisted on using this expression to designate the inability or refusal to think – to reflect upon what one is doing. Eichmann, she claimed, was not stupid, but was so entrapped in clichés and "language rules" that he lacked the imagination to stop and think.

Chapter 8 Evil, Thinking, and Judging

1 The massacre at Deir Jassim actually took place on April 8, 1948. Arendt (citing Magnes) mentioned this massacre in "Peace or Armistice in the Near East?," *Review of Politics*, 12/1 (Jan. 1950): 56–82; repr. in *JP*, 193–232. Lidice was a town in Czechoslovakia that was destroyed by the SS in June 1942 in revenge for the assassination of Reinhardt Heydrich. Heydrich had been Eichmann's superior officer, and was "the real engineer of the Final Solution" (*EJ*, 36).

2 Arendt used this phrase in "To Save the Jewish Homeland: There is Still Time," *Commentary*, 5 (May 1948): 398–406; repr. in *JP*, 178–92. She wrote: "Every believer in a democratic government knows the import-ance of a loyal opposition. The tragedy of Jewish politics at this moment is that it is wholly determined by the Jewish Agency and that no opposition to it of any significance exists either in Palestine or America" (*JP*, 184).

3 For their extended discussion of the upcoming trial, see especially their correspondence from the fall of 1960 until the beginning of the trial in April, 1961.

4 The subtitle, *A Report on the Banality of Evil*, did not appear in the *New Yorker* articles, but only when the articles were published in book form in May 1963.

5 For a discussion of the extensive criticism of *Eichmann in Jerusalem*, see *YB* ch. 8, "*Cura Posterior*: Eichmann in Jerusalem (1961–65)." See also Barnouw's *Visible Spaces*, ch. 6, "The Obscurity of Evil: Listening to Eichmann." For a balanced statement concerning Arendt's errors, see Hans Mommsen, "Hannah Arendt und der Prozess gegen Adolf Eichmann," introduction to *Eichmann in Jerusalem: Ein Bericht von der Banalität des Bösen*, tr. Brigitte Ganzow (Munich: Piper Verlag, 1986), i–xxxvii.

6 Jerome Kohn has brought to my attention an extremely revealing unpublished document in the Arendt archives. On Sept. 19, 1963, Samuel Grafton, who was commissioned to write an article for *Look* magazine about the reaction to *Eichmann in Jerusalem*, sent Arendt a series of questions. She agreed to answer them on condition that she would have the right to approve the article based on her replies. (To my knowledge, *Look* never published Grafton's article.) But there is a draft of a 13-page reply to Grafton's questions. In response to Grafton's question "At what moment should their community leaders have said to them [the Jewish people] 'Cooperate no longer, but fight!,' " Arendt answers:

> There never was a moment when "the community leaders [could] have said: 'Cooperate no longer, but fight!,' " as you phrase it. Resistance,

which existed but played a very small role, meant only: we don't want that kind of death, we want to die with honor. But the question of co-operation is indeed bothersome. There certainly was a moment when the Jewish leaders could have said: We shall no longer cooperate, we shall try to disappear. This moment might have come when they, already fully informed of what deportation meant, were asked by the Nazis to prepare the lists for deportation. The Nazis themselves gave them the number and categories of those to be shipped to the killing centers, but who then went and was given a chance to survive was decided by the Jewish authorities. In other words, those who co-operated were at that particular moment masters over life and death. Can't you imagine what that meant in practice? . . .

As for the justifications of this policy, there are many, the most important ones in the Kastner Report which appeared in Germany. It was common enough to think a) if some of us have to die, it is better we decide it than the Nazis. I disagree. It would have been infinitely better to let the Nazis do their own murderous business. b) With a hundred victims we shall save a thousand. This sounds to me like the last version of human sacrifice. Pick seven virgins, sacrifice them to placate the wrath of the gods. Well, this is not my religious belief, and most certainly is not the faith of Judaism.

I answered your questions with respect to this point, but I should like to point out that it was never my intention to bring this part of our "unmastered past" to the attention of the public. It so happened that the *Judenräte* came up at the trial and I had to report on that as I reported on everything else. Within the context of my Report, this plays no prominent role – either in space or in emphasis. It has been blown up out of all reasonable proportions. ("Answer to Grafton, Draft," in Arendt Archives, Library of Congress)

7 Concerning Denmark, Arendt writes:

The story of the Danish Jews is *sui generis*, and the behavior of the Danish people and their government was unique among all the countries of Europe. . . . One is tempted to recommend the story as required reading in political science for all students who wish to learn something about the enormous power potential inherent in nonviolent action and in resistance to an opponent possessing vastly superior means of violence. (*EJ*, 171)

8 Isaiah Trunk, *Judenrat* (New York: Stein and Day, 1972), 570.
9 Walter Z. Laqueur, "Hannah Arendt in Jerusalem: The Controversy Revisited," in *Western Society after the Holocaust*, ed. Lyman H. Legters (Boulder, Colo.: Westview Press, 1983), 118.
10 The German word *Gleichschaltung* can be translated literally as "co-ordination" or "cooperation," but this does not convey its ugly racist overtones of complicity and "cleansing."
11 These lectures are now being edited by Jerome Kohn. The first lecture was published in *Social Research*, 61/4 (Winter 1994): 750.

12 Canovan, *Hannah Arendt*, 158.
13 Hannah Arendt, "Personal Responsibility under Dictatorship," *Listener* (Aug. 6, 1964): 187.
14 Arendt elaborates on the sense in which evil is "thought-defying" in her 1965 lectures, "Some Questions of Moral Philosophy."

> Thinking and remembering, we said, is the human way of striking roots, of taking one's place in the world into which we all arrive as strangers. What we usually call a person or a personality, as distinguished from a mere human being who can also be a nobody, is actually what grows out of this root-striking process which is thinking. . . . If he is a thinking being, rooted in his thoughts and remembrances, and hence knowing that he has to live with himself, there will be limits to what he can permit himself to do, and these limits will not be imposed from the outside upon him but be as it were self-set; these limits can change considerably and uncomfortably from person to person, from country to country, from century to century; but limitless, extreme evil is possible only where these self-grown roots, which automatically limit the possibilities, are entirely absent; they are absent wherever men skid only over the surface of events, where they permit themselves to be carried away without ever penetrating into whatever depth they may be capable of, and this depth, of course, changes again from person to person, from century to century, in its specific quality as well as its dimensions. (Arendt Archives, Library of Congress)

15 Hannah Arendt, *TM*. This article was revised and incorporated in *LM*, 3–16.
16 Martin Heidegger, "The Question Concerning Technology," in *Basic Writings*, ed. David F. Krell (New York: Harper & Row, 1977), 296. For a critical discussion of this essay see my "Heidegger's Silence."
17 This passage is cited in Wolfgang Schirmacher, *Technik und Gelassenheit* (Freiburg: Alber, 1983), 25. The passage was translated by Thomas Sheehan in "Heidegger and the Nazis," *New York Review of Books*, June 16, 1988. The German original is: "Ackerbau ist jetzt motorisierte Ernährungsindustrie, im Wesen das Selbe wie die Fabrikation von Leichen in Gaskammern und Vernichtungslagern, das Selbe wie die Blockade und Aushungerung von Ländern, das Selbe wie die Fabrikation von Wasserstoffbomben."
18 See Sheehan, "Heidegger and the Nazis."
19 See my discussion of the significance of this phrase in "Heidegger's Silence."
20 Although I think that the mentality that Heidegger graphically portrays in his characterization of *Gestell* enables us to understand what Arendt means by "the banality of evil," it must be emphasized that Arendt strongly diverges from Heidegger concerning the issue of personal responsibility.

21 Seyla Benhabib suggests that "A better phrase than the 'banality of evil' might have been the 'routinization of evil' or its *Alltäglichung* (everyday-ness). Analogical thinking governs the logic of the everyday, where we orient ourselves by expected and established patterns and rules" ("Hannah Arendt and the Redemptive Power of Narrative," 185). Although Arendt did focus on how evil deeds became routinized, the phrase "the routinization of evil" does not capture her striking claim that such deeds lacked not only "evil motives," but any motives at all. Furthermore, it was not the orientation by "established patterns and rules" that she emphasized, but rather the ease with which such patterns and rules could be exchanged for new ones.

22 Arendt, "Personal Responsibility under Dictatorship," 186. See her discussion and rejection of cog theories in this article.

23 To cite one notorious example, I find it difficult to reconcile Eichmann's actions in Budapest during the spring and summer of 1944 with Arendt's portrait of him as someone who had "no motives at all" and as someone who "never realized what he was doing." By 1944 the only important European Jewish community that had been unaffected by deportation to death camps was in Hungary, where there were 750,000 Jews. When Eichmann and his staff went to Budapest in March of 1944 to organize a Jewish council, it was well known what "deportation" and "resettle-ment" meant (even to Jewish leaders). Yet Eichmann was able to swiftly organize a Jewish council and initiate mass deportations.

Arendt herself reports how after Budapest had been bombed by the Allies on July 2, Horthy gave the order to stop the deportations. Nevertheless, Eichmann did not obey "the old fool's order but, in mid-July, deported another fifteen hundred Jews." Eichmann even schemed to keep Jewish leaders from informing Horthy about this deportation. Arendt describes this as "one of the most damning pieces of evidence against Eichmann" (*EJ*, 201), yet fails to see it as evidence of Eichmann's fanaticism.

24 Arendt uses the following quotation from Heidegger as an epigraph for *The Life of the Mind*:

> Thinking does not bring knowledge as do the sciences.
> Thinking does not produce usable practical wisdom.
> Thinking does not solve the riddles of the universe.
> Thinking does not endow us directly with the power to act.

25 "Personal Responsibility under Dictatorship," 205.

26 Robert Bernasconi detects a similar tension in Arendt, in that she never quite justifies her claim that thinking has a *moral* side-effect, or by-product. Furthermore, he notes that in regard to evil deeds, Arendt was ultimately concerned not with thinking but with judging. See his

"Habermas and Arendt on the Philosopher's 'Error': Tracking the Diabolical in Heidegger," *Graduate Faculty Philosophy Journal*, 14/2 – 15/1 (1991): 3–24.

27 Arendt notes that Alcibiades and Critias were not content "with being taught how to think without being taught a doctrine, and they changed the non-results of the Socratic thinking examination into negative results." But even if we accept her interpretation, it only serves to underscore how thinking itself is not *sufficient* to liberate the faculty of judging. There is also a further perplexity when Arendt, in characterizing Socrates as a thinker, tells us: "Ugliness and evil are excluded by definition from the thinking concern, although they may occasionally turn up as deficiencies, as lack of beauty, injustice, and evil (*kakia*) as lack of good" (*TM*, 437).

28 Arendt, "Martin Heidegger at Eighty," 295.

29 Margaret Canovan perceptively illuminates the tensions exhibited in Arendt's appeal to Socrates and Heidegger as thinkers. She relates this to the larger theme of philosophy and politics. See "Socrates or Heidegger?", in *Hannah Arendt*, 268–74. See also my discussion of Arendt's understanding of judgment in "Judging – The Actor and the Spectator."

30 In "Some Questions of Moral Philosophy" she put the issue succinctly:

> The total collapse of conscience and morality, or rather of the age-old laws according to which men in our civilization ought to behave suggest that what we are talking about is indeed nothing but mores – customs and manners, adjustment to society: Conscience is nothing but the voice of society, of those who are around us.
>
> Against this: There were always a few with whom it did not work. And we are concerned in this course with these: What prevented them from acting as everybody else did?. . . .
>
> Those who resisted could be found in all walks of life, among poor and entirely uneducated people as among members of good and high society. They said little: the argument was always the same: No *conflict*, no struggle, the evil was no temptation. . . . they simply said: I *can't*; I'd rather die; for life would be not worthwhile when I have done it.
>
> Hence we are concerned with the behavior of common people, not of Nazis or convinced Bolsheviks, not with saints and heroes, and not with born criminals. For if there is any such thing as what we call morality for want of a better term, it certainly concerns such common people and common happenings. (Arendt Archives, Library of Congress)

31 Arendt tells the story of Anton Schmidt in her chapter entitled "Evidence and Witnesses." Just before this, she quotes the words of Zindel Grynszpan, a Polish Jew who moved to Hanover in 1911. In 1938 "catastrophe overcame him," and he was now asked to tell his "story" at the trial. This was one of the moments of the trial that stood out for

Arendt. After quoting his testimony, Arendt writes: "This story took no more than perhaps ten minutes to tell, and when it was over – the senseless, needless destruction of twenty-seven years in less than twenty-four hours – one thought foolishly: Everyone, everyone should have his day in court. . . . No one either before or after was to equal the shining honesty of Zindel Grynszpan" (*EJ*, 229–30).

32 Arendt, "Personal Responsibility under Dictatorship," 187.

Chapter 9 Concluding Remarks: Blindness and Insight

1 Hannah Arendt, "The History of a Great Crime," review of *Bréviaire de la Haine: Le IIIe Reich et les Juifs*, by Léon Poliakov, *Commentary*, 13 (1952): 304.

2 Arendt, "Collective Responsibility" in James W. Bernauer, SJ, *Amor Mundi: Explorations in the Faith and Thought of Hannah Arendt* (Dordrecht: Martinus Nijhoff, 1987), 46. For a discussion of Arendt's critique of Christianity, see Bernauer's article "The Faith of Hannah Arendt: *Amor Mundi* and its Critique-Assimilation of Religious Experience," in the same volume. Other articles in this volume examine Arendt's dissertation on St Augustine and her use of "Christian metaphors."

3 This passage, which so epitomizes the basic outlook of Arendt, is a source for the title of Young-Bruehl's biography, *Hannah Arendt: For the Love of the World*.

4 This is the phrase that Arendt used to describe Judah Magnes (*C*, 117), and echoes what she says about Heine (*JP*, 72).

Bibliography

WORKS BY ARENDT

Only works cited are listed here. For a more complete bibliography of Arendt's works, see Elisabeth Young-Bruehl, *Hannah Arendt: For Love of the World*. New Haven: Yale University Press, 1982.

Books

The Origins of Totalitarianism. New York: Harcourt, Brace, Jovanovich, 1951; 2nd edn, New York: Meridian Books, 1958; 3rd edn, rev., New York: Harcourt, Brace, Jovanovich, 1968.

The Human Condition. Chicago: University of Chicago Press, 1958.

On Revolution. New York: Viking Press, 1963.

Eichmann in Jerusalem: A Report on the Banality of Evil, 2nd edn. New York: Viking Press, 1965.

Between Past and Future. New York: Viking Press, 1968.

Men in Dark Times. New York: Harcourt, Brace, Jovanovich, 1968.

Crises of the Republic. New York: Harcourt, Brace, Jovanovich, 1972.

Rahel Varnhagen: The Life of a Jewish Woman, rev. edn, tr. Richard and Clara Winston. New York: Harcourt, Brace, Jovanovich, 1974.

The Life of the Mind. New York: Harcourt, Brace, Jovanovich, 1978.

The Jew as Pariah, ed. Ron H. Feldman. New York: The Grove Press, 1978.

Lectures on Kant's Political Philosophy, ed. with an interpretive essay by Ronald Beiner. Chicago: University of Chicago Press, 1982.

Essays in Understanding, 1930–1954, ed. Jerome Kohn. New York: Harcourt, Brace & Co., 1994.

Correspondence

Arendt, Hannah and Blumenfeld, Kurt, '. . . *in keinem Besitz verwurzelt,' Die Korrespondenz*, ed. Ingeborg Nordmann and Iris Pilling. Hamburg: Rotbuch Verlag, 1995.
Arendt, Hannah and Jaspers, Karl, *Correspondence, 1926–1969*, ed. Lotte Kohler and Hans Saner, tr. Robert and Rita Kimber. New York: Harcourt Brace & Co., 1992.
Arendt, Hannah and McCarthy, Mary, *Between Friends: The Correspondence of Hannah Arendt and Mary McCarthy, 1949–75*, ed. Carol Brightman. New York: Harcourt Brace & Co., 1995.
Arendt, Hannah and Scholem, Gershom, " 'Eichmann in Jerusalem': Exchange of Letters between Gershom Scholem and Hannah Arendt," *Encounter*, 22/1 (1964): 51–6. Repr. in *JP*, 240–51.

Books Edited by Arendt

Job's Dungheap, by Bernard Lazare. New York: Schocken Press, 1949.
Illuminations, by Walter Benjamin. New York: Schocken Press, 1969.

Articles

"Die jüdische Armee – der Beginn einer jüdisch Politik?" (The Jewish Army – The Beginning of a Jewish Politics?), *Aufbau*, 7/47 (Nov. 14, 1941): 1–2.
"From the Dreyfus Affair to France Today," *Jewish Social Studies*, 4 (July 1942): 195–240.
"The Jewish State, Fifty Years After: Where Have Herzl's Politics Led?,'', *Commentary*, 1 (May, 1946): 1–8. Repr. in *JP*, 164–77.
"We Refugees," *Menorah Journal*, 31 (Jan. 1943): 69–77. Repr. in *JP*, 55–66.
"Franz Kafka: A Reevaluation," *Partisan Review*, 11/4 (1944): 412–22. Repr. in *EU*, 69–80.
"The Jew as Pariah: A Hidden Tradition," *Jewish Social Studies*, 6/2 (Apr. 1944): 99–122. Repr. in *JP*, 67–90.
"Nightmare and Flight," *Partisan Review*, 12/2 (Spring 1945): 259–60. Repr. in *EU*, 133–5.
"Zionism Reconsidered," *Menorah Journal*, 33 (Aug. 1945): 162–96. Repr. in *JP*, 131–63.
"The Image of Hell," review of *The Black Book: The Nazi Crime Against the Jewish People*, compiled and edited by the World Jewish Congress, the Jewish Anti-Fascist Committee, the Vaad Leumi, and the American Committee of Jewish Writers, Artists and Scientists (New York: Duell, Sloan and Pearce, 1946) and *Hitler's Professors*, by Max Weinreich (New

York: Yiddish Scientific Institute, 1946), *Commentary*, 2/3 (1946): 291–5. Repr. in *EU*, 197–205.

"The Nation," Review of *La Nation* by J. T. Delos, *Review of Politics*, 8/1 (Jan. 1946): 138–41.

"The Concentration Camps," *Partisan Review*, 15/7 (July 1948): 743–63.

"Jewish History, Revised," *Jewish Frontier*, 15 (Mar. 1948): 34–8. Repr. in *JP*, 96–105.

"The Mission of Bernadotte," *New Leader*, 31 (Oct. 1948): 808, 819.

"To Save the Jewish Homeland: There is Still Time," *Commentary*, 5 (May 1948): 398–406. Repr. in *JP*, 178–92.

"Peace or Armistice in the Near East?," *Reviews of Politics*, 12/1 (Jan. 1950): 56–82. Repr. in *JP*, 193–232.

"Social Science Techniques and the Study of Concentration Camps," *Jewish Social Studies*, 12 (1950): 49–64. Repr. in *EU*, 232–47.

"The History of a Great Crime," review of *Bréviaire de la Haine: Le IIIe Reich et les Juifs*, by Léon Poliakov, *Commentary*, 13 (1952): 300–4.

"A Reply to Eric Voegelin," *Review of Politics*, 15/6 (Jan. 1953): 76–84.

"Philosophy and Politics," lecture from 1954, ed. Jerome Kohn, *Social Research*, 57/1 (Spring 1990): 73–103.

"Understanding and Politics" (originally entitled "The Difficulties of Understanding"), *Partisan Review*, 20/4 (1954): 377–92. Repr. in *EU*, 307–27.

"Totalitarianism," *Meridian*, 2/2 (Fall 1958): 1.

"On Humanity in Dark Times: Thoughts about Lessing" (lecture from 1959). In *MD*, 3–31.

"Action and the Pursuit of Happiness," in *Politische Ordnung und Menschliche Existenz: Festgabe für Eric Voegelin* (Munich: Beck, 1962), 1–16.

"Personal Responsibility Under Dictatorship," *Listener*, Aug. 6, 1964.

"What Remains? The Language Remains: An Interview with Günter Gaus" (translation of "Was Bleibt? Es bleibt die Muttersprache," in Günter Gaus, *Zur Person: Porträts in Frage und Antwort* (Munich: Feder Verlag, 1964), 13–32. In *EU*, 1–23.

"Some Questions of Moral Philosophy" (lecture from 1965), ed. Jerome Kohn, *Social Research*, 61/4 (Winter 1994): 739–64.

"Collective Responsibility" (1968), in *Amor Mundi: Explorations in the Faith and Thought of Hannah Arendt*, ed. James W. Bernauer, SJ, 43–50. Dordrecht: Martinus Nijhoff, 1987.

"What is Freedom?" (1968). In *BPF*, 143–71.

"Martin Heidegger at Eighty," New York Review of Books, 17/6 (Oct. 21, 1971): 50–4. Repr. in *Heidegger and Modern Philosophy*, ed. M. Murray, 293–303. New Haven: Yale University Press, 1978.

"Thinking and Moral Considerations: A Lecture," *Social Research*, 38/3 (Fall 1971): 417–46. Revised and incorporated in *LM*, 3–16.

"Hannah Arendt on Hannah Arendt" (1972). In *RPW*, 301–39.

Unpublished Papers

Hannah Arendt to Paul Brooks, Houghton Mifflin, New York, Feb. 13, 1948, in Arendt Archives, Library of Congress.

"Answer to Grafton, Draft" (1963), in Arendt Archives, Library of Congress.

"Some Questions of Moral Philosophy" (lecture series from 1965, first lecture ed. Jerome Kohn, *Social Research*, 61/4 (Winter 1994): 739–64), in Arendt Archives, Library of Congress.

SECONDARY WORKS

Allison, Henry E., *Kant's Theory of Freedom*. Cambridge: Cambridge University Press, 1990.

—— "Reflections on the Banality of (Radical) Evil: A Kantian Analysis," *Graduate Faculty Philosophy Journal*, 18/2 (Winter 1995): 141–58.

Anderson-Gold, Sharon, "Kant's Rejection of Devilishness: The Limits of Human Volition," *Idealistic Studies*, 14 (1989): 35–48.

Barnouw, Dagmar, *Visible Spaces: Hannah Arendt and the German-Jewish Experience*. Baltimore: Johns Hopkins University Press, 1990.

Bedford, Sybille, "Emancipation and Destiny," review of *Rahel Varnhagen*, by Hannah Arendt, *Reconstructionist*, 24 (Dec. 1958): 22–6.

Beiner, Ronald, "A Commentary on Hannah Arendt's Unwritten Finale," *History of Political Thought*, 1/1 (1980): 117–35.

—— "Interpretive Essay: Hannah Arendt on Judging," in Hannah Arendt, *Lectures on Kant's Political Philosophy*, ed. by Ronald Beiner, 89–156. Chicago: University of Chicago Press, 1982.

—— "Action, Natality, and Citizenship: Hannah Arendt's Concept of Freedom," in *Conceptions of Liberty in Political Philosophy*, ed. Zbigniew Pelczynski and John Gray, 349–75. London: Athlone Press, 1984.

Benhabib, Seyla, "Judgment and the Moral Foundations of Politics in Arendt's Thought," *Political Theory*, 16 (1988): 29–51.

—— "Hannah Arendt and the Redemptive Power of Narrative," *Social Research*, 57/1 (Spring 1990): 168–96.

—— "Models of Public Space: Hannah Arendt, the Liberal Tradition, and Jürgen Habermas," in *Habermas and the Public Sphere*, ed. by Craig Calhoun, 73–98. Cambridge, Mass.: M.I.T. Press, 1992.

—— "Feminist Theory and Hannah Arendt's Concept of Public Space," *History of the Human Sciences*, 6/2 (1993): 97–114.

—— "The Pariah and her Shadow," *Political Theory*, 23 (Feb. 1995): 5–24.

—— *The Reluctant Modernism of Hannah Arendt*. Newbury Park, Calif.: Sage Publications, 1996.

Benjamin, Walter, "Theses on the Philosophy of History," in *Illuminations*, ed. and introduced by Hannah Arendt, 253–64. New York: Schocken Press, 1969.

Bernasconi, Robert, "Habermas and Arendt on the Philosopher's 'Error': Tracking the Diabolical in Heidegger," *Graduate Faculty Philosophy Journal*, 14/2–15/1 (1991): 3–24.

Bernauer, James W., SJ, "On Reading and Mis-Reading Hannah Arendt," *Philosophy and Social Criticism*, 11/1 (1985): 1–34.

—— "The Faith of Hannah Arendt: Amor Mundi and its Critique-Assimilation of Religious Experience," in *Amor Mundi: Explorations in the Faith and Thought of Hannah Arendt*, 1–28. Dordrecht: Martinus Nijhoff, 1987.

Bernstein, Richard J., "Hannah Arendt: The Ambiguities of Theory and Practice," in *Political Theory and Praxis*, ed. Terence Ball, 141–58. Minneapolis: University of Minnesota Press, 1977.

—— "Heidegger on Humanism," in *Philosophical Profiles: Essays in a Pragmatic Mode*, 197–220. Cambridge: Polity Press, 1986.

—— "Judging – The Actor and the Spectator," in *Philosophical Profiles: Essays in a Pragmatic Mode*, 221–37. Cambridge: Polity Press, 1986.

—— "Rethinking the Social and the Political," in *Philosophical Profiles: Essays in a Pragmatic Mode*, 238–59. Cambridge: Polity Press, 1986.

—— "Heidegger's Silence?: *Éthos* and Technology," in *The New Constellation: The Ethical-Political Horizons of Modernity/Postmodernity*, 79–141. Cambridge: Polity Press, 1991.

Botstein, Leon, "Hannah Arendt: Opposing Views," *Partisan Review*, 45/3 (1978): 368–80.

—— "The Jew as Pariah: Hannah Arendt's Political Philosophy," *Dialectical Anthropology*, 8/1–2 (1983): 47–73.

—— "Liberating the Pariah: Politics, the Jews, and Hannah Arendt," *Salmagundi*, 60 (1983): 73–106.

Canovan, Margaret. *The Political Thought of Hannah Arendt*. London: J. M. Dent, 1974.

—— "The Contradictions of Hannah Arendt's Political Thought," *Political Theory*, 6 (Feb. 1978): 5–26.

—— "Arendt, Rousseau and Human Plurality in Politics," *Journal of Politics*, 45 (1983): 286–302.

—— "A Case of Distorted Communication: A Note on Habermas and Arendt," *Political Theory* 11 (Feb. 1983): 105–16.

—— "Hannah Arendt on Ideology in Totalitarianism," in *The Structure of Modern Ideology*, ed. Noel O'Sullivan, 151–71. Aldershot: Edward Elgar, 1989.

—— "Socrates or Heidegger? Hannah Arendt's Reflections on Philosophy and Politics," *Social Research*, 57/1 (Spring 1990): 135–65.

—— *Hannah Arendt: A Reinterpretation of Her Political Thought*. Cambridge: Cambridge University Press, 1992.

Cutting-Gray, Joanne, "Hannah Arendt's *Rahel Varnhagen*," *Philosophy and Literature*, 15 (1991): 229–45.

—— "Hannah Arendt, Feminism, and the Politics of Alterity: 'What Will We Lose if We Win?'," *Hypatia*, 8 (1993): 35–53.

Denneny, Michael, "The Privilege of Ourselves: Hannah Arendt on Judgment" (1979). In *RPW*, 245–74.

Disch, Lisa J., "More Truth than Fact," *Political Theory*, 21 (Nov. 1993): 665–94.

—— *Hannah Arendt and the Limits of Philosophy*. Ithaca, NY: Cornell University Press, 1994.

Dostal, Robert J., "Judging Human Action: Arendt's Appropriation of Kant," *Review of Metaphysics*, 37 (June 1984): 725–55.

Ettinger, Elzbieta, *Hannah Arendt and Martin Heidegger*. New Haven: Yale University Press, 1995.

Fehér, Ferenc, "The Pariah and the Citizen: On Arendt's Political Theory," *Thesis Eleven*, 15 (1986): 15–29.

—— "Freedom and the Social Question: Hannah Arendt's Theory of the French Revolution," *Philosophy and Social Criticism*, 12/1 (1987): 1–30.

Feldman, Ron H., "The Jew as Pariah: the Case of Hannah Arendt (1906–1975)" (1978). Introduction to *JP*, 15–52.

Flynn, Bernard, "Arendt's Appropriation of Kant's Theory of Judgment," *Journal of the British Society for Phenomenology*, 19 (May 1988): 128–39.

Forti, Simona, *Vita Della Mente e Tempo Della Polis: Hannah Arendt Tra Filosofia e Politica*. Milan: Franco Angeli, 1994.

Friedmann, Friedrich G., *Hannah Arendt: Eine deutsche Jüdin im Zeitalter des Totalitarismus*. Munich: Piper Verlag, 1985.

Gray, J. Glenn, "The Winds of Thought," *Social Research*, 44/1 (Spring 1977): 44–61.

—— "The Abyss of Freedom – and Hannah Arendt" (1979). In *RPW*, 225–44.

Habermas, Jürgen, "Hannah Arendt's Communications Concept of Power," *Social Research*, 44/1 (Spring 1977): 3–24.

Hansen, Phillip, *Hannah Arendt*. Cambridge: Polity Press, 1993.

Heidegger, Martin, "The Question Concerning Technology," in *Basic Writings*, ed. David F. Krell, 284–317. New York: Harper & Row, 1977.

Heller, Agnes, "Hannah Arendt on the 'Vita Contemplativa,' " *Philosophy and Social Criticism*, 12/4 (1987): 281–96. Repr. in *Hannah Arendt: Thinking, Judging, Freedom*, ed. Gisela T. Kaplan and Clive S. Kessler, 144–59. Sydney: Allen and Unwin, 1989.

—— "An Imaginary Preface to the 1984 Edition of Hannah Arendt's *The Origins of Totalitarianism*," in *Eastern Left, Western Left: Totalitarianism*,

Freedom and Democracy, ed. by Ferenc Fehér and Agnes Heller, 243–59. Cambridge: Polity Press, 1987.

Hilberg, Raul, *The Destruction of the European Jews.* Chicago: Quadrangle Books, 1961.

Hill, Melvyn A. (ed.), *Hannah Arendt: The Recovery of the Public World.* New York: St. Martin's Press, 1979.

Hinchman, Sandra K., "Common Sense and Political Barbarism in the Theory of Hannah Arendt," *Polity*, 17/2 (1984): 183–211.

Hinchman, Lewis P. and Sandra K., "In Heidegger's Shadow: Hannah Arendt's Phenomenological Humanism," *Review of Politics*, 46 (Apr. 1984): 183–211.

—— "Existentialism Politicized: Arendt's Debt to Jaspers," *Review of Politics*, 53/3 (Summer 1991): 435–68.

—— (eds), *Hannah Arendt: Critical Essays.* Albany, NY: State University of New York Press, 1994.

Honig, Bonnie, "Arendt, Identity, and Difference," *Political Theory*, 16 (Feb. 1988): 77–98.

—— "Declarations of Independence: Arendt and Derrida on the Problem of Founding a Republic," *American Political Science Review*, 85 (Mar. 1991): 97–113.

—— "Toward an Agonistic Feminism: Hannah Arendt and the Politics of Identity," in *Feminists Theorize the Political*, ed. Judith Butler and Joan W. Scott, 215–35. New York: Routledge, 1992.

—— *Political Theory and the Displacement of Politics.* Ithaca, NY: Cornell University Press, 1993.

—— "The Politics of Agonism," *Political Theory*, 21 (1993): 528–33.

—— (ed.), *Feminist Interpretations of Hannah Arendt.* University Park, Pa.: Pennsylvania State University Press, 1995.

Ingram, David, "The Postmodern Kantianism of Arendt and Lyotard," *Review of Metaphysics*, 42 (Sept. 1988): 51–77.

Isaac, Jeffrey C., "Arendt, Camus, and Postmodern Politics," *Praxis International*, 9/1–2 (Apr.–July 1989): 48–71.

—— "At the Margins: Jewish Identity and Politics in the Thought of Hannah Arendt," *Tikkun* (Jan.–Feb. 1990): 23–92.

—— *Arendt, Camus, and Modern Rebellion.* New Haven: Yale University Press, 1992.

—— "Situating Hannah Arendt on Action and Politics," *Political Theory*, 21 (1993): 534–40.

Jacobilti, Suzanne, "Hannah Arendt and the Will," *Political Theory*, 16 (Feb. 1988): 53–76.

Jay, Martin. "The Political Existentialism of Hannah Arendt," in *Permanent Exiles: Essays on the Intellectual Migration from Germany to America*, 237–56. New York: Columbia University Press, 1986.

Jonas, Hans, "Acting, Knowing, Thinking: Gleanings from Hannah Arendt's Philosophical Work," *Social Research*, 44/1 (1977): 25–43.

Kant, Immanuel, *Religion within the Limits of Reason Alone*, tr., introduced and with notes by Theodore M. Greene and Hoyt H. Hudson. New York: Harper & Row, 1960.

Kaplan, Gisela T. and Kessler, Clive S. (eds), *Hannah Arendt: Thinking, Judging, Freedom*. Sydney: Allen & Unwin, 1989.

Kateb, George, *Hannah Arendt: Politics, Conscience, Evil*. Oxford: Martin Robertson, 1984.

Knauer, James, "Hannah Arendt on Judgment, Philosophy and Praxis," *International Studies in Philosophy*, 21/3 (1989): 71–83.

Kohn, Jerome, "Thinking/Acting," *Social Research*, 57/1 (Spring, 1990): 105–34.

—— Introduction to Hannah Arendt, *Essays in Understanding, 1930–1954*, ed. Jerome Kohn, ix–xxxi. New York: Harcourt, Brace & Co., 1994.

Lane, Ann, "The Feminism of Hannah Arendt," *Democracy*, 3 (Summer 1983): 107–17.

Laqueur, Walter Z., "Rereading Hannah Arendt," *Encounter*, 52/3 (1979): 73–9.

—— "Hannah Arendt in Jerusalem: The Controversy Revisited," in *Western Society after the Holocaust*, ed. Lyman H. Legters, 107–20. Boulder, Colo.: Westview Press, 1983.

Lazare, Bernard, *Job's Dungheap*, ed. Hannah Arendt. New York: Schocken Press, 1949.

Lefort, Claude, "Hannah Arendt and the Question of the Political," *Democracy and Political Theory*, 45–55. Minneapolis: University of Minnesota Press, 1988.

Lévinas, Emmanuel, *Difficile Liberté*. Paris: Albin Michel, 1976.

Luban, David, "Explaining Dark Times: Hannah Arendt's Theory of Theory," *Social Research*, 50/1 (Spring 1983): 215–48.

Markus, Maria, "The 'Anti-Feminism' of Hannah Arendt," *Thesis Eleven*, 17 (1987): 76–87.

Miller, James, "The Pathos of Novelty: Hannah Arendt's Image of Freedom in the Modern World" (1979). In *RPW*, 177–208.

Mommsen, Hans, "Hannah Arendt und der Prozess gegen Adolf Eichmann," introduction to *Eichmann in Jerusalem: Ein Bericht von der Banalität des Bösen*, tr. Brigitte Ganzow, i–xxxvii. Munich: Piper Verlag, 1986.

Parekh, Bikhu, *Hannah Arendt and the Search for a New Political Philosophy*. London: Macmillan, 1981.

Pitkin, Hanna "Justice: On Relating Private and Public," *Political Theory*, 9/3 (1981): 327–52.

—— "Conformism, Housekeeping, and the Attack of the Blob: Hannah Arendt's Concept of the Social," paper presented at the 1990 American

Political Science Association. Revised and included in *Feminist Interpretations of Hannah Arendt*, ed. Bonnie Honig, 51–81. University Park, Pa.: Pennsylvania State University Press, 1995.

Ricoeur, Paul, "Action, Story and History – On Re-reading *The Human Condition*," *Salmagundi*, 60 (Spring – Summer 1983): 60–72.

Riley, Patrick, "Hannah Arendt on Kant, Truth and Politics," *Political Studies* 35 (1987): 379–92.

Rouset, David, *Les Jours de notre mort*. Paris: Éditions du Pavois, 1947.

Sartre, Jean-Paul, *Anti-Semite and Jew*. New York: Schocken Books, 1948.

Schirmacher, Wolfgang, *Technik und Gelassenheit*. Freiburg: Alber, 1983.

Schürmann, Reiner, "Le Temps de l'esprit et l'histoire de la liberté," *Les Études philosophiques*, 3 (1983): 357–62.

Sheehan, Thomas, "Heidegger and the Nazis," *New York Review of Books*, June 16, 1988.

Shklar, Judith N., "Rethinking the Past," *Social Research*, 44/1 (1977): 80–90.

――― "Hannah Arendt as Pariah," *Partisan Review*, 50/1 (1983): 64–77.

Silber, John, "The Ethical Significance of Kant's *Religion*," introductory essay to Kant's *Religion within the Limits of Reason Alone*, lxxix–cxxxiv. New York: Harper & Row, 1960.

Stern, Peter and Yarborough, Jean, "Hannah Arendt," *American Scholar*, 47/3 (1978): 1371–81.

Taminiaux, Jacques, "Arendt, disciple de Heidegger?," *Études phénoménologiques*, 73/4 (1962): 111–36.

――― "Phenomenology and the Problem of Action," *Philosophy and Social Criticism*, 11/3 (1986): 207–19.

――― "Heidegger et Arendt lecteurs d'Aristote," *Les Cahiers de philosophie*, 4 (1987): 41–52.

――― *La fille de Thrace et le penseur professionnel: Arendt et Heidegger*. Paris: Éditions Payot, 1992.

Toury, Jacob, " 'The Jewish Question': A Semantic Approach," *Leo Baeck Institute Year Book*, 11 (1966): 85–107.

Trunk, Isaiah, *Judenrat*. New York: Stein and Day, 1972.

Villa, Dana R., "Beyond Good and Evil: Arendt, Nietzsche, and the Aestheticization of Political Action," *Political Theory*, 20 (1992): 274–308.

――― *Arendt and Heidegger: The Fate of the Political*. Princeton: Princeton University Press, 1995.

Voegelin, Eric, review of *The Origins of Totalitarianism* by Hannah Arendt, *Review of Politics*, 15/6 (Jan. 1953): 68–76, 84–5.

Vollrath, Ernst, "Hannah Arendt and the Method of Political Thinking," *Social Research*, 44/1 (1977): 160–82.

――― "Hannah Arendt über Meinung und Urteilskraft," in *Hannah Arendt: Materialien in ihrem Werk*, ed. Adalbert Reif, 85–107. Vienna: Europa Verlag, 1979.

Young-Bruehl, Elisabeth, "Hannah Arendt's Storytelling," *Social Research*, 44/1 (1977): 183–90.

——"From the Pariah's Point of View: Reflections on Hannah Arendt's Life and Work" (1979). In *RPW*, 3–25.

——*Hannah Arendt: For Love of the World*. New Haven: Yale University Press, 1982.

——"Reflections on Hannah Arendt's *The Life of the Mind*," *Political Theory*, 10/2 (1982): 277–305.

Index of Subjects

abstraction, 5, 11, 26, 44, 78–9, 84, 182
action, 3, 5, 99–100, 134
    political 11, 22, 41–2, 198–9n
aletheia (truth), 106
American Jews, 114–15
American Revolution, 17, 100, 130–1
American Zionists, resolution (October 1944), 104, 107
"Amor Mundi," 188
anti-foundationalism, 4
anti-Semitism
    doctrines of eternal, 54, 55, 181
    political, 9, 10, 24–5, 45, 48–9, 54–7, 62, 63–70, 180
    as a political ideology, 46–70
    scapegoat theories, 54–5, 56, 181
    social, 24–5, 48, 62
anti-utilitarianism, 91–2, 202n
Arab Higher League, 114
Arab–Jewish councils *see* Jewish–Arab councils
Arabs, 104, 107–9, 114, 116–18, 124–5
Arendt, Camus, and Modern Rebellion (Isaac), 7
army, Jewish, 53, 57, 61, 181
assimilation, 42–3, 76–7, 124, 187
    German–Jewish, 9–10, 14, 17, 19–22, 24–5, 35
    social, 57, 103, 180, 186

Aufbau, 53
Auschwitz, 88, 154
Austria, November revolution, 127
"authentic" Jew (Sartre), 196–7n

Balfour Declaration (1917), 109
Balkanization, 121
Bestand (standing-reserve – Heidegger), 169–70
Between Past and Future (Arendt), 1, 8, 41
Biltmore Program (1942), 104, 107
"biological" metaphors, 148, 208n
blindness, and insight, 179–89
Bolshevism, 67
"bringing-forth" (Heidegger), 169
Brit Shalom (Covenant of Peace), 109–10
bureaucracy, 57, 75–6

Castle, The (Kafka), 39, 42–3
catalytic agent, Jewish question as, 9, 49–50, 69–70
causality, 51–4
"challenging-forth" (Heidegger), 169
chalutz (Jewish pioneer), 103
chosenness, claims to, 68, 187, 200–1n
Christianity, 15, 16, 185, 188

Index of Names